Y0-ACI-643

# THE INDIAN FILM

# THE INDIAN FILM

*by*

## PANNA SHAH

Wingate College Library

GREENWOOD PRESS, PUBLISHERS
WESTPORT, CONNECTICUT

101192

**Library of Congress Cataloging in Publication Data**

Shah, Panna.
    The Indian film.

    Reprint. Originally published: Bombay : Motion Pic-
ture Society of India, 1950.
    Originally presented as the author's thesis (doctoral
--Bombay University) under title: A social study of the
cinema in Bombay.
    Bibliography: p.
    Includes index.
    1. Moving-picture industry--India--Bombay.  I. Title.
PN1993.5.I8S5  1981      384'.8'0954      81-6268
ISBN 0-8371-3144-8 (lib. bdg.)              AACR2

Published in November 1950 by I. K. Menon for the
Motion Picture Society of India.

Reprinted from an original copy in the collection of the
Library, State University College at Purchase, New York

Reprinted in 1981 by Greenwood Press
A division of Congressional Information Service, Inc.
88 Post Road West, Westport, Connecticut 06881

Printed in the United States of America

10 9 8 7 6 5 4 3 2 1

*To*

MY FATHER
*who, by his encouragement, criticism and labour, has contributed so much to this book.*

# FOREWORD

It is very seldom indeed that one comes across a university in India which encourages a research student to take up the study of the motion picture industry. It is in the fitness of things that this was done by the University of Bombay—the birthplace of the film industry in India.

The present publication is the concise version of a thesis prepared by Miss Panna Shah for which she was awarded a doctor's degree by the Bombay University. The book gives a historical, sociological and economic survey of the industry, particularly in Bombay. It is a unique work of its kind in our country and I am sure it will prove to be of great help to any one who wants to know something about the growth of our Industry.

The Motion Picture Society of India has undertaken the publication of this book in the confident hope that it will serve to meet one of the long-felt needs of the Industry.

I congratulate Dr. Miss Panna Shah for the hard work she has put in for bringing out this book and I am sure her services will be thankfully acknowledged by every one in our Industry.

CHUNI LALL
*President, M.P.S.I.*

*Bombay,*
*August, 1950.*

# CONTENTS

# PREFACE

IN modern, civilized and machine-dominated society, man's leisure has been commercialized and the provision of entertainment for spare time hours has become a large scale business. In that business the film industry plays a major role, for the primary aim of the cinema, no matter what its critics say, is to entertain. And yet, the film is not only a leviathan in the sphere of entertainment; it has become the most potent single factor in modern life. Its influence, though largely unmeasured, is enormous.

Though the power of the film as a medium of creative expression, education and social significance is admitted, it is curious that so little should have been done to investigate its problems and capabilities. Hundreds of pictures are made every year, tons of newsprint commend them and millions of people see and are moved or thrilled by them. But there, in a way, the whole thing ends, for the films quickly disappear from sight and very little thought is given to this powerful but transient medium. One of the reasons for the dearth of significant literature is that films fade into the past with rapidity and are to be viewed again, if at all, with the greatest difficulty. Moreover, till recently, there was virtually no means of informing ourselves about this medium of expression which appeals to the greatest number of people.

The moving picture world is for ever changing and tends to cast into oblivion the things that it leaves behind. The investigator has to deal with the most evanescent form of expression, which is due not merely to the change of interest and taste on the part of the

audience but also to the change in technique of production which renders the most important films of the past
antiquated and incapable of conveying their full message
to succeeding generations.

In spite of these difficulties, in Western countries
some social investigations have been carried out. But
these efforts, however good in themselves, are far from
complete. They have only just touched the fringe of the
problem while the core yet remains to be probed.
Strange though it may seem, this industry of such gigantic dimensions—it ranks as the fifth largest in the U.S.A.
and as eighth in India—knows little about itself and has
done little systematic research on its product and the
acceptance of that product by the public. To questions
such as "What is the nature of the impact of the content
of motion pictures on the audience?" or "What are the
psychological needs of the audience?" and "Why do they
go to pictures?", there is little in the way of tested and
reliable answers. Diverse and often contradictory views
are held, based on a variety of assumptions about human
nature and the reactions of man to different social situations.

Even in matters of reliable statistical information,
there is a sad dearth of authoritative factual data. More
fiction than fact has found its way into the domain of
films resulting in much erroneous information being
spread. More often than not, this information is based
on nothing more than common talk or mere guesswork,
and given out with the hope that in the absence of proof,
it would not be easily challenged.

Today, in Western countries, this factual deficiency
is slowly but surely being remedied. The industry has
realized the value of sound data, and steps have been
taken to compile reliable and unbiased statistics. Yet
there is ample scope for future research. The economic
stature of the industry, an intelligent analysis of the product, the weekly attendance of the audience, their
psychological needs and the cinema's influence on them,
especially on the younger generation, and the scope for
non-theatrical films, all these factors and their problems
can be better solved with the help of reliable factual

material.

Though statistical and psychological research is a relatively new concept in the field of motion pictures, its significance is apparent. The value of accurate data has been repeatedly stressed and its application to important problems is indispensable to the progress of the industry as a whole.

Being fully aware of these difficulties, all the more great in this backward country, it was with hesitation that this vast subject of research was undertaken. With the exception of the enquiry undertaken by the Indian Cinematograph Committee appointed by the Government of India in 1927-28, no systematic and thorough sociological investigation of the Indian film has hitherto been made. The absence of all data, lack of facilities for research and poor response to field work have considerably limited the scope of the present volume.

Our producers, distributors and exhibitors, not used to social investigations, were reluctant to answer the questions put to them on the economic structure of the industry. There was next to no response from the industry. While most of them ignored the circular I sent, a few frankly admitted that they were not in a position to answer the enquiry, and one with a sense of humour replied that if he could answer all the questions, he would write the thesis himself. The only information secured was from the Motion Picture Society of India to whom I owe a debt of gratitude. But even this was not enough to fill the lacuna regarding the films of the early days.

The Government was next approached. To them, however, the thesis was 'a teaser', and, instead of supplying information, all they did was to say that there was hardly any literature on the subject and that I would have to draw heavily on my own imagination and observation! The only information they were able to supply was on the Information Films of India, a Government project of World War II.

Even the Censors' Office was non-co-operative. When approached for material, it refused access to the synopses of the stories of films certified by the Board on the ground that there was no precedent for such a step and no reason to establish one. The only recourse was to examine the reviews of films exhibited, in the old files of *The Times of India* and on the basis of this the analysis of the contents of films shown in Bombay since 1935 has been worked out.

Nor were film stars neglected. A questionnaire was circulated among the leading screen luminaries of Bombay Province in the hope of getting some idea about their profession and society's attitude towards it. But only a 20 per cent response was received.

On the important topic of the effect of cinemas, especially on juveniles, the college students of Bombay were contacted through a questionnaire. The students, however, not used to such social investigation, were inclined to take the whole thing very light heartedly, with the result that, in spite of three attempts, only 22.7 per cent replied.

The absence of all data and the indifference of the industry and the Government in this matter very clearly show that we have not yet realized the value of statistics and of research in this powerful medium. No doubt, now and again some stray figures are published and, in the absence of any other reliable material, have to be accepted for what they are worth. But who can vouch for their authenticity? They are, at best, mere approximations and can only serve as a substitute till more reliable data can be obtained.

In view of these handicaps, this book has only partially succeeded in accomplishing what it set about to do —to make a social study of the Indian film. Many are the failings and drawbacks of the present work but if it succeeds in rousing interest and leads to further research, it will have served its purpose.

I should like to take this opportunity to thank Dr. G. S. Ghurye, Head of the Department of Sociology, University of Bombay, for his able guidance of this work which was originally written as a thesis for the degree of Ph.D. of the Unversity of Bombay, and later condensed to the present book form. I should also like to express my thanks to the Motion Picture Society of

India for kindly undertaking to publish the book; to the various producers and distributors  for the stills supplied; to Mr. I. K. Menon for his assistance and co-operation; to Mr. Phiroze Mistry for his genuine interest and help in producing the book and  seeing it through the press and to my numerous other friends who, in one way or another, have helped with this book.

PANNA SHAH

*Bombay,*
*August, 1950.*

*1*

# THE PLACE OF CINEMA IN SOCIETY

THE rise and development of the cinema is one of the outstanding social phenomena of the twentieth century. It has come to occupy a unique position in our everyday urban social life. Over fifty years[1] of work, hope, despair, self-sacrifice and crookedness—a veritable whirlpool of all that is best and worst in human nature—have gone to the making of the film of today. Its birth was a flickering hardly noticed. Its future is still in the realms of the unknown. Its influences on peoples of wide and varied cultures throughout the whole of the civilized world is such that it would be rash indeed to dogmatize as to its real significance. Perhaps one of the most striking features of present day life is the ease — almost too great an ease, some people contend—with which we can get entertainment. And of all the means of amusing ourselves that are offered for our choice, none is more popular than the cinema. 'Going to the pictures' has become for many people not merely an entertainment, but a habit. Its little artificial world of persons and personalities, facts and fantasies is a topic of conversation and a matter for journalistic discussion of which the public never tire. For good or for bad, the cinema is an immense force which by the subtlety of its nature moulds the opinion of millions in the course of its apparently superficial business of merely providing entertainment.

[1] The moving picture as we know it today was publicly exhibited in the United States of America on April 23, 1896, and in India in June-July, 1896. See Lewis Jacobs, *The Rise of the American Film*, p. 3 and *The Times of India* July 7, 22, and 27, 1896.

The cinema as one of the foremost means of amusement has come to occupy an important position in our social life primarily because of the recent increase in leisure. At one time the privilege of a few, leisure has now become the right of all. This growth of leisure is due to certain economic and social changes brought about by industrialization, such as reduction of working hours, use of gas and electricity, increase in wages, development of communications and spread of compulsory, primary education.

These changed conditions have affected man's attitude to his work and his relationship with his family and society. Factory work now fails to supply to the labourer the rationale of his existence. To religion which formerly interpreted his world, he remains indifferent. The spontaneous relationship once assured to him by the family and the community has now disappeared. What is it that links him now with society? The answer is 'the machinery of amusement.'

It is pertinent to ask what exactly has been replaced in working class life by the cinema and other amusements and with what gain or loss? As regards the West there is no doubt that the cinema has to some extent taken the place of the old time music-hall and has driven out of existence the public houses of the last century. The talkies have also come into direct competition with the theatres but there had never been a large working class element among city theatre-goers. In the main, however, the cinema has created and filled an entirely new demand. The fact is that during the latter half of the last century the part of working class leisure now filled by the cinema was either non-existent—the working day being much longer — or to a large extent passed idly at the public house or street corner.[1]

In a world where relationships are in the main reduced to a cash nexus, the exploitation of leisure for profit is to be expected. Leisure being unorganized, commercial concerns have standardized recreational activities for personal or corporate profit. While some

[1] Sir Hubert Llewellyn Smith, *New Survey of London Life & Labour*, Vol. IX, p. i.

engaged in commercial amusements are interested in furnishing entertainment which will benefit the people at large, the profit motive is uppermost and programmes are conditioned by box-office returns.

The business of providing entertainment to the public has become a large scale and lucrative undertaking especially since World War I, and those interested have been unusually alert in supplying what people want, or at any rate what will attract them.

Even a cursory survey of the extent and variety of commercial amusements to be found in any big city today reveals their popularity. Measured by the number of people attending, commercial amusements reach more people and exert a much greater influence than is generally imagined. In fact as G. M. Trevelyan says: "News of Wellington's campaigns in Spain were not awaited with greater national eagerness than reports on the prospects of famous horse-races and prize-fights."[1] Hordes of people collected from all parts of the country, sometimes as many as twenty thousand spectators, to witness these events. Today many more often assemble to watch a Test match or a horse-race.

An analysis of one of the most popular forms of commercial amusement today—the cinema—will give a clue to the significance and place of all forms of entertainment in modern society.

To say that the cinema is popular is to utter a truism. It is *par excellence* the people's amusement. No other form of entertainment has regularly attracted so many people in recent decades. Under such circumstances it is of vital importance to analyse the reasons for its popularity; or in other words, to ask why do people go to the cinema?

There are many answers to that question. In a big city or a town it is one of the cheapest, most easily understood, and accessible forms of entertainment. While many visit it for pure enjoyment, or through force of habit, others find in it an escape from their humdrum lives into a world of luxury and make-believe.

[1] G. M. Trevelyan, *English Social History*, p. 503.

Motion pictures appeal to man's unconscious desires. They are a means of self-identification and wish-
fulfilment. To many they are a release from the frus-
trations of a dull day. They compensate them for the
deficiencies of real life. In the course of the film, the
spectator loses for a while his self-consciousness  and
identifies himself with some character on  the  screen
more or less unconsciously.

No matter why one goes to the cinema, the fact remains that it has become a most powerful factor in modern social life with immense potentialities for good or
ill through its widespread influence on the juvenile as
well as the adult mind.

The social power of the film lies in the subtlety of
its propaganda rather than in any particular theme or
story. One of the most significant social effects of the
cinema is that it makes for similarity of outlook and attitude among people of different occupations, incomes or
classes and in a lesser degree among different nations.
This does not imply that it is making those who belong
to different classes more friendly or different nations
more peaceful towards each other; but a greater aware-
ness now exists about the way of life of others than it
did before the growth of the cinema.

In most countries except Russia, the cinema is not
controlled by any one group in power. There is no deliberate policy expressed in films shown. But the assi-
milation of attitude and outlook among different classes
occurs none the less. The film to be a paying proposition must be viewed by many, and the kind of entertainment provided is what those in charge think is already
desired by a great number. No change of taste is intended to occur as a result of seeing films. Nevertheless if
one kind of taste is satisfied that kind becomes more dominant and fixed over large sections of society. The
result is an almost unconscious formation of certain
general tastes or ideas. Often, the undesigned result
of many films is to fix in a great number of minds fantastic and often mistaken notions about foreigners. However, some ideas derived from films are not bad, where
the producer's attitude has been more intelligent. On

the whole, films have widened the knowledge of our generation and added considerably to the interest of the majority.

The similarity of outlook the cinema brings about is to be found also in the common admiration for cinema stars. All over the world the same conventions are being introduced by film stars and one has only to watch the behaviour of the younger generation to see the effect of the cinema.

The motion picture is also a potent influence in moulding such relatively trivial things as dress fashions, hair styles and even speech. Talkies are tending to introduce into the ordinary language of an average person numerous American words, phrases and intonations.

The use of leisure in going to the cinema has also made some difference in the relation between the sexes for it has become usual for young men and women to take their entertainment together at the pictures. This may tend towards equality of status for women as well as towards a greater identity in the points of view of men and women. Seventy-five years ago the two sexes generally took their leisure separately. With the coming of the bicycle in 1880 and the motor car in 1890,[1] and more so with the coming of the cinema the opportunity for men and women to take their recreation together has increased considerably.

As regards the effect of cinemas on younger people two views are held. Some say it is bad, while others argue that not much harm is done. Psychologists and sociologists have discussed the effect of films on the physical and moral well-being of young people, and come to the general conclusion that the danger to them is on the whole slight except from the typical horror films.

Another much discussed problem which arises out of the social implications of the cinema is whether it encourages crime and delinquency especially among juveniles. On this subject diametrically opposite views are advanced. While some state that juveniles pick up from films ways and means of committing petty crimes, others argue that the cinema is a deterring agent, for

[1] *Ibid*, p. 560.

if it were not there they would be open to other greater dangers—an argument pathetic in its failure to realize that this is no defence of the cinema but merely a condemnation of conditions existing outside it.

Another aspect of the impact of the cinema is a dislike for work and a desire for luxury—the reaching after ease and comfort only to find them denied in the cold, hard world of everyday life. The patrons of the cinema experience for the space of two or three hours, the joys of fine clothes, rich food and elegant rooms. They enjoy all the comforts and luxuries that surround the rich; but when the two hours spent in the dream world are over they must scramble for a place on the bus or tram, eat a simple meal and hurry to bed so that next morning they will hear the alarm clock summoning them to another day of toil exactly like the last. Under such circumstances how can they avoid being disturbed when, witnessing the social ascent of the hero through his own efforts, they realize how unsuccessful they themselves have been? Despair and discontent must arise so long as what they see and absorb is greatly at variance with their daily lot.

On the whole, however, the cinema has done immense good. Its cheapness does not lead to the impoverishment of the people who go continuously. In a world as yet unfitted for creative leisure it provides a steady fill-up for otherwise empty hours, and thus must in the long run prevent much anti-social behaviour.

Thus the motion picture in a period of effective existence, incredibly short when considered in relation to its achievement, has become not only an entertainment of gigantic dimensions, but also the most potent single factor in modern life. Living as it does by universal appeal, its impact on modern society is widespread and varied. Today the cinema is so far advanced that it has reached the stage of an art form. Anthony Asquith regards it as the 'Tenth Muse'.[1] It is the twentieth century art—an art almost everyone loves. It combines sight and sound into a new form which belongs to our

[1] Anthony Asquith, 'Tenth Muse Climbs Parnassus', *Penguin Film Review* I, p. 10.

society and to our time. It is an art easy to transport, to share and to enjoy. Because of its basis of visual narrative, its essential spirit is less easily lost on the foreign screen than that of translated drama on the foreign stage. It is a medium capable of extremes of realism and fantasy, and has claimed its audience in every developed country of the world.

*2*

## THE AMERICAN FILM 1896—1949

THE story of the cinema from the early crude beginnings to its establishment today as one of the largest and most important art industries whose potentialities are matched only by its popularity, reads more like a romantic tale than a record of cold hard facts. Its annals abound in tales of adventure, of high endeavour, of hopes fulfilled, of bitter disappointment, of penury and of riches, though at the same time there is much in them that is dull and prosaic.

The closing years of the last century saw the birth of the film in the West. Man and science had succeeded in accomplishing the impossible—pictures which moved! It was on April 23, 1896, that the moving picture as we know it today was seen for the first time in America. *The New York Times* dated April 24, 1896, described its premiere as "wonderfully real and singularly exhilarating"[1] This early moving picture consisted of disjointed fragments which depicted motion such as a dance, waves of the sea and vaudeville comic routines. In those bygone days these were considered miracles, but before the movies reached the present state of perfection, much film had to churn through the crude clanking projectors of those early years.

It is very difficult to attribute the credit for the invention of the motion picture to any one person or group

[1] This is the date given by Lewis Jacobs in *The Rise of the American Film*, pp. 3-4, and by Roger Manvell in *The Film*, p. 13. Howard T. Lewis writing in the *Encyclopaedia of Social Sciences* Vol. XI and Iris Barry in her *Cycle of Seventy Films, Art in our Times*, p. 335 give 1895 as the year of the birth of the modern film.

of persons of any particular country. The real genesis of the cinema is similar to that of a great many other discoveries and inventions of social importance. Inventive ideas on the problem of making moving pictures sprung up almost simultaneously and apparently independently in different countries. If, however, one reads an American account of the subject, one will gather the impression that most of the credit is due to Thomas Alva Edison and other American inventors. In works written from the European side, stress is naturally laid on the achievements of Robert W. Paul, Cecil M. Hepworth and William Friese-Greene of England; of Louis and Auguste Lumiere, the Pathe Brothers and Leon Gaumont of France. The truth, however, is that it is impossible to attribute exact priority to any one person or group of persons. There is nothing clear cut and definite about the dates offered to us as to the sequences of the cinema's early development. It seems obvious from facts and also from the known history of so many other inventions that there were numberless other men working on identical lines of research, but whose names for one reason or another had no chance of coming into the limelight. This conclusion is strengthened by the fact that in a general way the invention was little thought of except as a kind of scientific plaything. In fact Edison thought so little of his 'Kinetoscope' that he had no idea of applying for patents until it was too late.

Even prior to 1896 moving pictures had been in existence in the crude form of peep-show cabinets at which one person at a time, paying his penny, could revolve a drum and give a motion picture effect to fifty feet of tiny pictures that passed before his eyes. These peep-shows were so popular that it was suggested to Edison that he should have the pictures enlarged upon a screen so that many people could watch them at the same time. He refused to listen because he thought that too many people seeing the picture at the same time would quickly exhaust the demand and the business could come to an end! Later on, however, the development of the projector made such a feat possible and established motion pictures as a new kind of group entertainment.

In England and in Europe these early performances aroused a great deal of interest and curiosity but there were very few who thought of the invention as having any future. People had got used to the ever recurring appearances and disappearances of all sorts of queer inventions. The cinematograph was looked upon as a scientific curiosity, a passing fancy which had no commercial future before it. Few realized that with this epoch-making invention, a new form of entertainment was born, and the foundations laid for one of the biggest industries in the world.

Strictly speaking there is no such thing as a picture which moves. What appears as movement is a succession of still pictures which stop for a fraction of a second before one's eyes and then move on. So quickly do they follow one another that the eye has not the time to distinguish each separate photograph, but records only an impression of the whole. Twenty-four separate photographs are projected on the modern cinema screen every second, the phase of movement recorded on each being slightly different from that of the picture which precedes it and from that which follows. The human eye cannot keep pace with them. What happens is that the image of each photograph remains impressed on the retina after it has actually left the screen with the result that it appears to blend into the next.

The early films were made in the streets. There were no studios but only crude laboratories behind the business offices. The making of those early pictures depended entirely on the ingenuity of the cameraman who was all in all. Photographic equipment available was unwieldy and primitive resulting in coarse prints. Consequently the first motion pictures only recorded simple movements, short skits or improvised incidents. The theatrical potentialities of the new medium were yet to be realized.

The contributions of George Melies and Edwin S. Porter mark the next important stage in the development of the motion picture. George Melies, a Frenchman, was the first cameraman to show individuality of technique. He discovered magic in the motion picture camera—turning it away from reality to fantasy. Regarded as "the dean of motion picture directors, the pioneer in film organization, the first movie artist,"[1] his innovations changed the whole course of film making.

Edwin S. Porter further developed George Melies's principles and was the first to discover that the art of motion picture depended on the continuity of shots and not on shots alone. His film *The Great Train Robbery* (1903), the first successful story film to be made in America, established the editing principle—whereby a story was told by cutting, recombining and arranging one shot after another, so as to give meaning to the whole—as the basis for future film development.

After Edwin S. Porter the industry rapidly expanded. Hitherto films had sought shelter here and there, in tents and in shops. But now a permanent home was found for them, significantly termed the 'Nickleodean'. Attempts at refinement were tried but on the whole the early cinemas were crowded and insanitary structures.

Motion picture production itself was far from advanced. It was permeated by stage technique. Scenes were always shot so that the whole setting was visible. Players faced the camera and moved horizontally. Every scene began with an entrance and ended with an exit. Action was slow, deliberate and exaggerated. To us today these conventions seem ludicrous but they were accepted standards then.

While the industry was rapidly expanding, competition was keen and inventions were not patented. Soon internal dissensions became rampant. They had important effects both artistically and economically. Competition focussed attention on self-improvement. The quality of motion pictures was raised and the feature film of multiple reels first imported from Europe, became an accepted fact by 1912. Hollywood was discovered and established as the home of motion picture production by 1913 and last but not the least the 'star-system' as a factor in profits, production and publicity,

[1] Lewis Jacobs, *The Rise of the American Film*, p. 32.

was originated by Carl Laemmle, the head of 'Independent' motion picture producers. This development progressively influenced the industry as years rolled by and it exists today as one of the major factors in film production.[1]

It was during this unsettled pre-war period that another pioneer, D. W. Griffith, blazed a new trail for the rest to follow. His greatness lies not in the films he made, nor in the stars he brought to fame, but in the fact that it was he who first discovered and laid down the basic principles of cinema technique and film art. He brought to the film new elements of form, a variety of resources and added at least two great productions *The Birth of a Nation* (1915), and *Intolerance* (1916), to motion picture achievement. The most revered and influential creator of his day, and perhaps of all motion picture history, he justified the new medium to the world.

The camera devices which every director uses today as a matter of course and without which the film as we know it would not be possible and which the public sees and accepts without a second thought, were first introduced by D. W. Griffith. As Leslie Wood says, "he created not only the essentially American film but laid down the rules of the game for all times."[2]

The years 1914-18 were a period of transition in the history of the American motion picture industry. When the war broke out American films constituted more than half of the world film production, and by 1917 they held a virtual monopoly of the world film market.[3] During the war boom the industry expanded rapidly and though at first it was ill prepared to serve as a war news agency, it was swiftly, mobilized for action' and used as a weapon of propaganda. Technically also the industry advanced. Many directors came into the limelight, including the world famous Charles Chaplin, the incomparable pantomimist, satirist and social critic, whose importance lies not in his contributions to the

[1] *Ibid*, p. 84.
[2] Leslie Wood, *The Romance of the Movies*, p. 138.
[3] Lewis Jacobs, *The Rise of the American Film*, p. 159.

film art but in his contributions to humanity. He will always be known for his social outlook, his insight into human nature and his pantomimic skill. Though not a technician, it is for these things that he is regarded as a screen artist. Unknown before 1914, by 1915 he was the screen idol of the world. He is a figure of fun to the masses who roar at his discomfort. To others, perhaps more sensitive, he is pathetic for in some ways he is themselves. For his actions, mistakes, self-deception and disillusionments are the very stuff of life.

The years 1919-29 mark the last decade in the annals of the silent film. Thereafter opens a new era in the motion picture history. The moving picture, the offspring of an unholy liaison between the magic lantern and the novelette, hitherto regarded as an ugly sister of the arts, was now recognized as an important member of the family.

Unrivalled by foreign films during the four years of war, American films had firmly established themselves at home and abroad including India, Western Asia and Africa. Hollywood had become the unquestioned motion picture centre of the world. Though technically flawless, the contents of the American films were trivial and shallow, so much so that while they were praised for their mechanical perfection, they were scoffed at for their low level of conception. In fact as Paul Rotha[1] observes, the American films of those days displayed an absence of good taste, intelligence and culture. They were easily made and as easily forgotten. Most of them were ephemeral in value.

While the industry was in this state, Hollywood was suddenly faced with foreign competition from European films far superior to many of its own productions. Outstanding films from Germany, France, Sweden and Soviet Russia roused American producers to the dramatic possibilities of the celluloid medium, and European talent was lured away to the U.S.A. with the bait of greater monetary gains.

Under the influence of European films and enriched

---

[1] Paul Rotha. *The Film Till Now,* pp. 79, 80, 144-5.

by European contributions, the workmanship of American motion pictures steadily improved throughout the postwar period culminating in the use of sound.

On August 6, 1926, Warner Brothers, a small company, produced the first picture *Don Juan* with sound equipment and followed it up in 1927, with their famous *The Jazz Singer*, the first film with synchronized music and dialogue.[1]

With the coming of sound, motion picture technique came to an abrupt halt. The industry was faced with a cataclysmic revolution and chaos was widespread. Film art was forgotten in the new craze for all talking and singing films. Early sound films were very crude. The dialogue was pompous and clumsy and pictorially speaking the first talkies were very dull. In fact technically and artistically the film lapsed to the elementary level of pre-war days.

Sound, however, was destined to remain, and once it was permanently accepted, rapid progress was made in perfecting its equipment and learning its artistic functions. The effect of the use of sound on every aspect of film making was far reaching and significant. "It altered some technique completely, modified others, quickened progress in all."[2]

The silent picture had spoken a universal language but with the introduction of dialogue all kinds of new problems with racial customs and accents were revealed in a terrifying array. Multi-lingual films, films with dialogue dubbed in foreign languages, and films with sub-titles were all tried, but with little success. And the problem of non-English speaking foreign markets remains unsolved even to this day.

Recovering from the Stock Market crash of 1929, the American film went forward to a decade of prosperity. Colour films were attempted. In 1935 appeared the first full-length colour film *Becky Sharp* and thereafter colour has taken its place as a permanent addition to film resources. "A considerable part of the

[1] Leslie Wood, *The Miracle of the Movies*, pp. 302-5.
[2] Lewis Jacobs, *The Rise of the American Film*, p. 433.

future of motion picture depends on advances in colour science" observes Lewis Jacobs.[1]

During the pre-war period many directors came into eminence, some of whom, even to this day, rank among the luminaries of Hollywood. Among all these, Walt Disney stands out "as the most distinctive and advanced of directors since the adoption of sound. He takes a position besides his fore-runners—George Melies, Edwin S. Porter, D. W. Griffith, the Germans and the Russians—as an important innovator and a great contributor to movie tradition. Though active only in the sphere of the animated cartoon, he nevertheless is more significant as a screen artist than any of his contemporaries."[2]

The disturbed and unsettled trend of national and international events during 1829-39 was reflected in the feature films and the news reels of this decade. The films became more serious in tone and focussed attention on economic and political corruption and maladjustments. Though the films reflected the times with greater reality, the treatment of this reality was often inadequate and meaningless.[3]

This was the state of affairs in the American film world, when the War broke out in 1939. The critical years which followed the fall of France in 1940 and, as far as America was concerned, especially after Pearl Harbour in December 1941, saw the motion picture mobilized for action. As stated in the Fourth Annual Report of the War Activities Committee: "The civilian audience at home, the uniformed audiences overseas, know that the industry accepted every assignment from the Government; completed every operation successfully, and gave of its time, its energy, its talent and its property beyond the call of duty."[4]

Not only were more and more films produced with war themes but the motion picture camera, especially the newsreel camera, went on active service to the front

[1] *Ibid*, p. 448.
[2] *Ibid*, pp. 453, 496.
[3] *Ibid*, p. 538.
[4] *Movies at War*, Vol. 4, Annual Report of the War Activities Committee, Motion Picture Industry, 1945, p. 1.

recording for posterity the pictorial story of the worst
upheaval in human history.

The end of the War in September 1945 and the celebration of the half-centenary of  the cinema in 1946
marked a new phase in the annals of the motion picture
industry.  In fifty years the mechanical contrivances of
Thomas  Edison,  Lumieres,  Friese-Greene,  Paul  and
others had developed into cameras and projectors capable of  entertaining the world whose  population  was
estimated to buy 235,000,000 seats a week.[1]  During
this period though the American film ranked (and still
ranks) supreme there  has  been  an  extraordinary  renaissance of British feature films since about 1940, so
much so that today they are rivalling some of America's
best products.  For this post-war expansion of British
films, J. Arthur Rank was largely responsible.  Under
his control the British film has made such rapid strides
in the field of international cinema holdings that it gave
rise to misgivings in some American quarters.  Trade
rivalries between the two countries have been settled by
agreement the ultimate outcome of which yet remains
to be seen.

In the films of today a high standard of technical
excellence has  become  a  commonplace feature.  The
facilities provided in a modern studio and the high level
of skill attained by qualified  technicians provide the
guarantee.  The result is that a picture has to be either
very badly made or very well made to fall outside the
general  run  and  provoke  comment   on  its  technical
merits.

What are the contents of the films of today?  Since
the war the men who make films have been exhibiting
more courage and have dared to venture into fields that
had heretobefore been considered taboo. Today writers
and directors have  returned  from the war with new
perspectives. They have realized that people want something besides the routine sort of story.  They want romance and adventure undoubtedly,  in addition  they
want realism, freshness and sparkle. Hence new themes
have  been  tried.  Shakespeare  has  been  brought

[1] Roger Manvell, *The Film*, p. 13.

to the screen. Films with psychological and similar themes which were at one time considered a trifle too strong have also appeared and proved very popular.

But outstanding films are rare. Generally speaking, from an artistic and social point of view the standard of American films has fallen. Richard Winnington complains of the bad films which have flooded the market. He says: "The cinema then, as represented by Hollywood, faces the turn of its first half century in the lowest possible condition of creative energy. . . ."[1] The total industrialisation of film manufacture from script to screen is largely responsible for this. Rarely does the writer see more than a vague ghost of his original conception after it has been picked at and mauled at every turn.

No less scathing in his comment is Emil Ludwig.[2] He says that Hollywood is to be condemned not only for destroying talent but for corrupting taste. It produces about 500 films a year, of which only five or six have any value. The merit of a film is judged by the box office and very rarely does an isolated critic venture to say in public that it is valueless.

In spite of what critics may have to say against Hollywood films of recent years, it cannot be denied that after fifty-three years of its existence, the film in Western countries can look back on its past achievement with pride. The film has endured and triumphed through its creative exuberance, not through its commercialism. From George Melies to Walt Disney it has developed its technique and enriched its powers of expression drawing greedily upon traditional arts as well as life for inspiration. But in every country the truly significant films which have marked the stages of progress stand out unique and apart from others. They are fit for comparison with the fiction, the painting or the drama of like date though they are utterly unlike them.

It would be foolish to minimize the immense contributions which America has made to the film's forward march. But in attempting to see what has been done

[1] Richard Winnington, 'Critic's Prologue', *Penguin Film Review* i, p. 28.
[2] Emil Ludwig, 'The Seven Pillars of Hollywood,' *Penguin Film Review* i, p. 95.

2

through many years and miles of celluloid it must be realized that advance has resulted always from the freest kind of international exchange and that many countries as well as many men have combined to confer upon the motion picture its peculiar importance and value in contemporary life.

*3*

## THE INDIAN SILENT FILM 1913-28

THE history of the film in India, from its imperfect and humble beginnings to its relatively high standards of perfection today, is a colourful record of the efforts and determination, hopes and ambitions, setbacks and despair of early pioneers who ventured forth into unknown and unchartered regions. No doubt their early experiments were failures but eventually their labours were crowned with success when, in 1913, the first Indian film, *Harischandra* was flashed on the silver screen. With it a new age in the sphere of mass entertainment opened, though few realized it then. Treated as an orphan by the Government, looked down upon by the higher classes in society, few took interest in this new art industry or realized its potentialities as a social force. Nevertheless it successfully overcame the initial difficulties and problems and has earned for itself a respectable place in our social life today.

There is little information to be had regarding the early days of the film in India. No authentic history of its rise and growth exists, nor are there any reliable statistics. In fact little interest was evinced in the motion picture till as late as 1928, when the Government and the industry were roused from their lethargy by the growing popularity of motion pictures among the masses. The Government appointed a committee which made a survey of the film industry in India and submitted its report which constitutes the only reliable source of information. Even this report gives little idea of conditions prior to 1921 and whatever little material one is able to gather about the previous history of the Indian film is sketchy and inadequate.

The rise and growth of the motion picture in the West and the curiosity it aroused, did not leave India unaffected. No sooner had the 'Cinematograph' made its appearance in Western countries, than within a few months 'this marvel of the century', this 'wonder of the world', as it was called, made its appearance in Bombay in June-July 1896. During that period, *The Times of India* reports that the Lumiere Brothers brought out a small machine and at Watson's Hotel (now Esplanade Mansion) gave three shows daily to the public at the admission price of Re. 1. The first show at the Novelty Theatre (site of the present Excelsior Theatre) took place on July 14, 1896. Here two shows a day were given and the admission fees ranged from 4 annas for the gallery to Rs. 2 for Orchestral Stalls and Dress Circle. Special boxes were even reserved for purdah ladies and their families. These were merely casual shows and no regular cinema performances were instituted till much later.

The very first cinema advertisement ever published in Bombay and in fact in this country, appeared in *The Times of India* dated July 7, 1896. Commenting on the advent of the cinematograph and on the nature of films exhibited it observed: "It is impossible to deny that the recent invention of Messrs. Lumiere Bros. is almost the greatest scientific discovery of the age. By its means life-size photographs are reproduced, every movement of the figure is accurate and despite the number of changes, accuracy is maintained. The figures are projected upon a screen and can thus be witnessed by a great number of spectators." The subjects depicted on the screen, such as the arrival of a train, sea bathers, London girl dancers, Parade of the Guard, Hyde Park, stormy sea, were reproduced in a very lifelike manner. "The distinctness with which each action of moving bodies was brought out showed to what an advanced stage the art of photography and the magic lantern had been brought. . . . The views being of a varied character found much favour, the more crowded scenes being applauded by the audience."

A year or two later an Italian named Signor Colonello, gave successful shows in Bombay. About the same time Mr. Jamshedjee Tata, the great industrialist, brought a cinema apparatus for private use and installed it in his home, Esplanade House. Soon after, some Europeans connected with the Paris-India Motor Car Co. of Hornby Road, opened a cinema show at the Novelty Theatre. They were followed by many enterprising firms and persons as for example, Messrs Clifton & Co., Photographers, who gave cinema performances at their studio in Medows Street in September 1897, P. A. Stewart, who held shows at the present Times of India building site and others like Khursedjee Baliwala, Morera, Edaljee Patel, Signor Limbo, who showed films of local interest as well as some scenes of the Boer War. These were the early pioneers who brought the film to India.

These early shows, however, were only sporadic attempts and regular shows commenced in Bombay and the rest of the country when M. Charles Pathe who had started a firm for the production of films and projection equipment under the Lumiere's patents in Paris in December 1897, opened a branch of the firm in Bombay in 1907. Thereafter with instruments and films supplied by Pathe, Messrs Colonello & Cornaglia who founded the Excelsior Cinema and Mr. P. B. Mehta who conducted his cinema under the name of America-India, commenced giving regular shows in their tents on the Esplanade Maidan.[1]

These were the first milestones in the history of the Indian cinema. Progress thereafter was very rapid. By 1910, many cinema halls had sprung up in cities where people flocked to see the foreign films. Even in towns, touring cinemas occasionally brought the thrills of the moving picture, though villages knew nothing about the new invention. Thus the film as a popular form of entertainment was an accomplished fact. Even

[1] *The Times of India,* July 7, 22, 27, 1896; *Ibid,* June 15, 21, 1948; *Ibid,* July 10, 1948.

then no one thought of producing an Indian film, till in 1913 Dadasaheb Phalke's first Indian film *Harischandra* was publicly exhibited. A landmark in the annals of Indian motion picture, this film earned for the producer the title of 'Father of the Indian Film Industry.'

D. G. Phalke was born at Trimbak near Nasik in 1870. From his early childhood he was interested in art and drama. In 1909 he went to Europe and learnt photo-engraving and photo-lithography, and for two years started and worked an art printing press. At that time foreign films were in great vogue, and once he saw a film based on the life of Jesus Christ. That show set his alert mind thinking and he visualized the image of Lord Krishna in the place of Jesus Christ. This idea soon became an obsession. On February 2, 1912 he sailed for Europe, returning within a couple of months. He brought with him a Williamson film camera, a printing machine and a perforator, for the raw films then available had no sprocket holes either for the camera or for the projector. Perforation had, therefore, to be done in a dark room foot by foot.

Having set up his 'studio', Phalke selected for production the story of Harischandra, from mythology. Financiers, however, were not willing to risk their capital in such a precarious business till they had some concrete examples of his ability. Phalke therefore had to pawn and sell his wife's ornaments so that he could produce a few typical shots for the financiers.

Raising money for production work, however, was not the only difficulty Phalke had to face. The next question that arose was who was to play the heroine of the story. Even courtesans and dancers thought it below their dignity to associate themselves with film acting. They jeered when told that film acting was an art. Ultimately, men had to be dressed as women, but even this was not easy as many refused to shave off their moustaches! Phalke's enthusiasm, however, was not damped by such adverse conditions. After much persuasion an actor was secured and eighteen months after his return from Europe, *Harischandra* the first full-length Indian picture was ready. It was 3700 feet long and was released to the public in 1913 at the Coronation Cinema, Sandhurst Road, Bombay. It was so popular that it proved a veritable gold mine.

One can imagine what a great event it must have been when Indian cinema-goers saw for the first time on the silver screen, a familiar story set in native surroundings and acted by people like themselves. This first enterprise was very successful and proved popular all over the country wherever it was shown.

It is a strange coincidence that *Harischandra* should have been presented at more or less the same time as Adolph Zukor presented the first multiple-reel feature film *Queen Elizabeth* which paved the way for the future feature films. Thus apparently as far as the origin of feature film goes, both East and West started together. The West however, advanced rapidly, while India lagged far behind.

The success of *Harischandra* encouraged Phalke to produce more films—*Bhasmasur Mohini* and *Savitri*. On his next visit to England he took his films along with him and had them screened there. They were admired and appreciated by the English audience and Phalke was congratulated on his skilful handling, good photography and spectacular background.

Between 1913 and 1918, Dadasaheb Phalke produced twenty-three films, the last of which was *Lanka Dahan*. It was in 1918 that Phalke was ultimately able to achieve his first dream of replacing Jesus on the celluloid by Krishna. In this film his daughter Mandakini played the role of the boy Krishna, incidentally becoming the first Indian juvenile actor. This film ran for ten months and was very popular wherever it was released. Following this came *Kaliya Mardan* in 1919, and after that for two years Phalke retired from film production due to difference of opinion with his partners. He was, however, recalled in 1923 and he produced *Sati Mahananda* and *Setu Bandhan*, two record-breakers of the time.

The life of Phalke has been one of romance and tragedy, for throughout his career fortune never gave him a fair deal. A pioneer in Indian film production, he worked twenty-one years and produced nearly a hundred films. Three-fourths of them he wrote, directed, photographed, processed and supervised personally.

The phenomenal success of Phalke's films did not leave enterprising men in other parts of India unaffected. More people were inspired to step into the production branch and Bombay's lead was soon followed by Bengal, the Punjab and finally Madras.

In Calcutta, J. F. Madan, a wealthy Parsi, originally from Bombay and owner of Elphinstone Bioscope Company, with a small crew of artistes and a cameraman, formed a producing unit. His first picture was *Nala Damayanti* released in 1917. It is interesting to note that the leading roles in it were played by Italians, namely, Signor and Signora Manelli.

During the decade 1920 to 1930 many other companies were formed in Bengal but only the Indian Kinema Arts founded in 1926 offered very serious competition to Madan and to a certain extent broke his monopoly in Bengal. In 1930, B. N. Sircar organized the International Film Craft which proved a successful venture and inspired him to establish the New Theatres Ltd. in 1931, the only producing company Bengal can be proud of today.

The Punjab was the next province to plunge into film production. In 1924, Sir Moti Sagar and Prem Sagar formed the Great Eastern Film Corporation. Their most important film *The Light of Asia* released in 1925, is a landmark in Indian film history. Based on the life of Gautama Buddha it was produced with the co-operation of a German firm, the Emelka Film Company of Munich. Himansu Rai, later to become famous as the founder of Bombay Talkies, directed the picture in collaboration with Frank Osten, but the technicians and the capital were mostly foreign.

*The Light of Asia* marks another important milestone in the industry's onward march. It was the first to be released abroad. It had its London premiere in 1926 at the Philharmonic Hall where, it is reported, it ran consecutively for over ten months. In a poll conducted by *The Daily Express* it was declared to be the third best picture of that year. By Royal Command the film was shown before King George V and Queen Mary. In all, 425 prints of the film were made for distribution all over the world. To the lot of the Great Eastern Corporation, however, fell only two positive prints for being exhibited in India to recover their investment of Rs. 90,000 in the making of *The Light of Asia*.

Undaunted, the Great Eastern Film Corporation launched its second venture, *The Love of a Moghul Prince*. It was released in 1928 but it was forestalled by the Imperial Film Company of Bombay releasing *Anarkali* based on the same theme, there being no copyright laws. Moreover the censors banned it in certain provinces, and this sounded the death knell of the Great Eastern Film Corporation.

Between 1925 and 1929 other film companies came into being but they had little success. The Punjab's main share in film production lies in the fact that from there many talented men and women have migrated south, especially to Bombay, where they have made their mark.

Till 1921, South India was getting an abundant supply of mythological pictures from Bombay and it had accordingly not entered into the race of film production. In 1921 was founded the Star Of The East Film Company and its first film *Bhishma Pratigna* was fairly popular. Other companies followed in its wake but most of them came to an untimely end.

Thus gradually the interest in film production started by Phalke in 1913 in Bombay spread to all corners of India. Many people tried their hand at this new scientific toy, some were successful while many lost all they had.

Not only Indians themselves but foreigners were also looking at India with interested eyes. It was the year 1911, significant in more respects than one, that brought the first foreigner to India in search of film material. Charles Urban of Kinema Colour Company of New York came with the purpose of making a short film of the Delhi Durbar and all the pomp and pageantry which went with Their Majesties' visit to India. Since then foreign producers have tried to exploit the East, but early foreign ventures like *The Sultaness of Love, Secrets of the East, Savitri, Shiraz,* however, were un-successful.

Even though the film industry was slowly but steadily spreading all over India, Bombay remained the hub of the industry, for the major part of production was centred there. In Bombay City and Province many companies sprang up, among which the important ones were, Oriental Film Manufacturing Company, Kohinoor Film Company, Ranjit Film Company, Imperial Film Company; Maharashtra Film Company, Kolhapur and Hindusthan Film Company, Nasik. These companies turned out many pictures. Mythology was their favour-ite subject and Ram, Krishna, Hanuman and other mythological deities came out from the cold printed pages of the Epics in a new visual form but bereft of speech, to entertain the teeming millions of India. In August 1920 the Oriental Film Manufacturing Company broke new ground by producing the first topical film *The Cremation of the Late Lokmanya B. G. Tilak.*[1]

Even though motion picture production had begun in India in 1913, the number of films produced was neg-ligible, and till 1921 most of the pictures shown were foreign. Import of foreign films had begun early and increased in volume from year to year. The early thrill-ers and sensational adventure films running into several instalments helped to convert hundreds of entertain-ment-hungry people into ardent film fans. It was be-cause of the growing popularity and influence of motion pictures that the Cinematograph Act was passed in 1918. Another milestone, this Act gave legal recognition to the industry, laid down certain fundamental rules regarding the place and exhibition of cinematograph films and, in place of previous arbitrary film censorship, set up Boards of Film Censors in Bombay, Calcutta, Madras, Rangoon and a few years later, in Lahore.

However, during the early years progress was very slow, for the trade and industry entirely depended on

[1] *Indian Cinematograph Year Book*, 1938, pp. 115-21.

foreign material, and were much affected by World War I. Consequently till 1919 the number of cinema theatres throughout the country was just over a hundred while in the production branch of the industry D. G. Phalke was practically the only one who contributed his small but ambitious quota of indigenous films. In fact the percentage of Indian to total footage of films examined by the Boards of Censors in India in 1921-22 and 1926-27 was only 9.57 per cent and 15.20 per cent respectively.[1] The chief concern of the trade at that time was the foreign film which, produced by well organized concerns and backed by sound finances, was fast establishing itself in the country as the following table shows.[2]

| Year | No. of foreign feature films | Footage of feature films examined in India. | Foreign feature films examined by the Bombay Board of Film Censors | Footage of foreign films examined by Bombay Board | Percentage of foreign films examined by Bombay Board |
|---|---|---|---|---|---|
| 1921-22 | 615 | 3,083,355 | 438 | 2,024,913 | 71.1 |
| 1926-27 | 775 | 4,316,996 | 564 | 2,549,084 | 72.8 |

Cinema theatres were also steadily on the increase as seen below.[3]

| Year | No. of cinemas all over India (excluding Burma) | Total seating accommodation | No. of cinemas in Bombay Province | Percentage of cinemas in Bombay Province | Seating accommodation in Bombay Province |
|---|---|---|---|---|---|
| 1921 | 121 | .. | 54 | 44.6 | .. |
| 1924 | 171 | .. | 54 | 31.6 | .. |
| 1927 | 251 | 174,350 | 77 (includes 20 in Bombay City) | 30.6 | 51,941 |

A realization of the immense commercial possibilities of Indian films quickened film production and film companies began to multiply rapidly. One company

[1] *Report of the Indian Cinematograph Committee*, 1927-28, pp. 184-5.
[2] *Ibid.*
[3] *Ibid*, pp. 179-80.

after another arose only to disintegrate, either through
internal dissensions or through competition with better
established concerns. There were fantastic successes and
failures, because many looked upon the films as a get-
rich-quick business.   However, some of these companies survived long enough to make a name for themselves.
Along with the rise of companies, production became
vigorous and Indian features which numbered only 63
in 1921-22 (of which 45 were produced in Bombay) rose
to 108 in 1926-27, Bombay's share being 96.[1]

In the early days of indigenous film production, the
pioneers were concerned mainly in coping with the increasing demand.   They gave little time or thought to
improving the technical side of the industry.   Consequently there was complete neglect and stagnation in
this aspect of production.

There were no studios worth the name.   Most of
the shooting was done in bungalow compounds.   It was
not till 1920 that artificial lighting was used.   Even the
actors were largely borrowed from the stage while only
dancing girls were available to act the feminine roles.
D. G. Phalke's attempts in securing a cast for his first
picture testify to the fact that film acting was looked
upon by society as something disgraceful.   It is therefore not surprising that Anglo-Indian women and sometimes foreign artistes were selected to play the leading
roles.

The whole process of Indian film production was
permeated by stage technique; curtains were used instead of sets, the gestures and actions of the artistes were
exaggerated and unrealistic and had a crude theatrical
touch and even the costumes were of the same hybrid,
tawdry variety as used by players in the theatrical productions of those days.

The stage also influenced the selection of themes
and stories for films. Mythological plays were made into
mythological films and the folklore and legends of ancient India were gone through in search of film material.
The year 1920 may be put down as marking the end of
what may be termed the exclusively mythological era of

[1] *Ibid*, pp. 184-5.

the Indian screen.  By then hardly an episode from the *Ramayan* or the *Mahabharat* was left which had not been filmed, and indeed some of the more popular legends had been produced over and over again.  While today there is a cry for sophisticated and modern pictures and one is inclined to regard mythological films with disfavour, one cannot deny that they did serve a purpose by establishing the screen as a popular medium of entertainment.  The vast mass of conservative Indians probably would not have taken to the innovation of cinema had they not been drawn to it not only by curiosity but also by their age-old interest in mythology and folklore. We cannot therefore accuse the producer of playing on the religious sentiment of the people.  Even in the West, in the early stages of film production,  Biblical themes were resorted to, though these were quickly discarded for something more popular and more suited to the film art.

In course of time, however, overdone mythology was not sufficient to satisfy the hunger of entertainment-starved masses, and a number of new producing concerns which came into being in 1919-20 were faced with a shortage of scenarios.  They wanted something different from the age-old mythological themes and therefore started a cycle of Rajput pictures which sought to win public favour by spicy tales of martial heroism and chivalry, presented with all the adventure and thrill of the Wild West film.  Rajput  history  and  legends were  ransacked  for  suitable  material,  and  when even  these  were  exhausted,  resourceful  producers  started  adapting  American  adventure  films  to the  Indian  scene  thereby  creating  the  'stunt film'.  To  appeal  to  popular  imagination  such films were packed with the most amazing exploits and adventures, impossible acts of heroism and superhuman feats of athletics.  This was the time when the hero fought an army of men single-handed, brandished a tin sword and always arrived on a galloping horse just in time to save the heroine from the clutches of the evil-looking villain.  Anyone who could ride and make a pretence of wielding a sword became a film star over-

night.  Several variations of stunt films were also very
popular and Douglas Fairbank's *Thief of Baghdad* created a vogue for similar action pictures.  These 'nerve
tinglers', as they were called, enthralled the uncritical
spectators.  The dare-devil stunts they contained were
crudely faked but to the enraptured audience any lack
of realism was unnoticeable.  The physical impact, the
mounting suspense, the death-defying leaps swept the
onlookers along with the story.  They stamped their
feet and often cried out in the spirit of participation with
the actors.

The next important step was the development of
social themes on the screen.  It is difficult now to trace
the origin of this term but in the language of the Indian
film industry, 'social' is still used to describe a film in
which the atmosphere, settings and costumes are modern, as distinct from a mythological or a historical film.

While the evolution of film content was taking place,
film technique was also making progress.  More and
better cinema houses were built and there was a demand
for films of a superior quality.   While it is no doubt
true that producers were motivated by a desire for quick
returns and minimum investments there were noticeable improvements in the equipment of the studios as
well as their products.  Indian films were getting an
encouraging response and the prospects seemed bright.
None the less financially and otherwise the real state
of the industry was completely chaotic.  Government
which was getting a good revenue from the industry had
very little idea about the exact scope and nature of the
motion picture in India.  As for the public, it was not
only ignorant about the industry but some sections of it
were definitely opposed to it and kept themselves scru-
pulously away from it.  Motion picture production was
thus left to the dictates of a few interested persons who
moulded the film according to their own experience and
narrow ideas.

In the history of the Indian film industry the appointment of the Indian Cinematograph Committee on
October 6, 1927, by the Government of India is an important milestone.  The Committee was appointed "to

examine and report on the system of censorship of cinematograph films in India and to consider whether it is
desirable that any steps should be taken to encourage
the exhibition of films produced within the British Empire generally and the production and exhibition of Indian films in particular."[1] The Committee visited
important centres and collected evidence from witnesses verbally as well as in writing. The latter was obtained through a questionnaire issued to responsible
members of the public. The findings of the Committee
were published in a Report, the only authentic source of
information available today.

On careful investigation, the Committee came to the
conclusion that the industry defective as it was in many
respects, was not altogether negligible and it was vital
that the Government should take early steps to guide,
control and utilize, in the interests of Indians, the
potentialities of the cinema. The Government, however, was apathetic. Consequently the Report was
shelved among forgotten documents. The only action
taken by the Government was to issue a resolution on
August 7, 1928, to the effect that "the Report should be
published for general information. . . . and the Governor-
General-in-Council has no doubt that the Report of the
Committee will prove of great value both as a comprehensive presentment of conditions now obtaining in
India and as material for the determination of future
policy."[2]

The industry's reaction to the Report was also not
encouraging. Due to a misunderstanding in the initial stages it was non-co-operative, and since none of
the suggestions of the Committee were accepted by the
Government it was looked upon as a sheer waste of
money. In fact, the industry's journal *Lighthouse* dated
July 30, 1938, went to the extent of saying that "the Report of the Indian Cinematograph Committee was buri-
ed because no word of protection for British films was
therein visible in pursuance of the ideal of Imperial Pre-

[1] Resolution passed by the Council of State on September 15, 1927. *Report of the Indian Cinematograph Committee, 1927-28*, p. xi.
[2] *Gazette of India*, Part I, August 11, 1928, p. 703.

ference which was the preamble of that Report."[1]

The press was divided in its opinion as to the value of the Report and its various recommendations. To *The Times of India*,[2] the Report provided "considerable amount of entertainment" due to some of its blundering remarks and it scathingly criticized the various recommendations put forth by the Committee. The two main proposals of the Committee, viz. the establishment of a Central Bureau under the Government of India and the scheme for providing cinema films with capital raised by loans from the general public, were partly disapproved, on the ground that the businessman did not want any Government interference in what had proved to be a thriving industry, though the suggestion to establish a Central Bureau for diffusion of knowledge was admirable if properly organized.

*The Bombay Chronicle*[3] on the other hand, approved of the above two recommendations and thought that the method suggested by the Committee for financing the new bodies sound and sensible. The only thing it disapproved of was the recommendation that the members of the Central Bureau should be nominated by the Government. In its opinion it would have been preferable to have the members elected by trade associations or the Central and Provincial legislatures.

In regard to the establishment of a Central Board of Censors, *The Bombay Chronicle* was all in favour of it provided the members were elected, but *The Times of India* was sceptical as to how it would function, and how the new censorship regulations would be taken by the industry.

On the question of giving preference to Empire films, the most debated question, these two leading papers took up opposite views. While *The Bombay Chronicle* was delighted that the Committee had refused to give any special preference or encouragement to films produced within the Empire, *The Times of India* felt that "the proposal to raise the import duty on Empire

1 *Journal of the Film Industry*, August 1945, p. 2.
2 *The Times of India*, August 8, 1928.
3 *The Bombay Chronicle*, August 8, 1928.

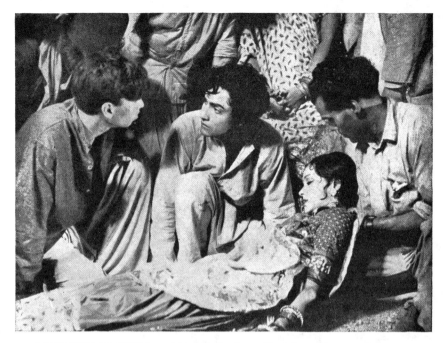

ACHHUT KANYA: *Directed by Frank Osten; featuring Devika Rani and Ashok Kumar; Bombay Talkies; 1936.*

AMAR JYOTI: *Directed by V. Shantaram; featuring Durga Khote and Chandramohan; Prabhat Film Co.; 1936.*

HARISHCHANDRA:
Produced and direct-
ed by D. G. Phalke
—1913.

(Top) Phalke re-
hearsing his actors
b e f o r e  shooting.

(Middle)  A  still
from the film.

(Bottom)  Phalke
editing the picture.

films along with others, was short sighted." The Indian film, in its opinion, could not exist without a large overseas market. It argued that if India would not co-operate with the rest of the Empire at its express invitation, there would be only one course open to the rest of the Empire—and that was to treat Indian films with the same strict unfriendliness and discouragement.

In spite of these differences of opinion the press was unanimous in its opinion that the Report contained a great deal of valuable and useful material admirably set forth. It, for the first time, presented a mass of information about the cinema in the country which revealed to the public, to the members of the industry and to the Government what an important problem the cinema had become, while the factual data it presented provided sound basis for discussion.

The appointment of a Committee at that juncture was indeed opportune, for at that time the industry, though still in its infancy, had reached a sufficient stage of development to enable a definite opinion to be formed regarding its quality and characteristics, its effects and possibilities. Moreover, it was entirely in Indian hands. Foreign interests, though watchful, had not established any control over it. Thus it was a time most suited for guidance and encouragement if the industry was to make any advance. The Report, however, did not affect the actual course of the industry because none of its recommendations were put into practice.

The task that was entrusted to the Committee was indeed very comprehensive. It was faced with many difficulties in the course of its investigations. The main difficulty which it experienced from the outset was the complete dearth of statistics and reliable information regarding the production, distribution and exhibition of Indian films and even to some extent regarding the import of foreign films. The departments of the Government of India and of various Local Governments had practically no information regarding these matters. Even in the industry itself there was the same dearth of accurate data. The material the Committee was able

3

to gather from different members within the industry was widely divergent. This complete dearth of reliable knowledge has been only partly remedied and still remains a major problem of the film industry today.

None the less, the Committee tackled the formidable task efficiently. It made its investigations as widespread and comprehensive as it could and based its conclusions on the general impression formed from the considerable amount of evidence which had come before it.

Making a survey of the conditions then prevailing in the industy the Committee found that though there was a fairly large proportion of indigenous film production, it was not generally known to the Government or the public. In fact the number of feature films produced in India was in excess of the number of films produced in the United Kingdom during the same periods. For example, during the years 1925, 1926 and 1927 the number of feature films produced in England was 34, 26 and 48 respectively. The approximate number of feature films produced in India was 70 in 1924-25, 111 in 1925-26 and 108 in 1926-27.[1] Though Indian films formed an appreciable percentage of the total and were very popular with Indian audiences, the majority of films exhibited were foreign, especially American which formed nearly 80 per cent of the total imported films.

It is impossible to compare the 'screen time' then devoted to Indian films with the time given to foreign films as no data are to be had. Some indication, however, of the extent to which Indian films were shown can be given by the number and footage of our films examined by the Boards of Censors. Between 1921 and 1927 there had been a gradual increase in our film production, but it was not uniform. The footage of Indian film to the total footage examined had also registered an increase. It was 9.57 per cent in 1921-22, 11.06 per cent in 1923-24, 16.05 per cent in 1925-26 and 15.26 per cent in 1926-27,[2] the rest being foreign footage. These figures, however, do not give any indication of the

[1] *Report of The Indian Cinematograph Committee*, 1927-28, p. 29.
[2] *Ibid*, pp. 184-5.

'screen time' involved as one film may be shown in ten cinemas while another may be shown in fifty. Moreover, several copies of the same film may be circulated, and there is always a tendency to show Indian films for longer continuous periods than western films. For example, in Bombay and other cities an Indian film if it is popular often has a run of several weeks in the same cinema. Besides, some cinema houses show exclusively foreign films. All these factors mar the possibility of judging accurately the 'screen time' devoted to indigenous productions.

During the same period there had been an increase in the number of imported films from 1320 in 1921-22 to 1429 in 1926-27 with a corresponding increase in the footage from 3,711,283 to 4,920,427.[1] These figures, however, do not give an accurate idea of the increase because for the years 1921 and 1922 those figures are unusually large owing to the fact that when the Cinematograph Act was passed in 1918 a very large number of films were put before the Boards for examination and were given a certificate at a nominal charge of one rupee often without examination.

Though fourteen years had elapsed since the inception of indigenous films, producing agencies in India in 1927 were still comparatively small and with the exception of Madan Theatres Ltd, Calcutta, were either privately owned or partnership concerns. The capital invested did not ordinarily exceed Rs. 200,000. The majority of the producers were neither experienced businessmen nor well-qualified technicians nor men of culture. Most of them had acquired their knowledge through experience. Some companies had a few trained directors and technicians, but the training had generally been of a desultory character. In spite of these handicaps, it is indeed creditable that they should have achieved as much as they did. At the same time it must be said that had they been better trained and better equipped our films today would not have been so technically and artistically inferior to those of the West. In

[1] *Ibid.*

1927-28 there were twenty-one producing concerns in India. Of these, two were situated in Indian States, viz. the Maharashtra Company at Kolhapur, and the Lakshmi Pictures Company at Baroda. Bombay was the centre of the producing industry. There were 13 producing agencies in Bombay Presidency including the one at Kolhapur. Calcutta was the other centre where there was an appreciable amount of production. Here there were four companies, the most important being Madan Theatres Ltd. Lahore had two producing concerns but they were mostly given to the production of a few topical, educational and public utility films for Government. In 1927 there was no film production in Madras, though a few films had been produced there in the past. Of these 21 companies only 8 or 9 kept up a steady output; the rest produced intermittently and in small numbers. In regard to the large number (as compared to the total output) of producing concerns in India, it is interesting to note that in the U.S.A., although there are a great many smaller producers, the bulk of pictures are produced by a very few, perhaps seven or eight companies.[1]

Till 1927-28 Indian films had made little technical progress, for most of the studios were bare and ill-equipped. The Committee inspected 13 of them and found them primitive, consisting of one or two areas walled with high screens and with a glass roof or merely a framework with curtains for diffusing the light. Attached to these studios were rooms where films were developed, printed, titled and edited. As for artificial lighting only two or three producers employed arc lamps, the 'technicians' had no knowledge of how to use them and intended learning through experiment. While in the West artificial lighting was regarded as indispensable in the shooting of scenes, in India a system of reflecting mirrors was used, which was not as efficient as artificial lights. All the companies did not develop and print their own negatives because they did not know how to do it nor did they have the necessary equipment. The technical staff consisted essentially of a director or

1 *Ibid*, pp. 31-2.

directors, and cameramen. Most of them had no training. There was also a tendency for one man in the
studio to perform several functions probably due to the
paucity of trained men.

In spite of the facilities that India offered for film
production with its sunshine and natural scenery, technical and financial difficulties curtailed the average output of studios. In 1927, only one company had an average annual output of 15 pictures; four or five companies
had an output of 10 to 12 pictures and the rest produced 4 or 5 pictures or even fewer.[1] They readily
found a market for their production as the demand was
very great and the audience uncritical.

On an average about three prints were made of a
picture. The life of a print varied  enormously but it
generally lasted 150 days[2] shown daily, though of course
much depended on the care and skill of the operator and
the condition of his projector.

In 1927-28 the cost of production had not reached
the mammoth proportions as it often does now, for the
average cost was about fifteen to twenty thousand rupees
per film.[3] This was so because labour was cheap,
salaries of actors and actresses and even film stars were
low, and to appeal to the masses elaborate production
or a high standard of art and technique was not necessary. The gullible and ignorant audience would swal-
low anything provided it was a picture which moved!
Generally if a picture was a good box-office hit its cost
of production was recovered rapidly in Bombay and
cther key cities, and thereafter the returns dribbled in
from other mofussil centres. The returns varied. Large
gains were made on some of the more successful films
though of course nothing in comparison with the incredible amount made by some American producers. On
an average there was a good margin of profit.

Even though the business was a profitable one,
Indian capital was shy and not easily forthcoming to

[1] *Ibid,* p. 35.
[2] *Ibid.*
[3] *Ibid,* p. 26.

finance the producer. Consequently the producer had often to wait for the returns of one picture before he could undertake another. Generally the producer got the required money either by loans obtained at a usurious rate of interest or awaited the returns on his previous production. Apart from the general apathy of the public and the number of film failures, the unscrupulous business methods of the producers evoked little respect from the public.

To make matters worse, it was very difficult to obtain artistes to take part in films. There was no lack of talented men and women, but generally women from higher social classes were not attracted to the profession of film acting which they considered disreputable. Most of the actors and actresses were untrained. Some intelligent ones had picked up their metier by studying Western films, while the rest simply depended on the director who often knew as little as they did. The various photographic tests carried out in America before an actor or actress was deemed suitable for film acting were unknown in India where producers and directors had little choice in making the selection. Large studios kept a permanent staff of actors and actresses whose salaries ranged from Rs. 30 for a good actor or actress to Rs. 700 to Rs. 800 for a film star,[1] in strange contrast to American conditions where during the boom period following World War I, salaries of film stars, along with other factors of production, reached gigantic proportions.

The general backwardness prevailing in Indian production was also to be found in the distribution section of the film industry. There was no organized system of distribution. It was undeveloped and the methods followed were far from uniform.

Foreign films were imported and distributed by four major concerns, namely: Universal Pictures Corporation Ltd., Pathé India Ltd., Madan Theatres Ltd., and Globe Theatres Ltd. The former two were in Bombay and the latter two in Calcutta. These four companies supplied most of the Western films exhibited in the

[1] *Ibid,* p. 33.

country. Universal Pictures supplied 85 cinemas, Pathé about 100, Madan 85 and Globe 35.[1]

The distribution of Indian films was in most cases undertaken by the producers themselves who negotiated directly with the exhibitors. Only a few of the Indian producers employed a distributing agency. In such cases the distributor was under an obligation to distribute only pictures of a particular company and himself often advanced the money to the producer.

The block booking system, under which the exhibitor who wished to obtain certain good pictures of recognized box-office value was compelled to accept with them a few inferior films, was to some extent prevalent in India also, but was not as great an evil as it had become in America. Thus the exhibitors had little choice and in smaller towns they booked their films from the reception given to pictures at their first release in important cities.

As regards exhibition, the number of permanent cinemas was 251, while there were about 35[2] seasonal cinemas mostly in hill stations which were open only for a part of the year. There were numerous halls which were occasionally used for cinema performances but these have been excluded from the above figures, as it was impossible to estimate their exact number.

In addition to these permanent cinemas there were an indefinite number of travelling cinemas. Provincial Governments estimated the number at about 111.[3] These travelling cinemas visited big fairs and smaller provincial towns where there were no picture houses. They sometimes hired local halls but more generally carried with them their own tents and benches in bullock carts. They halted for varying periods at the centres they visited and their admission charge was two annas and often even an anna. Ordinarily, they exhibited old, second-hand Western films purchased very cheaply and often in very bad condition. Very seldom

[1] *Ibid*, p. 26.
[2] *Ibid*,p. 179.
[3] *Ibid*, pp. 24-5.

were Indian films exhibited by them. Most of these cinemas were poorly organized, badly equipped and unprofitable concerns.

The number of permanent cinema houses though limited, showed a progressive increase from year to year. From 121 in 1921, the number more than doubled to 251 in 1927. Even in the number of cinemas, Bombay Province headed the list with 77 permanent cinemas in 1927. Next came Madras with 43, United Provinces with 28, Bengal 26, Punjab 22, Central Provinces 15, Bihar & Orissa 13, North-West Frontier Province 10, Delhi and Assam 3 each and about 11 others in cantonments situated in Indian States. Out of these, 67 were in provincial capitals and the rest in the smaller provincial towns.[1]

From the above figures, it is obvious that the number of cinemas in the country was very small compared to the population. There were 251 cinemas with a total seating accommodation of 174,350 for a population of 248,000,000 i.e. one cinema for every 988,048 of the population. Compared to other countries this number was woefully small. For example, the U.S.A. and Great Britain had 20,500 and 3,700 cinemas respectively for a population of 120,000,000 and 47,146,506 i.e. approximately one cinema for every 5,857 and 12,740[2] people respectively.

This shows very clearly that the cinema played a most insignificant part in the life of our country and there was ample scope for expansion. Moreover, cinema shows were very sparsely attended. The small number of cinemas and low attendance are explained partly by the poverty of the people, partly by the fact that the great majority resided in villages where a film very rarely found its way, and partly by the fact that Indians were not as 'movie conscious' as the people of the West.

Here a distinction must be drawn between Western and Indian cinema houses, i.e. between picture houses which showed exclusively foreign films and catered

[1] *Ibid*, pp. 179-80.
[2] *Ibid*, pp. 19, 65.

mainly for Europeans, Anglo-Indians and educated Indians and those theatres which showed exclusively Indian films and catered wholly for Indian audiences. A few of the former existed in almost every city and showed only foreign films. Of the 213 cinemas regarding which information was available, 56 showed foreign films exclusively, 4 showed Indian films while 153 showed both.[1]

The number of cinema houses being very small, the market for Indian films was very limited. The type and class of films produced here had no prospect whatsoever of a market in the U.S.A. or England. A few Indian films found a market in places where there was an appreciably large Indian population, as for example in Ceylon, East Africa and South Africa.

The existing cinema houses left much to be desired. The large, luxurious auditoriums and buildings, common in cities of the West after 1918, did not exist in India. There were a few comfortable, well-fitted theatres, but the majority of them were cheap, unpretentious constructions which somehow served the purpose. The admission fee ranged from three annas to two or three rupees with special charges for boxes. The price of seats in cinemas showing foreign films was generally higher. The music varied according to the class of the audience who patronized the hall. In those cinemas frequented by Europeans and educated Indians, Western music was generally provided by means of a piano or a small orchestra; while in those patronized exclusively by Indians, Indian music regaled the audience.

L'Estrange Fawcett describing the condition of the smaller cinemas in Britain says: "The music is bad, the attendants incompetent, the equipment of the building out of date, the seats uncomfortable. It is marvellous what the public will endure and how the entertainment purveyor drives them..."[2] No description could be more apt than this one for the conditions prevalent

[1] *Ibid*, p. 181.
[2] *Ibid*, p. 66.

in picture houses showing Indian films in 1927.

Though the cinema in India had made some progress, it had scarcely touched the fringe of the vast rural population. Those who attended the cinema were generally inhabitants of cities and larger towns. Only to a very slight extent was the rural population affected through the travelling cinema. The composition of the audience varied according to the part of the country as well as the particular locality in which the cinema was situated and according to which class it belonged i.e. whether it showed Indian or foreign films. It is, therefore, not possible to lay down any classification of an average audience which would be true for the country as a whole.

No survey of the conditions prevailing in the Indian cinemas just before the coming of the 'talkies' would be complete without a mention of the kinds of films shown and their respective popularity. Both Western and Indian films were widely exhibited. There was no prejudice against Western films which were much enjoyed and appreciated. In fact, certain types of Western films appealed to all classes and communities. The spectacular films featuring Douglas Fairbanks, Harold Lloyd and Charles Chaplin had a universal appeal and were enthusiastically received in every cinema. The most popular foreign feature film of those years was *The Thief of Baghdad* with its oriental setting and starring Douglas Fairbanks.

The taste of educated Indians who had a knowledge of English and were acquainted with Western ideas was akin to those of Europeans, and generally the same films —whether love stories, comedies or whatever they may be — which were popular in the West were appreciated by this section of the community. The bulk of the population, however, enjoyed films with plenty of action, especially comic and adventure films, but found no attraction in the more sophisticated love stories. Being unable to read the captions which were generally in English, they derived their main pleasure from watching the action and stunts. If there was plenty of action they could follow the sequence of events, were quick to grasp the significance of scenes and pick up the main thread of the story.   Loud applause was often heard from the pit when the hero administered summary justice to the villain or rescued the heroine in the nick of time.   Even today, the majority of our audience at an Indian film are not so sophisticated as not to applaud when a particular scene appeals to them.   On the other hand, the love story depending for its appeal on some matrimonial entanglement or other complications of an entirely alien social life, was quite unintelligible to an audience of this class.   At one time the 'serials' which consisted of a series of sensational and thrilling episodes—fighting, kidnapping, escapes, rescues with a lavish employment of motor cars, aeroplanes and submarines were the most popular type of films with the masses.   Gradually, however, they were supplanted by Indian films.

Indian feature films, in spite of their crudity, were very popular with the masses. Most of the pictures produced were either mythological, religious, historical or 'social' dramas including stunt films. Mythological films like *Krishna Janma* not only had a special attraction for the uneducated but appealed to Hindus of all classes throughout the country. Films of a historical or quasi-historical character were also popular.   The so-called historical films (where history was often fictitious) were, however, very stereotyped and unconvincing.   Indian history is rich in romantic stories many of which are suitable for film adoption, but they had not been drawn upon partly due to lack of financial resources and partly due to dearth of capable script writers.   There was also the additional difficulty of showing certain Muslim historical characters on the screen, as it was liable to rouse objection from Muslims, even though the fact represented may have been historically correct; for example, Queen Raziya not observing purdah.   Such objections whether justifiable or not, strictly circumscribed the scope of the producers.

Social themes in which the atmosphere, setting and dress were modern were also popular, but their appeal was limited by provincial differences of customs and dress. In this type of film there was a tendency not only to borrow plots and incidents from Western novels but also to imitate Western films, both in action and treatment. This crude imitation of foreign films was neither pleasing nor successful.

Comedies and satires did not then exist in the Indian film world though comic scenes were sometimes introduced.

Apart from other production problems, there was the additional difficulty of language. An Indian film had little chance of success unless the sub-titles were in the regional language of the area in which it was shown. It is no doubt true that Western films were popular though they did not have vernacular captions, but an Indian film was expected to have titles in different provincial languages, and that was the reason why it was preferred. No doubt a considerable portion of the audience was unable to read its own vernacular, but it was usual for those who could, to read out aloud for the benefit of others. It was, therefore, necessary to have titles in four or five regional languages, with the result that the film suffered in its presentation and became lengthy and costly.

On the whole, Indian pictures were crude in comparison with Western films in all respects. They were defective both from an artistic as well as from a technical point of view. Plots and scenarios were indifferent and lacked originality. The action was wooden and unexpressive. Scenes of fighting and struggles, profusely introduced to appeal to the popular taste, were weak. Episodes were long drawn out and action was slow. Composition and photography were poor; and generally films were too long and boring.

In spite of its obvious inferiority, the Indian feature film was very popular especially with the uneducated and semi-educated classes. To the educated Indians, however, used to superior foreign films, indigenous films compared very unfavourably. Nevertheless, a suitable Indian picture drew a much larger audience than a foreign film.

As Indian films were generally more popular it goes without saying that in cinemas which showed both Indian and foreign films an Indian film was ordinarily more profitable than a Western film. Although an exhibitor paid more for an Indian film, his gross receipts were greater owing to much larger attendance. The crowds which flocked to see an Indian film were indeed remarkable. Exhibitors, however, could not always obtain Indian films as the demand was great. And it was very difficult to obtain the better productions, which commanded relatively higher prices than ordinary foreign films.

As regards news and topical films, they were exhibited only in first class cinemas. The most widely exhibited were the Pathé Gazettes (British) which were imported in considerable numbers. The footage of these Gazettes which passed through the Boards of Censors was 217,480 in 1925-26 and 243,982 in 1926-27.[1] Extremely few Indian newsreels and topical films were exhibited. The first Indian topical was *The Cremation of the Late Lokmanya B. G. Tilak* produced by the Oriental Film Manufacturing Company, in 1920. This lead was not followed by other companies for there was no demand for such films which were, therefore, not profitable. J.F. Madan, however, produced a few, both for home consumption and export and found them profitable, no doubt because of the facilities he had for exhibition in his large circuit of theatres. Generally speaking, attempts to produce topical Indian newsreels were not successful.

A study of the survey made by the Indian Cinematograph Committee in 1927-28, in spite of all its limitations, brought to the forefront many aspects, problems and defects of the Indian film industry which had hitherto been concealed from the gaze of the public, the Government and also from many members of the industry itself. Drawing general conclusions from the facts as they existed then, it can be said without hesitation that

[1] *Ibid*, p. 25.

while the industry had made some progress, the need
for improvement was indeed very great if the films were
to continue their hold on the general mass of the public.

With the appointment of the Cinematograph Committee ends one phase in the history of the cinema in
India.   It is indeed a strange coincidence that an attempt to stabilize the Indian film industry should have
been made at the very time when the cinema was on the
threshold of a new age.   In fact, in the whole history
of motion pictures, the years 1927-29 are very significant
for they mark the death of the silent era and the birth
of the 'talkies'.   A cataclysmic revolution had taken
place in the industry for, henceforth, sound and spoken
dialogue were incorporated as permanent elements in
the movies.   The Indian film was faced with a problem
of how to meet these new changes with the poor equipment it had.   But in spite of initial difficulties it gradually adapted itself to the changing circumstances, and with
the production of the first talkie, *Alam Ara,* in 1931, a
new page had been written in the annals of the motion
picture in India.

# 4

## THE INDIAN FILM 1931 - 49

THE advent and establishment of sound as a major and permanent factor in the motion picture technique of the West, and the production of the first Indian talkie *Alam Ara* in 1931, have already been noted. While the American and European film had reached a state of maturity when sound first invaded the motion picture domain, the Indian film was still in its infancy when circumstances compelled it to adopt the innovation. Nevertheless, it proved itself equal to the task, for *Alam Ara* produced in Hindustani by the Imperial Film Company of Bombay, featuring Master Vithal and Zubeida and directed by Ardeshir M. Irani, was a great success. The public which was taken by storm, packed the Majestic Cinema, Bombay, to suffocation on the opening night, March 14, 1931. A landmark in the history of Indian film, this picture paved the way for future Indian talkies.

### PERIOD OF TRANSITION 1931-35

Encouraged by the success of the first talkie, other companies followed suit. Madan Theatres Ltd. produced *Shirin Farhad* featuring Kajjan and Nissar which was an even greater success than *Alam Ara*. Next came the Prabhat Film Company with its two masterpieces, *The King of Ayodhya* produced both in Hindustani and Marathi and *Jalti Nishani* produced in Hindustani.

These early pictures established the talkie vogue in India and started a new phase in the development of the Indian film.   In a couple of years the entire Indian output turned into one hundred per cent talking and singing film.

In the other provinces of India producers were adopting this novel technique. Sind which had hitherto hardly ventured into the industry came forward in 1933 with the production of *Insan-ya-Shaitan* by the Eastern Arts Production.   It was made at the Imperial Film Company's studio at Bombay under the direction of Moti Gidwani and was a great success.   Equally successful was its next picture *Prem Pariksha* (1934) but its greatest triumph was *Bharat-ki-Beti* (1935). The company did not, however, continue long in the field of production and went into liquidation in 1936.

During this period at least twenty other companies had been established but only three of them were partially successful.

In the Punjab also, the course of events was the same as in Sind. Many companies emerged, but most of them failed.   Finally some of  the  more  enterprising young men moved to Bombay where they started production on their own.

Bombay was the major centre of production and by the end of 1934 talking picture production had reached its peak with 86 companies in Bombay and Maharashtra alone.  Of these 86, however, only 12 were based on foundations firm enough to withstand the onslaught of time.   These were Ranjit Movietone, Wadia Movietone, Saroj Movietone, Prakash Pictures, Paramount Film Company, Huns Pictures, Bombay Talkies, Prabhat Film Company, Saraswati Cinetone and Kolhapur Cinetone.   Only Bombay Talkies  and  Prabhat Film Company had really efficient and good studios.

Bengal too had its string of producers, but the most noted company which was later to  establish  a  high standard in film production was New Theatres Ltd. The superior quality of its pictures *Puran Bhakt, Chandidas* and *Devdas* (all released in Bombay in 1935) and *Dhup*

*Chaon* (released in Bombay in 1936) set the public cla-
mouring for a better class of pictures from other producers also.

During the film's silent days, South India had hardly entered the field of production, though it was a rich
market for films produced in the other parts of India.
Since the introduction of sound, however, a keen necessity was felt to produce films in South Indian languages.
Production was started simultaneously in Tamil and
Telugu, but as South India had no studios, the films were
shot at the producing centres in Western and Eastern
India· It was, however, found that taking artistes and
technicians to distant shooting centres was too expensive. Local studios were therefore opened at Madras,
Bangalore, Coimbatore and Vizagapatam reaching a
total of fifteen in about a couple of years.

In the first few years of its existence the talkie in
India had to pass through the same ordeal as the early
sound pictures in other countries. The stage
element reigned supreme in the studios and the early
productions were more in the nature of photographed
theatrical scenes than motion pictures.

Talkies brought in their wake a fresh set of problems which the industry had to face in addition to the
already existing ones. Provincialized talkies no doubt
limited the market for Indian films, but at the same
time they created a fresh urge in others to produce films
in their own language. In this way the film penetrated
to untrodden regions, as is evident from the example of
South India.

It is generally admitted that the coming of sound
has greatly affected the international character of the
motion picture. In India the absence of a common
language has seriously hampered the free circulation of
films. In the days of the silent film the language difficulty was overcome by providing titles in the vernacular
of the area in which the film was shown. Not so with
the talkies. Due to the diversity of language the same
film had often to be produced in more than one language
thereby greatly increasing its cost of production which

4

was even otherwise, four to five times the cost of a
silent picture. Indian pictures were produced in Hindustani, Gujerati, Marathi, Urdu, Tamil and Telugu
though of course the great majority of them were produced in Hindustani which was understood by a large
number of people.

Even the foreign films exhibited in India were hard
hit. Hitherto their action, understood by all, attracted
audiences. Now, however, the English dialogue limited
their appeal. Foreign films had to face serious competition for the great majority of Indian audiences preferred to see the indigenous film. Europeans and educated
Indians, however, who understood the English language
continued to patronize foreign films.

### PERIOD OF CONSOLIDATION 1935-39

In spite of the innumerable difficulties and problems which beset the Indian film, the cinema habit in
general and the popularity of the Indian film in particular was manifestly on the increase. The number of feature films produced in India, the number of imported
films and the number of cinema houses rose considerably as the following table[1] shows—

|  | 1926-27 | 1931 | 1935 |
|---|---|---|---|
| Number of Indian feature films produced and exhibited | 108 (Silent) | 328 (300 Silent) | 240 (7 Silent) |
| Foreign films exhibited in India | 775 (Silent) | 322 (Talkies) | 383 (Talkies) |
| Motion Picture Theatres in India | 251 | 419 | 660 |

Thus by 1934-35, Indian talkies had firmly established themselves. The silent film was rapidly dying
out as is evident from the fact that only 7 out of the

[1] *Report of the Indian Cinematograph Committee*, 1928, pp. 185, 179;
B. V. Dharap, *Motion Picture Year Book*, 1940, pp. 2-3, 144-6, 213-5.

total of 240 Indian pictures produced in 1935 were silent. Thereafter no silent pictures were produced in India or imported from abroad and to meet these new conditions almost all the cinema houses were converted for sound projection.

Hitherto hardly any film journalism was in existence. Now film journals started coming into vogue, the most important of which was *Filmindia*. *The Times of India* which had so far completely ignored the existence of Indian films started taking an interest in them and reviewing them. The Motion Picture Society of India though inaugurated in 1932, was formally registered in 1934 and its journal, started in 1935, was another important publication serving as a link between the public and the film industry. The talkies had thus definitely come to stay and from 1935 to the outbreak of World War II in 1939, the Indian film industry continued its steady progress.

In the field of production the industry was active. It being a fascinating and alluring occupation, new companies sprang up in important cities. Many of these concerns, however, were started by persons with no experience and little or no capital of their own. These mushroom establishments, during their short existence, exploited the unemployed artistes and technicians and, instead of doing any good, brought discredit to the industry as a whole. The number of producing units increased from 21 in 1926 to 110 in 1936, and the capital invested in the three branches of the film industry was Rs. 50,000,000. The industry gave employment to about 25,000 people.[1] These figures, compared with the figures of 1926, show the rapid strides the Indian film had taken during this decade, but when compared with the achievements of the West, bring forcefully to one's mind the possibilities of expanding the cinema in our country. For example, in Great Britain in 1934, there were 4,305 cinemas with a seating capacity of 3,872,000 and a weekly cinema attendance of 18,500,000. The number of feature films produced was

[1] B. V. Dharap, *Motion Picture Year Book* 1940, pp. 2-3.

190 and the gross box-office receipts amounted to
£41,000,000.[1] If this was the position in a country with
a population only one-seventh that of India, one can well
imagine the immense possibilities there were for the
Indian film.

Though South India had entered the field of production rather late, by 1937 film production in Tamil and
Telugu had made as great a headway as that in any other
vernacular except Hindustani, which  for all purposes
was considered an all-India language. These Tamil and
Telugu pictures were very popular in their own regions,
with the result that foreign and Hindustani pictures
suffered a setback though good Hindustani pictures such
as *Achhut Kanya, Amar Jyoti, Sant Tukaram* and
*Duniya-na-Mane* did command an extensive market.

Even though production was spread all over India,
Bombay was the main centre of the industry. Of the 110
producing companies in 1936, 61 were centred in the
Bombay Presidency. Of these 54 were in Bombay City,
3 in Poona, 3 in Kolhapur and one in Nasik.[2] Many of
these concerns distributed their own films. There were
19 studios in Bombay in 1936.[3]

Though film production had improved, Indian
capital still fought shy of it, and financiers were not willing to invest in what they regarded as a risky venture.
The few who did, demanded exorbitant rates of interest
which throttled business. This together with the
narrow-minded policy of producers, prevented the industry from making great improvements.

In spite of this serious handicap, Indian producers
were not deterred from making innovations. In 1937,
Wadia Movietone made an attempt to synchronize
Indian songs with the American silent picture *The Thief
of Baghdad*. Keeping the original film and its cast, they
introduced Hindustani songs and Indian dances and released it under the title of *Sulemani Shetranji* as a
morning show at the Palace Cinema. This was an un-

[1]The Arts Enquiry, *The Factual Film*, pp. 198-9; *Journal of The Motion
Picture Society of India*, June-July 1936, p. 5; *Ibid*, June 1937, p. 209.
[2]*Journal of the Motion Picture Society of India*, March 1936, p. 29.
[3]*Ibid*.

precedented and unique event in the history of Indian motion pictures. Though a significant landmark, this film did not make any lasting impression for no other similar attempt was made and the trend of the Indian film was unaffected.

Another important milestone was marked by the film *Kisan Kanya* produced by the Imperial Film Company of Bombay and directed by Moti B. Gidwani. This company which gave us our first talkie, had been experimenting in colour photography for some time and, in December 1937, *Kisan Kanya* the first full length Indian picture in cine-colour was released in Bombay. Though not a box-office success it marked a new step forward in Indian film technique. Later, in 1938, another picture, *Mother India*,[1] was released in colour and it was a great success. Colour photography, however, was too expensive for the Indian producers. These early attempts were not, therefore, followed up with better equipment or greater effort. Colour photography was abandoned and producers continued with the production of monochrome pictures.

Indian producers were also making experiments in another field, namely, cartoon films. On November 15, 1935, a cartoon short in Hindustani was released at the Majestic Talkies, Bombay, along with the feature film *Swapna Swayamwar*. It was the first of its kind and the first in the series by Herr Bodo Gutschwager, a specialist in trick photography formerly of the Ufa studios of Germany. The cartoon was entitled *Lafanga Langoor* or *The Merry Monkey*.[2] It is indeed regrettable that no further account is to be had about that first cartoon or its sequel, if there was any. In fact, cartoon production did not figure on Indian producers' schedules again till 1938 when *The Times of India* dated April 2, 1938, announced: "An Indian Mickey Mouse may soon make his bow to the film-goers. Experiments at producing cartoons of the Walt Disney type are, it is learnt, being made in Bombay, in view of the successful development

[1] *The Times of India,* November 12, 1937.
[2] *Ibid,* November 15, 1935.

of this type of film entertainment in the West.

"During the last few months  half a dozen special artists have been experimenting on the evolution of the Indian contemporaries of Mickey Mouse  and  Donald Duck and it is understood that already a thousand feet of successful colour cartoons have been made.   These artists have been working on behalf  of a Bombay film company which is hoping to produce cartoons based on Indian folklore and other stories. For  this  purpose a separate company has to be floated and in the course of a few months it is expected that the first all-Indian cartoon will be seen on the screen." Over  a  decade  has elapsed since that statement was made.  The  scheme seems to have fizzled out because cartoon production is too expensive and too difficult  for  our  producers  to undertake. The *Journal of the Film Industry,* the official spokesman of the industry hastened to assure the critics that "the moment these (cartoon) films  can  return  a minimum of profits, Indian film producers, businessmen as they are, will not hesitate to embark on this venture as well."[1]

It is only recently that fresh effort has been made in this line.  In July 1948, an Indian cartoon film *Ek Sadi Bad* was released at  the  Royal Opera House, Bombay. Produced in Bombay by the Indian Cartoon Pictures, it aims at giving a humorous insight into the India of the year 2047.  Though clumsy and crude in its animation, it is indeed creditable that some attempt  should  have been made in spite of all difficulties, lack of resources and equipment.

Thereafter on August  26,  1949,  was  released another cartoon entitled *The War that Never Ends* produced by the Government of India's film unit. It stresses the need for an intensive  drive  against  disease  and emphasizes the necessity for cleanliness.

The steady progress that the Indian  film had been making reached its climax with the recognition of the picture *Sant Tukaram* at the Fifth International Exhibition of Cinematograph Art, Venice, on August 10, 1937.

[1] *Journal of the Film Industry,* March 1941, pp. 4-5.

Produced by Prabhat Film Company, directed by V. Damle and S. Fatehlal, starring Vishnupant Pagnis and based on the life story of Maharashtra's greatest saint, this film was ranked among the three best pictures of the world. For the first time in the annals of the motion picture, an Indian film had come into the limelight. Prior to this, India had sent its film *Amar Jyoti*, also produced by the Prabhat Film Company, to the Fourth International Exhibition at Venice in 1937, but never before had an Indian film won such a distinguished honour in an international field. *Sant Tukaram* was not only an important landmark in the history of Indian film, it was an outstanding box-office success.

Side by side with the advance in film production, methods of distribution were also progressing. Independent distributors came into existence for the exploitation of films which in the old days had to be done by producers themselves. Indian films were distributed outside India in such places as East Africa and South Africa, Fiji and Mauritius Islands, Federated Malay States, Iraq and The West Indies — in fact wherever there was an appreciably large Indian population. In practically all these places, except probably the last, stunt pictures appeared to be the most popular. With the exhibition of films outside India, the market for the indigenous product expanded.

Many more new markets could have been tapped in Europe and in the U.S.A., for the success of *Sant Tukaram* at the International Exhibition at Venice had roused interest in Indian films, particularly cultural and documentary films. Nothing, however, was done and no Indian film was sent to the West till 1941.

During the first nine years of the talkies' existence in India, film exhibition had undergone considerable progress. The number of cinemas had increased three-fold from 419 in 1931 to 1265 in 1939.[1] This rise, however, seems insignificant when compared with figures in other countries. For example, in Russia the number of cinema houses had increased from 1953 in 1924 to 29,163

[1] B. V. Dharap, *Motion Picture Year Book*, 1940, pp. 213-5.

in 1934 representing a fifteenfold increase within a decade.[1]

Moreover compared with Western countries, for example, Great Britain and Germany, in 1936 even the seating accommodation in our cinema houses was very limited, with the result that the number of people per seat was very large, as can be seen from the following table.[2]

| Country | Approximate Number of Cinemas. | Total seating accommodation | Average seating accommodation per cinema house | People per seat |
|---|---|---|---|---|
| Great Britain | 5,000 | 4,500,000 | 900 | 11 |
| Germany | 5,302 | 1,943,049 | 366 | 32 |
| India | 910 | 750,000 | 825 | 466 |

Though quantitatively cinema houses had increased rapidly since the Cinematograph Committee reported in 1928, with the exception of a few houses and those too showing foreign films, most of them were cheaply and rapidly constructed. As *The Times of India* commented, most of the Bombay picture houses were fifteen years behind time. Their exteriors were ugly and interiors lacked comfort. There was no air-conditioning and the seats were hard and uncomfortable. From buildings of this order, the Regal Cinema, opened in October 1933, the Eros, opened in February 1938, and the Metro Cinema in June 1938, stood out unique. In comfort, style and finish they were the last word. They surrounded their patrons with luxury, wealth and splendour, and came close to the super cinema houses of the West. Even to this day the Eros, Regal and Metro are not only the three biggest cinema houses in Bombay — Eros has a seating capacity of 1114, Regal 1225 and Metro 1491 — but also three of the best theatres in the City. To this was added another magnificent cinema,

[1]*Journal of the Motion Picture Society of India,* November 1937, p. 434.
[2]*Ibid,* p. 435.

the Liberty, in March 1949, with a seating accommodation of 1100.

Foreign producers, not deterred by their earlier unsuccessful attempts to produce films in India, renewed their efforts at capturing the Indian market with the advent of the talkie. Though foreign talkies continued to flow into India regularly, it was found that the Indian masses preferred films in their own language. Realizing the potentialities of the Indian market and the possibilities of film production here, E. D. Leishman of R.K.O. Radio Pictures Ltd. said in 1934 that his company was prepared to make one or more pictures in India with a suitable subject and a universal theme.

Other American film magnates, thinking that it was better to have their own theatres here, started by taking over and converting old cinema houses for showing exclusively their own pictures. For example, in December 1935, Central Cinema on Charni Road, Bombay, was opened to show exclusively Metro-Goldwyn-Mayer films, and in January 1936, the Royal Opera House which had undergone many vicissitudes in the course of its existence, was converted as the first release cinema house in Bombay for Warner Brothers, First National pictures.

By October 1936, however, the cinema houses in Bombay had again changed hands. There was a general tendency to confine English films to the Fort area. The Central Cinema decided to show only Indian films and the Royal Opera House instead of being the first run cinema house for Warner Brothers became the first release centre for Bombay Talkies. Thus M.G.M. shifted to the Empire and 20th Century-Fox moved from the Empire to the Regal. This reduced the first run English houses in Bombay City from seven to five.[1]

Not satisfied with having secured a few cinema houses exclusively for their own products, one of the foreign companies—Metro-Goldwyn-Mayer—proposed to erect a new theatre of its own in Bombay and become an exhibitor of its own products. The Indian

[1] *The Times of India,* October 10, 1936.

film concerns were perturbed by this encroachment on
their domain and a vigorous protest was made in the
press and elsewhere.

Despite the strong public opinion against it, the
Government granted the necessary permit for the building of a cinema house at Dhobi Talao. Sir Phiroze
Sethna, the then President of the Motion Picture Society of India, said in this connexion: ". . . this question,
local as it may seem, apparently constitutes essentially
an all-India problem inasmuch as it amounts to
foreigners' inroad on one major section of the Indian
film industry viz. exhibition.... This venture will not
merely be in competition with the indigenous exhibitors
but generally and definitely tend to be a monopoly of
exhibiting all super American productions....the proposed American venture constitutes a serious menace to
the Indian film industry."[1]

It is also interesting to note that in Britain at about
the same time, a storm of protest was raised by the
British public against the proposed control of the Gaumont British Film Company by the powerful American
combine of M.G.M. and 20th Century-Fox. Due to intense agitation in the House of Commons and in the
press a considerable portion of the new company's stock
was made available for sale to the British public with
a view to keeping the control in the hands of the British.

Not satisfied with merely having a share in the
exhibition of films, American producers realized that
extensive markets awaited films with Indian settings.
In May 1937, therefore, one of the major producing concerns in America sent an Art Director to study Indian
settings, so that any company producing films with Indian locale would have sets which might resemble appreciably the original, while some concerns, with a view
to authentic presentation, were seriously considering
the possibility of shooting films in India.

Not only Hollywood, but the British film industry
was also planning to raid the Indian market by building
studios and cinemas here. This plan, however, never

[1] *Journal of the Motion Picture Society,* September 1936, pp. 5, 7, 8.

materialized for it was shelved with the outbreak of World War II.

It is indeed significant that while on the one hand the English were crying themselves hoarse against the American domination of their home film market they expected, on the other hand, another country to tolerate the idea of their intrusion into its home market without the least protest.

Before proceeding further, a few words must be said about the foreign films exhibited in India, especially in Bombay. During the period 1934-39, George Arliss' pictures set the vogue for screen biographies. Greville Bain, commenting in *The Times of India,* remarked: "The films are becoming something of a (misleading) dictionary of world biography. Private lives are becoming transcendingly public at a great rate. Crowned heads have had considerable vogue and the records are being ransacked for celebrities who can be the subjects of good pictures and better publicity. We have seen Catherine, Christina, Cleopatra, Nero, Voltaire, Rothschild and a host more. In the near future we will see many more besides....

"No doubt these biographical pictures are very tempting to the producer and director. They mostly offer scope for picturesque background. George Arliss who may be considered something of a pioneer in the present fashion has made a great commercial success of it, and no doubt the public enjoys seeing Cleopatra and Nero almost in the flesh. But serious and conscientious historians must be driven to frequent apoplexy."[1]

The film public, it was said, demanded better films —more intelligent, more imaginative, more subtle and more wholesome than the ones that were shown. Yet, curiously enough, it was the public which defeated its own desire, for the success of a film was judged by its box-office record. It was the only barometer which producers had of judging public taste. Investigation revealed that melodramas were most popular. It seems that the public of those days liked its films with a strong

[1] *The Times of India,* December 29, 1934.

flavour.

Even though the Hollywood product was often trite and shallow, the audience preferred American to British films. Generally speaking American films were more entertaining than English pictures, and hence even the advertisements of the latter were ignored. Even today the prejudice against British films is strong, although it is disappearing gradually as a result of the recent release of a number of impressive and superior British films.

What about the Indian films of the early thirties? Though film production had grown into one of the most flourishing industries, from a technical point of view conditions were most unsatisfactory. Lack of efficient men and money made it impossible to produce films of a high order. Slapstick comedy, crude melodrama, stunt pictures and mythological films replete with magic tricks formed the mainstay of film production, though a few stories by well-known writers were also screened.

Thus far had the Indian film progressed when the year 1939 dawned. A milestone in Indian film history, this year marked the celebration of the silver jubilee of the industry.

During the first week of May 1939, Bombay was the venue of a film exhibition and congress held to celebrate the silver jubilee of the Indian film industry. The exhibition bore testimony to the great strides the industry had made since its humble inception in Bombay City twenty-five years previously. The aim of the congress was to assist those engaged in the different branches of the industry to confer and plan together for future progress.

On its twenty-fifth birthday the Indian film ranked eighth among Indian industries, and the third largest film industry in the world.[1] There were about 75 producing companies whose annual output averaged about 200 feature films. To screen these there were a little over a thousand cinemas (1,265) in the country with a

[1] B. V. Dharap, *Motion Picture Year Book of India* 1940, p. vii; Roger Manvell, *The Film*, p. 175.

population of over 350,000,000. About 200 of these theatres were devoted exclusively to foreign films.[1]

Even after twenty-five years the Indian film industry was in a very disorganized condition. Though a profitable business, it had many faults such as unsound financial methods, technical handicaps, a plethora of poor quality films which did not compensate for a few good ones, very few and unsuitable cinema houses and great divergences in methods of distribution.

All these defects were capable of being remedied with more concerted action and rationalization, and with that aim the Motion Picture Congress was convened. To start with, what was needed was to place the producing concerns on a secure financial basis. They could then work according to their schedule without being compelled to sell the rights of their pictures even before they were produced as happened very often in the past. More trained technicians and experts were needed to cope with the increasing rate of production and to produce a better grade of film to attract a more cultured and educated audience.

Distributors needed to be organized. Only then would they cater better for the needs of exhibitors who in their turn could build more cinemas and capture the immense, untapped markets. For while the British and American productions had a world-wide market, Indian films had perforce to depend mostly on the home market. Thus, great as had been the strides in the past generation, the pace of progress had to be accelerated if the Indian film was to gain international recognition.

## WAR PERIOD 1939-45

While motion picture producers were making ambitious plans for the future, little dreaming what the next few months were to bring, Hitler was carrying out his sinister designs in Central Europe.

The contribution of the American film to the war

[1]Chandulal Shah, Welcome Speech at the Indian Motion Picture Congress, May 8, 1939, pp. 5, 15.

effort of its country was immense. The Indian film was in its infancy when World War I broke out. It did not, therefore, have to face major problems. World War II, however, affected the growing industry. How did the industry fare during these war years?

Practically, for the first two and a half years, the Indian film industry was not much affected by the international struggle that was going on. Production continued apace. With the war boom many small independent producers came into existence. Bombay continued to be the main centre of production. There were approximately 125 producing concerns and 50 studios. Although exact figures are not available it was estimated that roughly about Rs. 830,000,000 were invested in the production, distribution and exhibition branches of the Indian film industry. Of this, the amount invested in production and distribution was estimated to be Rs. 30 million, that invested in the construction and equipment of studios was about Rs. 10 million and about Rs. 43.7 million in the equipment of cinemas. The film industry gave employment to about 15,000 people. On these, it was estimated that 4,000 were employed in production, mostly as artistes and technicians, 4,500 were employed in distribution mainly as clerks and about 5,600 were employed in exhibition. The foreign income of Indian films was about 5 per cent while the remaining 95 per cent was recovered from India itself. The amount paid to the Central Government and Provincial Governments in the form of taxes was over Rs. 10,000,000—generally speaking Indian films paid about 33-1/3 per cent of the total income as taxes to Government.[1]

The Indian Motion Picture Producers Association reviewing the year 1940 found that the number of films produced in India in 1940 was 162, of which 9 were in two versions. Of these, 77 were in Hindustani, 35 in Tamil, 18 in Bengali, 12 in Telugu, 10 in Marathi, 8 in Punjabi and one each in Urdu and Malayalam. These 162 films marked a slight though not a very encouraging

[1] *Journal of the Film Industry,* September 1940, p. 4. *Ibid,* November 1940, p. 4.

improvement on the 154 pictures released in 1939. These figures reveal that the majority of films produced were in Hindustani; that about 51 per cent of indigenous production was centred in Bombay Presidency, 30 per cent in South India, 16 per cent in Bengal and 3 per cent in the Punjab.[1]

The story of film production in 1941, as disclosed through the pictures of that year, is not a happy one. Against the 162 films of 1940, there were no more than 137 in 1941, a decrease of 25 films. The descending curve which began from 172 films in 1936 dropped to 147 by 1939. The year 1940, however, brought about a recovery to 162 films, but this was only temporary as by the end of 1941, production had dropped down to 137.[2]

The production of films in Hindustani fell from 90 in 1936 to 51 in 1941.[3] This fall is not easily explicable because more people understand Hindustani than any other language, and therefore Hindustani films have a wider market and a better chance of success.

Although on an average about 44 Tamil and Telugu films had been produced annually since 1939, even in 1941 these films, with rare exceptions, hardly showed any improvement in technique, content or presentation. The market for these films was so restricted that there was hardly any scope for improvement. The story of Bengali and Marathi films was the same, though they too had increased in number since 1939. No doubt the market at their disposal was wider but it offered little chance for betterment. The only way open to provincial producers to raise their standard was to widen their market by producing films in Hindustani along with provincial films.

As regards production activity, Bombay, even though it held the leading position with 44 per cent of the total production, had ceased to tower over the Punjab, Bengal and Madras put together; between them they

1 *Ibid*, January 1941, p. 4.
2 *Ibid,* January 1942, pp. 15-8.
3 *Ibid.*

commanded 56 per cent of the total production of 1941.
This was due not so much to increased production in the
other three centres as to diminished output in Bombay,
partly due to the riots in the middle of the year and partly due to lack of screen space which prevented 11 Hindustani and 4 Marathi pictures from being released.

Of the 61 pictures released in Bombay, only 40 came
from established producers—established in the sense
that they had studios of their own or had produced at
least three pictures in succession without suspension of
production. In fact, there were as many as 16 independent picture producers in Bombay, 7 in Bengal, 3 in the
Punjab and 24 in South India, making a total of 50 independent producers,[1] the merit of whose individual contributions to the industry was, to say the least, dubious.

The year 1942 saw the war at the very gates of
India. The film industry felt its full impact in the restrictions placed on the import of raw films, chemicals
and machinery. The Government promulgated an order
on May 15, 1942, restricting the length of feature films
to 11,000 feet and trailers to 400 feet. These restrictions
made the year 1942 a very anxious period. Nevertheless,
the number of pictures completed and certified during
that year was 165. This number exceeded not only the
figures of the previous war years 1940 and 1941, which
were 162 and 137 respectively, but was greater than the
1939 output of 147 and more or less equalled the 1937
figure of 166.

If the effect of the war were to be judged in terms
of the number of films produced, it might well be said
that the conditions in the industry in 1942 were no worse
than those in the peace time years of 1937 or 1939. It
was possible to maintain the same level of production
because of the greater economy practised in the consumption of raw material, the imports of which had
fallen by 20 per cent due to the war.

As regards provincial production, Bombay was still
leading; 64 per cent of the films were made in Bombay,
21 per cent in South India, 12 per cent in Bengal and

[1] *Ibid.*

3 per cent in the Punjab.

By producing more pictures than the rest of India put together, Bombay regained her paramount position which she had lost in 1941. This increase in output was partly due to the decrease of production in South India and Bengal following air raids in those regions.

In Madras, the chief centre of production in South India, the evacuation of people into the interior resulted in considerable loss to the various branches of the industry. Production companies ceased to function for a time, distributing firms withdrew to the interior and the income of exhibitors in the city dwindled considerably. In the course of the year after normal conditions were restored, business was resumed, but there was a fall in the total number of films produced from 43 in 1939 to 33 in 1942.

As the war continued unabated, the difficulty of obtaining raw films became more acute. The Government, in order to conserve raw stock, introduced a system of licensing on July 17, 1943, whereby a strict embargo was placed on the production of new films and even on the making of new prints of duly certified pictures except under a licence from the Government. Moreover, by an order under the Defence of India Rules promulgated on September 15, 1943, the exhibition of 2,000 feet of 'approved' propaganda film was made compulsory in every cinema programme. These new measures though they affected the number of new films produced—which fell to 149—did not influence box-office receipts. In fact the collection at the box-office during the year was unprecedented in the history of the Indian film industry. This fall in production, however, was due not entirely to paucity of raw stock. It was a normal phenomenon that had manifested itself every alternate year during the four years of the war and even during pre-war years. The only serious drop in production due mainly to the war was in South India as already noted.

During this period Bombay maintained her ascendency in production with as many as 99 pictures or 66.5 per cent, the remaining 50 pictures being distributed

5

among Bengal 27 or 18.1 per cent, South India 20 or 13.4 per cent and the Punjab 3 pictures or 2 per cent.

The full impact of the various Government orders restricting the length of films, conserving raw stock and making compulsory the exhibition of 'approved' films was felt in the years 1944 and 1945. The number of pictures produced fell considerably, but box-office receipts were still high. By no stretch of the imagination can it be said that this increased revenue was due to any rise in the standard of pictures. Inflation, a general rise in the standard of living especially among the working classes, increase in wages, larger employment, the entertainment requirements of the armed forces—these were the important factors that led to an increase in returns. Added to these was the fact that a lesser number of pictures were produced to cater to the largely increased needs of the people without any material increase in the number of cinemas available for release of pictures resulting in a larger return per picture. The net income of the industry, however, was proportionately not as great, for a large part of the income went in meeting the heavy costs of production and enhanced taxation. The following tables give an idea of the state of production till December, 1945.[1]

### Number of Pictures Censored

| Year | Bombay | Bengal | Punjab | Madras | Total |
|---|---|---|---|---|---|
| Pre-control average for 3 years 1940, 1941, 1942 | 81 | 27 | 9 | 37 | 154 |
| 1943 | 100 | 27 | 5 | 17 | 149 |
| 1944 | 85 | 18 | 5 | 16 | 124 |
| 1945 | 60 | 18 | 4 | 17 | 99 |

[1] *Ibid,* May 1946, p. 19.

### Number of Pictures Censored According to their Languages

| Languages | 1942 | 1943 | 1944 | 1945 |
|---|---|---|---|---|
| Hindustani | 99 | 98 | 88 | 73 |
| Bengali | 15 | 20 | 12 | 9 |
| Marathi | 13 | 7 | 5 | .. |
| Punjabi | 3 | 3 | 1 | .. |
| Sindhi | 1 | .. | .. | .. |
| Marwari | 1 | 1 | .. | .. |
| Arabic | .. | 1 | .. | .. |
| Tamil | 21 | 11 | 13 | 12 |
| Telugu | 10 | 4 | 5 | 4 |
| Kanarese | 2 | 4 | .. | 1 |

In regard to provincial production, in the years 1944 and 1945, Bombay maintained her leading position with 68.6 per cent and 60.6 per cent of total production during 1944 and 1945 respectively.[1]

Rounding the corner of the war and all the obstacles it imposed, the Indian film industry faced a very uncertain future. Having drifted through over thirty years of its existence without any fixed plan or intention, constantly asking for help from Government, but never getting it, the Indian film emerged out of the dark years of the war with few bright prospects for the future.

In Bengal studios were almost dead. Producers there seemed to have lost their early initiative and enterprise. The old and known artistes began migrating from Bengal to regions where they would be able to make money. In such circumstances Bengal held out no hope to the future of the film industry.

In South India production was crude and primitive. Producers there did not care either for quality or art, but existed because they supplied a provincial need.

The Punjab lacked organization and discipline to raise the Indian film from its rut of stagnation. Thus, neither South India nor the Punjab could be depended on. That left only Bombay. But even here during the years of war, the greed for money had tempted most of the producers to sacrifice art. Undoubtedly, a continuous stream of pictures flowed every year but they

[1] *Ibid*, February 1946, p. 14. *Ibid*, May 1946, p. 9.

made no pretence of being either artistic or intellectual in content.

The fact that the Indian film industry was steadily developing is proved by the gradual increase in the number of cinema houses in the country. Within the decade 1931-40, the number of cinemas had increased from 419 to 1265 permanent cinemas and 500 touring cinemas. By the end of 1941, heavy taxation sent some exhibitors into liquidation, and the number of permanent and seasonal theatres were respectively reduced to 1,136 and about 400.[1] By 1943, however, things had improved a bit with 1,460 cinemas[2] rising to approximately 1,700 in 1946.

With its vast and increasing population, India continues to offer a huge potential market for films, but so far the cinema has been mainly an urban entertainment. The fringe of the vast rural population has been hardly touched and can only be reached by mobile units. Men at the helm of the indigenous industry should, therefore, devote greater attention to the expansion of film exhibition in villages where people have few diversions. Opening up of theatres in the interior would create a wider outlet for the films produced, many of which cannot be released through lack of space.

Though the number of cinema houses had been increasing since the outbreak of the war, exhibitors were also hit by abnormal conditions. Production and exhibition of advertisement slides were curtailed, thereby depriving the exhibitor of a part of his income. The number of shows in cities with a population of 100,000 or more was restricted to three a day, and in towns with a population below that to two shows a day in order to economize in electricity, fuel, raw stock, chemicals, and to reduce the general wear and tear on equipment.

The war also encouraged profiteering in cinema tickets. Profiteers found a high measure of prosperity in the never-ending crowds at the cinemas. Industry and

[1] *Ibid,* November 1940, p. 4; *Ibid,* October 1941, pp. 15-7; B. B. Dharap, *Motion Picture Year Book of India* 1940, pp. 213-5.
[2] *Journal of the Film Industry,* April 1943, p. 14.

Government, however, failed to take adequate steps against this evil. In Central Provinces, the Punjab and Delhi, Government issued orders that tickets could be sold by and purchased only from approved persons but this did not effectively stop the illegal resale of tickets.

To add to all this, distributors were charging the exhibitors high rentals. Occasionally they insisted on as much as 70 per cent of the collection except in key cities such as Bombay.[1] This was not all. The compulsory exhibition of 2,000 feet of 'approved film' under rule 44A of the Defence of India Rules from September 15, 1943, not only took up a part of the screening time of the exhibitors much against their wishes, but they had to pay rental to the Government.

Despite these handicaps, the exhibitor appears to have been one of the greatest beneficiaries of the war boom because, due to the inflation, the average worker had the required money to go to the cinema — a luxury which perhaps he had not enjoyed previously or only very rarely.

While Indian producers were struggling with the difficulties of war time, foreign films steadily poured into the country and many of them were box-office successes. American and British film magnates were once again planning to raid the Indian market. During the latter part of the war and immediate post-war years, newspapers were rife with reports that capitalists in the United Kingdom and the U.S.A. were keenly interested in exploiting India as a field for their future film activity. It was reported that an organization had already been formed in Great Britain not only to secure theatre monopolies in India but also to establish distribution circuits and production units. In America, Darryl Zanuck, Vice-President of 20th Century-Fox Corporation said: "To meet the expanded demand for films, the major producers in time must come closer to their patrons. I can well visualize the day when the major film companies will have plants in India, China, in Latin America and in other lands where movies have become a part of the

---

[1] *Ibid*, April 1945, pp. 3-5; *Ibid*, December 1945, pp. 5-6.

daily life of the people. This, I am sure, will make for better pictures in that they will be more authentic and therefore appeal more readily to the people in the countries where they are produced."[1]

Some of the ambitious plans of foreigners were to:

(i) Build a chain of modern theatres in all towns of India—1,200 during the first year and gradually increase the number to 5,000 in five years, if found necessary.

(ii) Acquire control over the distribution of important Indian pictures to feed the theatres during intervals when foreign films were not shown.

(iii) Build up-to-date production studios and laboratories ostensibly to train Indians in the modern technique of production but ultimately to acquire complete control over Indian production.

(iv) Finance independent Indian producers with a view to controlling their activities and products.

(v) Dub foreign productions with Hindustani dialogue with the help of Indian artistes in order to make such pictures acceptable to Indian masses thereby competing directly with the local product. Walt Disney was the first to announce the dubbing of his cartoons in Hindustani, the first one being *Bambi*.

What would be the effect on our industry if all these foreign plans were to materialize? From the national point of view the idea of foreigners competing with us in our own country is to be deplored. From an artistic and industrial point of view, however, such competition might prove beneficial. Vigorous competition is needed to rouse our producers from their lethargy and shake their present self-complacency. Our producers with a few exceptions have, in spite of numerous opportunities, never made an attempt either to better the contents of films or to raise their standard. They are sitting back

[1] *Filmindia*, March 1946, p. 32.

smugly on the money they made during the war and unless they are faced with the serious competition of superior production in their own field they will have no incentive to better their output.

While foreign films have a decided hold on the Indian market, there is hardly a foreign market for Indian films. No doubt Indian films are exhibited in Malaya, East Indies, South Africa and East Africa where there is an appreciably large Indian population, but these places do not in the strict sense of the word constitute a foreign market as perhaps no non-Indian in these parts ever visits an Indian picture except sometimes out of curiosity. But both from a cultural and commercial point of view, a foreign film market is essential if the Indian motion picture industry is to develop its potentialities.

The biggest limitation to a venture of this type is, however, finance. No studio in India can afford to risk the large sum involved in producing an Indian picture which would be popular in foreign countries. No financier would finance such a production unless a return on his investment was ensured. To add to it, Indian pictures of the current type would have no foreign market unless their standard was considerably improved.

Another difficulty is the problem of language. Films in Hindustani with English titles cannot be as successful as those with English dialogue. So far our producers have ventured to make only two films with English dialogue—*The Court Dancer* (1941) produced by the Wadia Movietone and *The Story of Dr. Kotnis* (1946) produced by V. Shantaram. The English version of the latter, however, has so far not been released in India though it is reported that it will be released in the U.S.A. some time in the near future. *The Court Dancer* though sent abroad in 1941 was never released in the U.S.A. except in a few unimportant towns. In India itself that film was far from successful. Its English dialogue was crude and incongruous. It is, therefore, not surprising that it failed abroad also. Beverley Nichols writes: "Even *The Court Dancer* can't be called an unqualified success. It has some poetical photography, but to Western eyes, its popular star Sadhona Bose is regrettably heavy on her feet, and its English dialogue is startlingly jejune."[1]

In strange contrast to the film in the U.S.A. and Great Britain, the war did not affect the contents of Indian films. Out of the 89 films censored by the Bombay Board of Film Censors in 1944, only two films dealt with war themes. In 1945, also, there were only two films produced with war themes out of 67 censored by the Bombay Board. Prior to 1944 no war feature films were produced in India.

The use of films for training illiterate servicemen, however, was well exploited by the Directorate of Military Training. Inaugurated in June 1941, the Indian Services Film Unit known as 'Combined Kinematograph Services Training and Film Production Centre' (CKS for short) made films in 35 mm. and 16 mm. size for training servicemen as well as rehabilitating them after demobilization. Disbanded in June 1947, this Unit is reputed to have made approximately 300 films in 14 languages[2]—more than any other similar unit in the world—a record to be proud of.

Another beneficent result of the war was that it gave the much needed impetus for the production of Indian newsreels. Before 1942, no Indian newsreel was produced. From 1942, Indian newsreels gradually began appearing rising from 6.3 per cent of total newsreels exhibited in 1942 to 58 per cent in 1946. At first produced by 20th Century-Fox, they were taken over by the Indian Government only in 1943 under the title of Indian News Parade. These newsreels though not entirely satisfactory, were a step forward in the right direction towards developing another aspect of the film industry in India.

[1] Beverley Nichols, *Verdict on India*, p. 104.
[2] Major S. T. Berkeley-Hill, "Films in Uniform", *United Services Institution Journal*, October 1948, pp. 387-91.

## Post-war Period 1945-49

The end of the year 1945 saw the termination of hostilities. The Indian film, now free from restraints, burst forth into prolific production. Many enterprising individuals and firms encouraged by the box-office returns during the period of the boom took to production in the hope of quick returns, with little thought to the future.

Although the war was at an end, the problems created by the war were not solved by the return of peace. Scarcity of raw film, lack of studio space, high cost of materials, heavy salaries and other expenses continued, and there was no knowing when the cost of production would come down. To add to it, the rates of interest demanded by financiers were exorbitant, and as no new cinema houses had been built the problem of release of films was as acute as before. In fact, more films were produced than could be released, so much so that while prior to the war only 150 pictures were produced annually on an average, in 1946, 195 pictures were made of which about 150 were produced in Bombay alone.[1]

At the rate at which films were turned out, it was not surprising that within a few months after the war, the market was glutted and box-office receipts fell rapidly. In up-country small towns, the fall was as great as 50 per cent, while in larger towns there was a fall of 30 to 40 per cent in the gross collections. The prices of pictures came down like the proverbial landslide and those who started making pictures in a hurry were left repenting at leisure.

Many independent producers, unable to meet their cost of production, cut down expenses and production schedules. One unfortunate result of this state of affairs was further deterioration in the standard and quality of films, for, in their anxiety to cut down costs, many producers took to cheaper productions especially stunt pictures.

What were the factors responsible for this retro-

[1] *Journal of the Film Industry,* January 1950, p. 51.

gression in the film industry?   Probably the most important single factor responsible for this was the large number of independent producers  the value of whose individual contributions to the industry  was  dubious. The unorganized, loosely knit industry was further handicapped by lack of finance.  High rates of interest and unscrupulous business methods held up the progress of the industry and no serious attempt was made to improve the quality of pictures.  This problem could have been solved by setting apart  a certain amount of resources available for research and general improvement.

The inherent weakness of industry was further aggravated by unfavourable circumstances.   The war had no sooner ended than the outbreak of communal disturbances in September 1946,  threw  out of gear the entire film  trade  resulting  in  irreparable loss to the industry.

In spite of this, the year 1946 saw an increase in film production from 162 in 1940 to 197 with a corresponding increase in Hindustani films from 78 to 151 respectively.[1]  75.6 per cent of this production was centred in Bombay Province.

The years 1947 and 1948 saw a further increase in production to approximately 278 and 263 films of which about 181 and 146 respectively were made in Bombay.[2]

In 1947-48 the UNESCO carried out a survey on the technical needs in press, film  and  radio  in  seventeen countries of the world including India and Pakistan, and revealed to Western eyes some interesting facts about India's little known film industry.[3]

Not only is the Indian film industry the second largest in the world but its three main producing groups located in the West, the East and the South form more or less three independent industries about  as large as any in Europe.  Nevertheless, Bombay is the main centre of the film industry in India with an average of about

[1] Ibid, February 1946, p. 14; Ibid, June 1947, p. 5.
[2] Ibid, January 1950, p. 51.
[3] UNESCO Report of the Commission on Technical Needs in Press Film & Radio, following Surveys in Seventeen Countries and Territories, p. 267.

63 per cent of production centred there since 1940. Of
the Rs. 150,000,000 invested in the film industry as
a whole, about 80 to 90 millions or 53 per cent is
invested in Bombay alone. There are about 400 producing companies in India, 60 per cent of which are located
in Bombay Province. All told there are 67 studios in
India; 22 in Bombay, 19 in Madras, 13 in Calcutta, 3 in
Madura and 2 each in Poona, Mysore, Kolhapur, Coimbatore and Salem.[1] They are all owned by Indians and
no foreign capital is invested in them. Some are used by
their owners while others are hired out. There is no record of the exact number of stages but on an average
each studio has two stages. All the studios are, in general,
reasonably well equipped. Many of them have their own
laboratories and all have their own recording rooms.

There are about 25 laboratories in India of which 15
are in Bombay Province, 5 in Calcutta, 2 in Madras, 2 in
Coimbatore and 1 in Salem.[2] Most of them are attached
to studios, but a few independent ones execute outside
orders. Three laboratories in Bombay and one in Calcutta do reduction and 16 mm. work.[3]

On an average India produces about 250 feature
films, the average cost of each being Rs. 300,000.[4] These
films are distributed through regional distribution circuits which divide the whole of India in five fairly dis-
tinct areas grouped around the main production centres.
These are: the Bombay Circuit (Bombay Province,
Kathiawar and Goa) with over 460 cinemas; the C. P. &
C. I. Circuit (Central Provinces and Berar, Central
India, Khandesh and Rajputana) with over 200 cinemas;
the North Circuit (United Provinces, Delhi, East Punjab
and Kashmir), with 280 cinemas; the South Circuit
(Madras Province, Hyderabad, Mysore, Travancore &
Cochin) with over 700 cinemas, and the Bengal Circuit
(West Bengal, Bihar and Orissa and Assam) with more
than 300 cinemas.[5]

[1] *Ibid.*
[2] *Ibid.*
[3] *Ibid.*
[4] *Ibid.*
[5] *Ibid,* p. 266.

There are over 400 distributing companies and agencies, all privately owned. Of these, ten represent foreign concerns—nine American and one British. On an average, about 225 American and 25 British[1] films are distributed. Occasionally, a French or a Russian film is exhibited. There is very little commercial 16 mm. distribution. Foreign film distributors practise block and blind booking while Indian films are in general booked individually and blind. Indian films are exported regularly to Pakistan, Burma, Ceylon, Malaya and irregularly to East Africa, Mauritius, Iran, South Africa and Aden. The biggest importer of Indian films is Pakistan[2] which is still dependent on India for her supply of films.

The partition of the country in August 1947 and its immediate aftermath, affected the film industry considerably. Cinemas were closed as curfews were imposed, and producers found that a large part of their market no longer existed particularly in the big cities of the north and especially in the Punjab where many cinemas were either destroyed, damaged or occupied by refugees. Though conditions have now returned to normal, finance is still shy. However, with a vast population still untouched by films there is a great scope for development and expansion.

Apart from the increased rate of production the years 1946 to 1949 are important for some significant events in the Indian film world.

The Indian film industry had since a decade attained the position of the eighth major industry in the country, but hitherto its existence had been completely ignored by the Government. The taxes that the industry paid to the Government, the activities of the Motion Picture Society of India and above all the part played by the film during the war, roused the Indian Government and made it realize that if the industry was to make progress, a technically trained personnel and research were absolutely essential. Government, therefore, formulated, in 1946, a scheme for the estab-

[1] *Ibid.*
[2] *Ibid.*

lishment of a Film Council and Institute on the lines of the Cinematograph Council in Great Britain. General conditions at the time, however, caused the scheme to be shelved. According to the plan a Film Council composed of representatives from all sections of the industry together with Government officials, University professors and members of the general public, was to have acted as a liason body between the industry and the Government. A Film Institute was to be established under the Council to train technicians, undertake research and experiments and carry out surveys. The total cost was to have been Rs. 1,000,000.

April 19, 1946, marked another significant milestone in Indian film industry. Ranjit Movietone having completed the production of 100 films celebrated the release of its next picture. To have to its credit a hundred talkies in the short space of 15 years was no small achievement for a producing company. Not only has Ranjit Movietone given us a hundred pictures but also some of India's leading stars and directors. Some of the popular stars who have risen to fame under the Ranjit banner are: Gohar, Madhuri, Khurshid, Mumtaz Shanti, Leela Chitnis, Sulochana, Mehtab, Sadhona Bose, Snehaprabha, Mazur Khan, Chandra Mohan, Saigal, Wasti, Ishwarlal, Motilal, Surendra and many more besides.

With a hundred films to its credit and still producing films to meet the tastes and trend of modern filmgoers, Ranjit Movietone has stood the supreme test of time and one can appreciate this fact better when one recollects the number of film companies which have come and gone.

Another outstanding event in film history occurred in November 1946 when film delegates from all over India met in an All-India Film Conference at Bombay. The last time when the industry had met in 1939, many resolutions had been passed but they remained in cold storage due to abnormal conditions. This had made many lose faith in the value of such conferences. It was, however, forgotten that it was in a festive mood of celebrating a silver jubilee that the film industry had assembled then, while in 1946, it assembled to deliberate on many vital problems confronting the industry such as:

(i) The formation of a federal body of all cine-organizations in the country.

(ii) The setting up of the Film Council and the Film Institute even if the Government did not sponsor them.

(iii) The founding of a bank or an insurance company to look after the financial interests of the industry and provide insurance facilities in every province.

(iv) The threatened invasion of the indigenous film industry by foreign interests.

(v) The collection of statistical information relating to the industry.

(vi) The setting up of a machinery for settlement of disputes.

(vii) The rationalization and future development of the industry.

Though delegates from all parts of India were expected at the Film Conference, the disturbed conditions prevailing in Bombay then prevented many from attending. The Conference had a fair measure of success as many important resolutions were carried unanimously and it was decided that as the Motion Picture Society of India was the oldest and premier cine-organization in India, its constitution should be modified and it should be regarded as the authoritative federation of all cine-organizations in India.

In regard to financial matters it was reported that the industry was paying 40 to 45 per cent of its gross collections as taxes to the Government, but since the war boom was over it was considered necessary that the taxes should be reduced at least to the pre-war level.

About the threatened foreign interests encroaching upon coveted fields of our film industry, it was suggested that no member of the industry should encourage or co-operate directly or indirectly with the activities of foreigners and that the Government should prohibit the dubbing of foreign films into Indian languages.

May 1, 1949, marked another milestone in the Indian film's onward path. On that day the Cinematograph (Amendment) Act, 1949, received the Governor-General's assent[1] and came into force on September 1, 1949, in Bombay. Under the new Act the Censors Boards are authorized to issue two types of certificates for films. 'A' for exhibition only to adults above the age of eighteen and 'U' for universal exhibition. Mothers, however, are permitted to carry children in arms under three years to any film irrespective of whether it has an 'A' or a 'U' certificate. This new amendment aims at preventing some of the harmful influences of the cinema on children and adolescents. Though enacted with the best of intentions, it is too early as yet to pass any judgment on it.

Two months later the film industry struck. For a long time to come the trade, the press and the public will remember June 30, 1949, as a special day in the annals of the motion picture in India. All cinemas remained closed on that day as a protest against the taxation policy of the Government. Never before had the film world united so well and so surely on any issue, and their eloquent protest, though apparently fruitless, will undoubtedly have effect in future when this question comes up before the Enquiry Committee.

On July 5, 1949, a unique event took place in the Indian film world. The Cinevoice Indian Motion Picture Awards Committee held its first annual award function and distributed 'Oscars' for the best performances of 1947. The recipients were:

Filmistan Ltd. for its picture *Sindoor*.

Kishore Sahu for the best director (*Sindoor*).

Mubarak Merchant for the best actor in his role in *Renuka*, and

Hansa Wadkar for the best actress in her performance in *Matwala Shair (Ramjoshi)*.

A commendable venture, this was the first time that

[1] *The Journal of the Film Industry*, August 1949, p. 31; *Ibid*, April 1949, p. 7.

the industry and the public as represented through the readers of *Cinevoice* had collaborated in giving awards. Though, no doubt, the ballot procedure followed as regards the final decision was not entirely satisfactory, nor was the 'Cimpa' Committee thoroughly representative, it cannot be denied that a good beginning was made in the right direction, a beginning which some day may pave the way for constituting a representative Indian Academy of Motion Picture Arts and Sciences.

Another landmark in the Indian film world was the release on December 16, 1949, of *Ajit*, a colour film produced and directed by M. Bhavnani. Photographed on Kodachrome 16 mm. film and subsequently blown up to standard size by the Ansco process in U.S.A., this was India's second colour film after a lapse of twelve years. Featuring Monica Desai, Premnath and Nayampally, it was based on 'Snilloc's' popular novel *Asir of Asirgarh*. Though its theme is too familiar on the Indian screen, the novelty of colour was a welcome departure which marked a new phase in the story of the Indian film.

The post-war period with its greater facilities for travel, has encouraged trips to Western countries especially America, the land of big business and big money. Many film magnates have tried to explore the possibilities of exhibiting their films abroad. However, so far, with the exception of V. Shantaram's *Shakuntala* which was released at the Art Theatre, New York on January 4, 1948, and ran for two weeks, no other Indian film has been publicly exhibited in that country, although reports of private shows for the benefit of U.S. film executives and for propaganda purposes have not been wanting. Newspaper reports give the impression that the Americans are anxious to see our films but there the tale ends. Whether or not our pictures are suitable for exhibition in the U.S.A. is another matter.

Immediately after the termination of hostilities, the first group of Indians to go to America was headed by K. S. Hirlekar who stated in the *Report of the Indian Film Industry's Mission to Europe and America* that they had been sent by the industry with the approval

SANT
TUKARAM:

*Directed by V. G. Damle and S. Fateh-
lal; featuring Vishnupant Pagnis and
Gouri; Prabhat Film Co.; 1937.*

DUNIYA NA
MANE:
*Directed by V. Shantaram; featuring
Shanta Apte and Vasanti; Prabhat
Film Co.; 1937.*

PADOSI:
*Directed by V. Shantaram; featuring
Mazhur Khan and Jagirdar; Prabhat
Film Co.; 1941.*

and support of the Government of India. However, the *Journal of the Film Industry* reports that originally an official delegation was to be sent, but as many nominees were unable to leave India the Indian Motion Picture Producers' Association recommended that Government should "give facilities to others who desired to proceed in their individual capacity."[1]

Commenting on such visitors the *Hollywood Reporter* dated August 29, 1945, observed: "Producers, directors and technicians from many countries feel that by making a pilgrimage to Hollywood they can overcome their own lack of knowledge and that when they return home they will have a magic wand to help them make motion pictures that look like the product of our best producers, directors and cameramen.

"How little these delegations actually learn has long been a secret to all but the hundreds in Hollywood who steer the groups around studios—and to the delegations themselves who return home knowing little more, but impressed with the necessity of making their associates think they have suddenly become wise."[2]

Baburao Patel criticized the visit of the Indian delegation as "a mere waste of time and money,"[3] for the Indian film industry has not yet been able to put on the screen all that it already knows about film production for some reason or another. Moreover, the delegates never really learn anything. The secret of the commercial success of American films is not divulged to foreigners, who are only entertained and given publicity.

Not deterred by these discouraging reports, V. Shantaram accompanied by his wife and his friend and screen writer, Dewan Sherar, paid a visit to America in November 1946, with the intention of securing a release for some of his films there.

As a result of Shantaram's mission, Arthur Mayer and Joseph Burstyn, Inc. of New York, distributors of

[1] *Ibid,* December 1946, p. 10.
[2] *Filmindia,* November 1945, p. 47.
[3] *Ibid.*

6

foreign films, entered into a deal with him for distribution in the United States and Canada, three of Rajkamal Kalamandir's popular features *Shakuntala*, *Parbat Pe Apna Dera* and the English version of *The Story of Dr. Kotnis*. To suit American audiences these films were cut down to 8,000 or 8,500 feet and the number of songs were reduced to not more than three. Brief English titles were super-imposed on Hindustani films to help the American audiences to follow the story.

This was the first American deal of its kind with regard to Indian films, and it reveals the high regard American distributors have for Shantaram's products. In fact, *Shakuntala*, when released in New York, was a box-office hit and was acclaimed by the press and the public.

Indian films have also been appreciated in other foreign fields. Chetan Anand's film *Neecha Nagar* won signal honours at the World Film Festival held at Cannes in October 1946. The film was awarded the Grand Prix of the International Film Festival. Of the 47 films shown at the Festival, *Neecha Nagar* was one of the four selected by the International Federation of Film Journalists. The other three were *Maria Candelaria* (Mexico), *Brief Encounter* (England) and *L'Epreuve* (Sweden). The prize went to *Brief Encounter* in the final count.[1]

The Government of India selected the *Story of Dr. Kotnis* for exhibition at the International Cinematographic Exhibition which was held at Venice in August-September 1947, and the three films *Story of Dr. Kotnis*, *Ram Rajya* and *Shah Jehan* were selected for exhibition at the Canadian National Exhibition, Toronto, held in August 1947.

An outstanding film made during this period was *Dharti-ke-Lal* or 'Children of the Earth' starring Anwar Mirza and Tripti Bhaduri and presented by the Indian Peoples Theatre Association. Though a feature film, it was akin to a documentary in its method of approach and treatment. Produced and directed by K. A. Abbas,

1 *The Times of India*, October 18, 1946.

it was based on the Bengal Famine of the summer of 1943. It was released at the Capitol Cinema, Bombay, during the last week of August 1946, but the outbreak of communal riots in September prevented it being a box-office success. A copy of the film was sent to U.S.S.R. and had its preview at the Soviet Ministry of Cinematography in March 1949.[1] This was the first time that an Indian film was seen in Moscow.

*Kalpana* is another film which has won laurels abroad. It is reported to have shared the prize for 'exceptional qualities' with some films from the U.S.A. at the Second World Festival of Film and Fine Arts, held at Brussels between June 20 and July 10, 1949.[2]

The year 1949 was replete with film festivals held in various parts of the world. India decided to participate in most of them. Among the films which were selected for screening at international exhibitions, the one which won triple honours was *Meera* produced by T. Sadasivam in Hindustani and featuring the renowned singer M. S. Subbulakshmi. It was selected by the Government of India for screening at the Fourth International Film Festival at Prague, Czechoslovakia in August 1949, at the Tenth International Exhibition of Cinematographic Art at Venice in August-September, 1949, and at the Canadian National Exhibition at Toronto.[3] Other films which were selected were *Chandralekha* produced by S. S. Vasan for exhibition at the Fourth International Film Festival at Prague, Czechoslovakia, in 1949[4] and *Chotta Bhai* produced by New Theatres Ltd. for screening at the Canadian National Exhibition, Toronto.[5]

The next question to consider is the position of foreign films in India? By the term 'foreign films' is meant almost entirely the American product. For over thirty years now, American films have enjoyed an almost undisturbed monopoly in India, as in all the countries

[1] *Journal of the Film Industry*, April 1949, p. 17.
[2] *Ibid*, August 1949, p. 30.
[3] *The Times of India*, September 5, 1949.
[4] *Journal of the Film Industry*, July 1949, p. 18.
[5] *Ibid*, August 1949, p. 30.

of the world.    The percentage of films that have come
from other countries has been more or less negligible as
the figures on the opposite page show.

The nearest rival to Hollywood has been England;
but until J. Arthur Rank and, before him, Sir Alexander Korda entered the British film industry and raised
the standard of its films, these could not be compared
with the technical and artistic excellence of the
American product.

The films of Soviet Russia though artistically very
fine, have not yet found a place in the Indian market
and have certainly not been commercialized to the extent which would constitute a threat to the American
monopoly of films in India.    Thus of the foreign films
exhibited in India about 75 per cent are American and
the remaining 25 per cent are mostly British.

It is predicted by some that in future the number
of foreign films imported into India will dwindle.    There
is, however, no likelihood of this, unless exhibitors'
hands are forced by the international monetary situation.    The demand for good pictures whether Indian or
foreign will always be there, and unless our producers
raise their standard they will be left far behind in this
race for quality and excellence.    To add to it, with the
vast market of England greatly circumscribed, American
film magnates are endeavouring to cater for the special
needs of the countries in which they hope either to
retain or find lucrative markets.    This can best be done
by opening producing centres in foreign countries.
Hence their eagerness  to establish producing units in
India and make films in Hindustani.

In this respect two efforts need special mention.    In
mid-1948 Bishen Sen, Managing Director of East & West
Film Production (London), a concern founded by emi-
nent Indians and Britishers with the aim of making films
with Indian themes, Indian atmosphere and if possible,
Indian capital, made public a plan to produce a film in
technicolour about the immortal story of the Taj Mahal.
The interior scenes were to be shot in England while
the exterior scenes would be done here.    It was reported

FEATURE FILMS IMPORTED INTO INDIA 1928-47*

| Country | 1928 | 1929 | 1930 | 1931 | 1932 | 1933 | 1934 | 1935 | 1936 | 1937 | 1938 | 1939 | 1940 | 1941 | 1942 | 1943 | 1944 | 1945 | 1946 | 1947 |
|---|---|---|---|---|---|---|---|---|---|---|---|---|---|---|---|---|---|---|---|---|
| U.S.A. | 1 | 40 | 193 | 268 | 292 | 310 | 305 | 304 | 313 | 309 | 298 | 297 | 268 | .. | .. | 231 | 242 | 273 | 247 | 208 |
| U.K. | .. | .. | 11 | 53 | 45 | 91 | 90 | 76 | 78 | 79 | 55 | 35 | 25 | .. | .. | 18 | 23 | 30 | 29 | 28 |
| France | .. | .. | 1 | .. | 1 | .. | .. | .. | .. | .. | 1 | .. | .. | .. | .. | .. | .. | .. | .. | .. |
| Germany | .. | .. | .. | 1 | 4 | 5 | 2 | 1 | .. | .. | 2 | 8 | 2 | .. | .. | .. | .. | .. | .. | .. |
| Italy | .. | .. | .. | .. | .. | .. | .. | .. | 1 | .. | 1 | 6 | .. | .. | .. | .. | .. | .. | .. | .. |
| China | .. | .. | .. | .. | .. | .. | .. | .. | .. | 1 | .. | 1 | 2 | .. | .. | .. | .. | .. | .. | .. |
| Russia | .. | .. | .. | .. | .. | .. | .. | .. | .. | .. | 2 | 1 | 1 | .. | .. | 5 | 25 | 9 | 6 | 11 |
| Czechoslovakia | .. | .. | .. | .. | .. | .. | .. | .. | .. | .. | .. | 1 | 1 | .. | .. | .. | .. | .. | .. | .. |
| Egypt | .. | .. | .. | .. | .. | .. | .. | .. | .. | .. | .. | 1 | 1 | .. | .. | .. | .. | .. | .. | .. |
| Turkey | .. | .. | .. | .. | .. | .. | .. | .. | .. | 1 | .. | 1 | .. | .. | .. | .. | .. | .. | .. | .. |
| Jerusalem | .. | .. | .. | .. | .. | .. | .. | .. | .. | .. | .. | .. | .. | .. | .. | .. | .. | .. | .. | .. |
| Miscellaneous | .. | .. | .. | .. | .. | .. | .. | .. | .. | .. | .. | .. | .. | .. | .. | .. | .. | .. | 1 | .. |
| Total | 1 | 40 | 205 | 322 | 342 | 407 | 397 | 383 | 392 | 391 | 359 | 351 | 299 | 169 | 197 | 254 | 290 | 312 | 283 | 247 |
| Percentage of American Films .. | 100 | 100 | 94.2 | 83.3 | 85.6 | 76.0 | 77.0 | 79.4 | 79.8 | 79.0 | 83.0 | 84.6 | 90.0 | .. | .. | 91.3 | 83.6 | 87.4 | 87.4 | 84.4 |
| Percentage of British Films .. | .. | .. | 5.37 | 16.45 | 13.15 | 22.3 | 22.7 | 19.75 | 19.9 | 20.2 | 15.3 | 10.0 | 8.4 | .. | .. | 7.1 | 7.94 | 9.63 | 10.22 | 11.35 |

*B. V. Dharap, *Motion Picture Year Book of India* 1940, pp. 144-6. (Separate figures for the years 1941 and 1942 were not available.)

that Laurence Olivier and Vivien Leigh would in all probability star in it while it would be directed by William Dieterle.[1]

A few months later, a newly formed company, the Oriental International Film Corporation, U.S.A., announced a plan to make films in India in the English language for world-wide distribution. They are to be financed by Indian capital. Most of the shooting will be done in Bombay and Poona studios. The pictures are not expressly meant for Indian consumption though probably they will be shown in Asia also. The theme for the first film will be probably selected from actual cases in the files of the Indian Criminal Investigation Department.[2]

These new enterprises are a challenge to our producers. The gauntlet has been thrown and the result of the combat is awaited with much interest.

What about the contents of the foreign films released here after the war? Judging from a cursory survey of some of the best foreign films of 1946 to 1949 it can be said that psychological dramas and well-known classics have become increasingly popular; that musical romances dealing with the lives and works of famous musicians have been profitable themes and that realistic themes and controversial problem pictures have come into their own.

Whatever be the merits or demerits of the foreign films shown in India, they reveal that the screen is slowly but surely leaving the boy-meets-girl tradition far behind. A great many of the foreign producers seem to have realized that to produce a film for financial profits is not enough, and that to be really outstanding, films cannot be divorced from the realities of life.

Soon after the end of the war, American and British film executives were once again mooting the possibilities of producing films in foreign countries. Newspapers were rife with reports that foreign film leaders were planning to extend their markets. Eric A. Johnston, President of

---

[1] *The Illustrated Weekly of India,* June 13, 1948; *The Bharat Jyoti,* June 23, 1948.
[2] *Sunday Standard,* August 29, 1948; *The Bharat Jyoti,* August 29, 1948.

the Motion Picture Producers Association of America, is reported to have said that it would be one of his aims to increase foreign business which represented 35 to 50 per cent[1] of the industry's gross income. According to him the 'mass dynamic market'[2] of Egypt, India, Middle East, China and South America were ripe fields and could be made to yield important revenue. They are not concerned with what would happen to the indigenous film industries of those countries. They are actuated by purely business motives and as far as India is concerned, it is this threatened plan to swamp the Indian film, which has caused panic among many people in our industry.

Before passing any verdict on foreigners or on the agitation of our producers, it would be proper to examine carefully the details of the proposed plans. It has been reported by the press that foreign distributors are planning to distribute and exhibit sub-standard 16 mm entertainment, educational and documentary films all over the country. With 16 mm films it would be possible to reach the remotest corners of India as sub-standard films have advantages over standard films in capital investment, transport facilities and safety measures.

Not merely in the field of 16 mm films but in the standard films also, foreign interests intend to enter into direct competition. It is reported that a new technique of film presentation, 'Narration', has been developed to make films more intelligible and hence more enjoyable. Where people of foreign countries cannot understand the English sound track, a large number of people can understand the American film with their own mother-tongue spoken by a commentator who explains the English dialogue right from the screen. A few of the first films with this 'Narration' are *Madame Curie, Gaslight,* and *Tarzan Escapes.* Apart from narration, foreign concerns intend dubbing their films into Indian languages with a view to screening them to non-English speaking peoples. In fact, for the development of the 16 mm market American organizations will have to

---

[1] Nora Laing, "Young India Studies Movie Technique", *The Illustrated Weekly of India,* September 7, 1947.
[2] *Ibid.*

dub their films into Indian languages, but they propose to dub some of the standard size films also. In fact, since 1944, about 26 foreign films[1] dubbed or narrated in Hindustani, have been examined and certified by the Board of Bombay Film Censors but most of them have not yet been commercially released. One notable exception, however, is the release of the Hindi-Urdu dubbed version of Sir Alexander Korda's famous Arabian Night fantasy *Thief of Baghdad* under the title of *Baghdad Ka Chor* at the Excelsior Cinema, Bombay, in August 1948. This was not the first time that this picture had been dubbed. As noted earlier, Wadia Movietone had made an attempt in 1937. The box-office success of the current version would mean serious encroachment on the home market, and would also pave the way for similar ventures in future. Of course, a great deal depends on the success of other films, for it cannot be denied that much of the popularity and success of this picture is to be attributed to its oriental theme and cast which featured the Indian-born Hollywood film star, Sabu. But would films with more sophisticated themes the appeal of which lies primarily in intrigue or psychological conflict, set in an alien social background, be as successful? This is a point worth consideration.

The Indian film has real cause for alarm; as it is, foreign films take away about 20 per cent of the total revenue, and if the dubbed versions are successful they would take away a large share of the box-office returns which ought legitimately to belong to Indian films.

This threat of foreign infiltration whether it be of a lesser or greater magnitude, can only be met in one way. Instead of sitting and lamenting over their lot or asking for Government protection, our producers should better their products and meet the foreigners in open competition. There is no point in saying that we have not got the resources. In spite of limited resources and equipment a few isolated instances have shown what really can be done by men with ideas. What has been done by a few can be done by many more if only they would not make

[1] *Journal of the Film Industry,* December 1948, p. 18.

monetary gain their prime consideration. Besides, our producers hold the trump card for they know the public taste better than their competitors across the ocean. Undoubtedly, we have much to learn from the foreigners, and it must be frankly recognized that there is much in the American film from which the Indian industry derives inspiration. To the educated film-goer it offers a standard of comparison. It is by educating the consumer and not by keeping him in ignorance that an industry can hope to thrive.

Foreigners interested in securing releases for their films in India may well think  of  building a chain of theatres, for even today the position of cinema houses in India is far from satisfactory. There  are  about  2,000 cinemas of which 1,700 are permanent 35 mm cinemas, the rest being mobile units. There are about 375 in Bombay Province and 53 in Bombay City.[1]   They have a total seating capacity of about 1,400,000 and an estimated yearly attendance of 200,000,000.[2] The average seating capacity of an Indian cinema house is about 700.  In Bombay City itself the seating capacity of cinemas varies considerably from the smallest number of 395 in Prakash Cinema situated on DeLisle Road to 1491 in the Metro at Dhobi Talao.  While the former is exclusively an Indian picture house the latter is exclusively foreign.  Of the 53 cinema houses in Bombay City 10 show foreign films and 43 show Indian films; two cinemas showing Indian films occasionally show foreign films  and  nine others show foreign films on Sunday mornings only.  Compared to the vastness of the country's population these figures

[1] Figures supplied by different authorities do not always tally.  The IMPPA gives the number of all-India theatres as 1700, 373 Bombay Presidency and 50 Bombay City.  B. V. Dharap gives the figures as 1618, 220 (excluding East & West Khandesh Districts which according to film distribution convention are included in C.P. & C.I. circuit) and 50 respectively. The Publicity Manager of United Artists says that the all-India figure is 1500 and 50 in Bombay City.  The manager of the 20th-Century Fox Corporation (India) Ltd. gives the number as 1,600 India, 600 Bombay Presidency and 48 Bombay City.  An unofficial enquiry made through the Bombay Provincial Government has revealed the number of cinemas in Bombay  City  as  53.  The UNESCO *Courier* Vol. 1 No. 6, July 1948, and UNESCO Commission on the Technical Needs in Press Film & Radio say that there are about 2,000 cinemas in India.
[2] UNESCO *Report of the Commission on Technical Needs in Press Film & Radio, Following Surveys in Seventeen Countries and Territories*, p. 265.

are indeed insignificant and absolutely inadequate to
meet the needs of the expanding industry. While India
and Pakistan with a population of about 400,000,000
have no more than 2,000 cinemas, the U.S.A. with a
population of about 130,000,000 (the estimate of the
1950 census is 150,000,000) has 17,000 cinemas and
Great Britain with a population of approximately
50,000,000 has as many as 5,000 cinemas.

In view of this urgent need, the industry sent a de-
putation to Government,  but there was considerable
agitation in the press against granting permission to con-
struct new cinema houses.  Apart from objections against
individual applications, the general objection raised was
that cinemas should not be constructed near educational
institutions, religious places, women's institutions, very
thickly populated areas and where there was traffic con-
gestion.  Another objection raised was that building
material should not be used for the construction of
cinemas when there was such an acute housing shortage
in the city.  The Government of Bombay though it has
given permission for the construction of fifteen more
cinema houses in Bombay City and Suburbs, has not yet
released any building material for them.

Apart from the inadequate  number of cinemas in
India most of those in existence are far from satisfactory.
They vary from air-conditioned buildings to bug-ridden
sheds with wooden benches, while the villages are served by mobile units.

In many small towns, dark, dingy, dirty houses with
poor sound equipment, without any ventilation or air
and without any sanitary arrangements are ironically
termed 'picture palaces'! Most of our cinemas today are
not in the least picturesque. Generally they are housed in
old buildings and those that are new remain clean only
for a short while. Then they get disfigured with dirt and
with streaks of red *paan* stains. Not merely this, but re-
freshments instead of being provided outside, are supplied in the auditoriums, and the hawkers selling nuts,
lemonade, soda and what not, clutter up the aisles adding
to the indiscipline and pandemonium. Besides, the seats

are hard, uncomfortable and bug-ridden. They are never dusted or cleaned or sprayed with some insecticide as these things are unknown to an average Indian showman. In many cinema houses seats are not numbered with the result that once a show is over and the doors are opened for the next show, there is a regular scramble, and often might is right.

That is not all. The box office scramble is the worst of all. Conditions vary from city to city and province to province. Some people earn a regular livelihood by selling tickets at a premium. Having obtained a ticket, it is a greater trial to push one's way through the surging crowd of humanity shoving and fighting to get inside the cinema house.

There is usually a world of difference between a cinema showing foreign films and one showing Indian films. In Bombay, for example, which is the most important release centre for films, while there are some very good cinema houses for foreign pictures, there is hardly a good theatre for Indian pictures barring the Liberty Cinema.

Among the audience at Indian films, there are crying babies, men who must explain the story to their womenfolk; musical people who must sing or keep time with the hero or heroine!

And what about the films themselves? Before Bombay audiences have the pleasure of seeing the films for which they have paid, they are compelled to see against their wishes gaudy, ill-designed and unimaginative advertisement slides. As the income from these slides is an overriding consideration, the management might charge higher rates for exhibiting them and discriminate in the matter of good taste.

After having endured all this, what entertainment does the audience get? Generally speaking, as far as Indian films go, the tragedies are too heavy and the comedies just miss being funny. There are many incongruities in presentation. The stars are lifeless, slow moving and highly theatrical in their action. Last but not least, Indian films lack realism and are tediously

long. Twelve to fourteen reels is nothing unusual for an
Indian film, but the pity of it is that most of the films are
not interesting enough to warrant that length. The few
that are interesting also tend to drag in parts from
where footage could be easily eliminated with advantage.
While the Government order restricting the length of the
film to 11,000 feet was in force, the Indian films—with
the exception of a few such as *Kismet, Shakuntala* and
*Ram Rajya* which were exempted on application by the
producers—were compelled not to exceed the limit.
Since the withdrawal of that order, however, Indian
films have gone back to their previous length. Undoubtedly a few outstanding films every year would necessarily be long, but the average Indian film should be cut
down to about 9,000 to 10,000 feet. In fact, once again
the Government of India is planning to revive the 11,000
feet restriction. A proposal to that effect is under consideration.

Taking stock of our pictures released since the
advent of sound, what is to be noted is that our producers still go in for stereotyped subjects produced in the
same way. The rut which our average producer has got
into, is the habit of forming a foregone conclusion that
because a certain story was a success at the box office
and was applauded by critics and fans, every story of the
same type would necessarily succeed. Nothing could be
further from the truth. Just because years ago *Pukar*
produced by the Minerva Movietone became a sensational box-office hit, others started a chain of historical
pictures, such as *Shahenshah Akbar, Sikander, Babar,
Humayun, Mumtaz Mahal, Shah Jehan,* many of which
failed to be popular. The success of *Sant Tukaram,* a devotional picture produced by Prabhat Film Company
was followed by other similar themes in *Tulsidas, Surdas,
Narsi Mehta, Bhakta Dhruva* and *Meera.* The success of
*Laila Majnu* has given us a spate of love themes, such as,
*Sohni Mehwal, Romeo and Juliet, Wamaq Ezra, Shirin
Farhad.* Some of these films were miserable failures.
The success of *Shakuntala* and *Ram Rajya* has brought
*Prithviraj Sanyukta, Lakha Rani, Krishna Leela, Ratna-*

*vali* and so on.   All this goes to show that the majority of our producers do not think on original or creative lines.  They imitate too often and fail as often, and yet refuse to learn lessons from their failures.  The result is that the more critical and discriminating audience avoids Indian films.

With few exceptions, most producers are quite satisfied with their stories because the majority of the audience accepts what is given.  There is no attempt on their part either to raise the standard of production or employ talented and capable writers of screen stories. The smug complacency of many of our producers in this matter is hard to imagine, and until something is done to rouse them it will be our unfortunate lot to witness insipid stories, badly treated.

Another regrettable feature of our films is the lack of realism.  Though film fans are not very critical in their attitude, they are certainly intelligent and not so much under the spell of the silver screen that they can be fooled into believing every impossible shot.  Many mythological films and stunt pictures are replete with spiritual miracles and impossible situations, such as the hero fighting a band of robbers single-handed and coming out of the fight unscathed or a man jumping from a roof-top and escaping unhurt.

Undoubtedly something can be said in defence of stunt films.  From a commercial point of view they are cheaper to produce and popular with certain sections of the population.  Even Western countries produce adventure thrillers, but a large number of such pictures cannot contribute towards the improvement of production. Apart from this, if stunt films are to be produced, surely they could be kept within the bounds of reason, and not packed with incidents and scenes which even the least critical may find hard to believe.

Even the amorous episodes in our pictures are often unrealistic and ridiculous.  The theme of boy-meets-girl, they fall in love, boy's love wanes, he falls in love with another girl, the first girl commits suicide leaving the boy free to marry the other girl, is common

on our screen and exploited by many producers.   But
such embarrassing and sticky sentiment is not appreciated by the audience which often expresses its disapproval
by whistles and catcalls.

The Indian screen has done all it can to cloak and
camouflage its romantic  episodes  to the point  of unconvincing artificiality.   They are boring and seem to
be cast in the same mould.   For example, in a typical
romantic interlude, a boy and a girl are shown meeting
in a garden or on the banks of a river either under the
full moon or with a pair of love birds billing and cooing
on a nearby tree.   The girl gazes at the boy and he
approaches her.   She then runs away from him either
out of modesty or to show the deftness of her feet!   An
instant later he goes in pursuit.   One would imagine
they were  playing hide and seek or competing in a
hundred yards race, and when they ultimately meet,
the hero stands a little away and bursts into a pathetic
wail which one is asked to believe is a love song!

The reason why such scenes lack realism is that a
few imaginative directors capable of doing something
better seem to be restricted through fear of the censors,
while the majority of producers are incapable of handling such scenes successfully.   They have no foresight
and even the backgrounds are monotonous. The 'lovers'
always walk on the same river bank, run over the same
artificial bridge and sing under the same  man-made
moon; the direction is the same and the method of approach is the same.   Where can there be charm when
there is no vision?   Moreover, kissing is never shown
on the Indian screen.   Censorship regulations do not
permit it.  Kissing in public, though a common Western
habit and as such shown frequently in foreign films, is
alien to our social habits and since the screen cannot
afford to be much ahead of the sentiment of society,
kissing scenes are omitted.

What about our mythological films?   Some people
are apt to belittle mythological films but V. G. Damle,
writing in defence of them says:  "I believe in the need
for mythological films.   I believe they have a mission

and I believe in that mission. . . . By mythological films, I mean those stories whose historical authenticity is partly or wholly open to question, but which through tradition are popularly accepted in good faith as true.

"A common factor of these stories is the part played by miracles. It must be remembered that these stories are an inseparable part of the faith of an overwhelming mass of the Indian public and there is nothing in them that is derogatory to basic standards of morality. Indeed, they are directed expressly towards the moral aim. They form an important, integral part of India's cultural heritage.

"I cannot recall a single social story that has brought to the screen a man more warmly human than Tukaram or a boy more spiritedly juvenile than Gopal Krishna.

"Pictures like *Tukaram, Gopal Krishna* and *Dnaneshwar* more nearly represent the social genius of India than most of the so-called 'social' films. They present deep-seated moral and spiritual ideals through personalities not merely idolized but also idealized through centuries. They symbolize the Golden Age which most nations and faiths believe existed and which most religions hope to bring about. As such symbols, their influence on the public mind is wholly wholesome and definitely desirable."[1]

Without the least intention of running down these pictures one cannot help feeling, however, that mythology is overdone on our screen. There is no aspect or incident from the Epics which has not been filmed over and over again. No doubt mythological films appeal more to our people in view of the inherent religious traditions of the average Indian. But as S. Radhakrishnan says, "We are getting too much of this mythology. We should retain all our ancient ideals but they must find out parallels in the life of modern people and the modern conditions. The industry must give to the nation pictures around our daily life and its social and economic problems.

[1] Prabhat Special Supplement, *The Times of India,* September 9, 1939.

"India's history both medieval and modern will
supply any number of themes for biographical pictures.
Travelogues, documentaries, newsreels and shorts such
as they produce in America must now be started here."[1]

There is no dearth of material in our country.
India is a land which hums with stories which, with
imagination and talent, could be converted to screen
scripts, and there is little reason for us to fall back upon
American plots which do not fit in with our environment or to harp on bygone deeds of valour or ancient
superstition which do not fit in which the fast-changing
times.

No critical survey of Indian films would be complete
without a mention of humour, music and dance as represented on the screen.

D. C. Patole writing in *The Times of India* stringent-
ly criticised the low standard of humour prevalent in
Indian talkies.   Humour as represented in Indian films,
is generally a story of absurd situations, preposterous
acting and jokes which  refuse to go off at the right
moment or refuse to go off at all like a damp squib.
Scenes which are meant to be farcical frequently end
by being ludicrous and the intelligent audience fails to
be amused.

Humour is not considered seriously as an integral
part of the plot in Indian films.   It is utilized only to
relieve the strain of heavy situation in a long drawn-
out and tedious drama.   Very often it is used to add
length to a film for no Indian picture can be possibly
less than 10,000 feet.

Producers have   a few artistes who   go through
their limited stock-in-trade in different films.   Many
think that if they introduce a scene in which a man is
wearing a sari, they are depicting a very funny situation indeed.   Often a manly comedian with a luxuriant
moustache is shown impersonating a woman and this
though it may amuse a section of the audience fails to
appeal to the more discriminating ones.

A few of our artistes have tried to imitate western

[1] *Filmindia,* March 1942, pp. 59-62.

comedians but failed miserably in their efforts.

Often, idiocy, stupidity and madness are made the basis of laughter in many films with little variation, and though this seems funny to children and to some grown-ups, it appears ridiculous to most adults.

To have humour in a picture it is not necessary that it should be comic. Fun can creep into any story. Again, to be humourous it is not necessary for our actors to act like drunkards, imbeciles or buffoons. A man can be normal and yet be humourous. He may never laugh, and yet keep the audience in fits of laughter with witty, brilliant repartee. That is what Clifton Webb does with his scathing tongue. The audience laughs at Charles Chaplin or Danny Kaye not because they exaggerate their actions but because they look so out of place in a given set of circumstances and are ludicrous when they attempt to be dignified.

In Indian films, music, especially vocal music, plays a significant part. A picture without songs is an unheard of thing, and no film without good music can be popular at the box office. Hence a producer has to sprinkle songs generously if he is to make his picture a paying proposition. In fact, every few minutes there is a song without any consideration as to whether it is essential to the story or not. On the least provocation, our film heroes and heroines burst into song, often in the most incredible situations. Though songs are the main attraction in an Indian film, too many of them are apt to disturb the tempo of the story, hold up development and make the film needlessly long.

As music is very often made the prime consideration, actors and actresses are frequently chosen for the central roles for their singing ability. Little thought is given to their suitability for such roles. Consequently miscasting occurs quite often in Indian films.

All Indian pictures, no matter of what type they are, have songs. Biographies, mythological and historical pictures, adventure thrillers, love stories and musicals are all replete with songs to appeal to the popular taste. Since each film must have six to eight songs,

7

some even more, music directors often rehash melodies from old pictures.

While we have sedulously aped the West in many respects, we should have realized also that songs are not considered an essential feature in all films produced in the U.S.A. and Great Britain.  This does not mean that our pictures should be devoid of songs, but songs should find a place in motion pictures only in so far as they correctly fit into the development of the theme.  There is no doubt that a picture produced with correct psychological appeal would succeed even without songs.  Besides, the power of incidental music in building up a situation is not fully exploited on the Indian screen.

Another striking feature of our film music is that it is in a class by itself.  It is neither oriental of the classical type nor occidental, but has a blend of both. It is to be regretted, however, that the latter element is often a very preponderating one.  Many a time the opening chords or the instrumental accompaniment is a cheap imitation of some western music.  Why should this be so?  When we have such a heritage of music why should music directors have to borrow from the West?  Is not an oriental piece a more fitting accompaniment to an Indian scene than a concocted piece of noise which is a cheap imitation of some western tune, however popular the latter may be?

The devotees of classical Indian music are also very critical of film music. It is said that film music has ruined our great musical traditions and that classical music is falsified to create film music which is cheap, hybrid and vulgar. Undoubtedly, classical music is elevating, sublime and spiritual, but its very quality limits its appeal, and though it was tried on the screen by a few directors, it was not as successful as folk and provincial songs and even some of the concocted melodies unabashedly stolen from foreign records.

Even though classical music has not been much used in the past, there is a great scope for it as has been demonstrated by the success of the film *Meera* featuring the renowned classical singer of the South, M. S. Subbulakshmi.

It is an undeniable fact that film music has some times been good, very often bad and indifferent; but this is inevitable considering that it is essentially meant for the man in the street and that about two thousand songs are being composed every year. In spite of these handi- caps film music, in the main, has been breaking new ground and evolving new tunes, combinations and to a certain extent, even rhythm.

Though much can be done, it seems that unless we have efficient music directors, well-read and talented lyric writers, singers with really good voices, and unless we learn to suit our songs and our music to every mood and aspect of a situation, our film music cannot rise out of the rut of stagnation into which it has fallen today.

What is true of music is true, though to a lesser degree, of dance sequences. They are the main attrac- tions on which the film producer usually relies to make his film popular. There was a time when an Indian dance shown on the screen was but a fleeting shadow of the real thing. Since then there has been an ad- vance, but there is still much scope for improvement.

As seen today, the film dance sequences lack variety and beauty. They form a style by themselves — a mix- ture of Bharat Natyam-cum-Kathak-cum-what-you-will. Dances are included with the main aim of adding a little sex-appeal to the picture and little thought is given to their suitability or appropriateness to the theme of the story.

In this connexion mention must be made of Uday Shankar's film *Kalpana* released in February 1948 simul- taneously in nine theatres in India of which five were in Bombay. It was the first full-length dance fantasy to be produced in India. So far no dance picture had been produced for the simple reason that it was very expensive. The problems that besieged Uday Shankar were great. There was no studio sufficiently large enough to facilitate the shooting of magnificent and superb dances. The problem of sets was equally great but he solved the problem and evolved a scheme which

was as simple as it was grand. The scheme was based
on the use of different blocks of squares, cubes, semi-
circles and sectors. *Kalpana's* seventy to eighty dance
sequences are incomparable in their rhythm, beauty
and grace.

A unique landmark in the annals of the Indian film,
it is a picture which deserves special mention for attempting a new theme. Its greatest drawback, however,
is its faulty editing. Uday Shankar who conceived, designed, produced and directed it seems to have been
reluctant to cut his work drastically, with the result that
it gives the impression of hasty, jerky narrative and
hurried glimpses at a kaleidoscope of haunting beauty
twirled too fast. The confused medley of ideas, the
autobiographical references and the difficulty of understanding the significance of the various dances, did not
make the film a popular success. Nevertheless, it marked not only an important step forward in the progress
of the Indian film but showed clearly that the screen
could very beautifully portray Indian culture as represented through dance and music. The beauty and
significance of it would have been heightened if it had
been in colour. Even then it really deserves to be ranked among the film classics.

Today, in the atomic era, while things are moving
fast and planning is going on furiously in many industrial circles, the Indian film industry seems to be self-
complacently static. There is no serious or organized
effort on the part of our producers to improve their lot.
The growth of the Indian film industry to the present
stage has been not only unconscious but unorganized
and haphazard. But it can no longer be ignored. It
is too potent a force which must either uplift or degrade.
It is thus in the fitness of things that at this stage when
we have reached another milestone in the history of
our industry, the Government of India should undertake a thorough investigation into the prevailing conditions. An Enquiry Committee has been appointed
consisting of six members of which two are members of
the film industry, two are members of the Constituent

Assembly, one an official and one an educationist. Its terms of reference are to enquire into the growth and organization of the industry and indicate the lines of future development, to examine what measures should be adopted to enable films in India to develop into an effective instrument for the promotion of national culture, education and entertainment, to enquire into the possibility of manufacturing raw film and cinematographic equipment in India and indicate what standards should be adopted for the import of raw film and equipment.

The industry has expressed some discontent at not being consulted before the appointments were made as also about the competence of the Committee to look into the vital problems of the industry.

Nevertheless, at the moment everyone interested is waiting to see how things will shape and what will be the outcome of this enquiry on which will depend the future of the Indian film.

# 5

## FILMS AND FILM-GOERS

EXTENSIVE research work done in the West estates blishes beyond question that the attitudes, emotions, behaviour and sleep of children and young people are influenced by the cinema. The nature of these effects depends on the contents of the motion pictures seen and the way in which the viewer reacts to these contents. If children and adults, especially young adults, are affected by what is shown on the screen, it is important that an analysis of their attendance at and of the contents of the motion picture be made to show the nature of the stimuli producing these effects.

Who attends the cinemas? Children or adults? Labourers or professional men? Men or women? What social group or groups are most attracted to the films? These are debatable questions. As far as Western countries are concerned the answer is that nearly everybody sees films. Children and youth are the most enthusiastic movie fans. Alice Mitchell speaking of the U.S.A. says that practically all children of all classes go to the movies. The frequency with which they go is determined by such factors as home environment, parental supervision, direct interest and finance. Some go only occasionally and when accompanied by parents and other adult members of the family. A large number go when and how they choose. But they all go as a matter of course.[1] Edgar Dale's enquiry conducted during the year 1929-30 supports the Chicago investigation of Alice Mitchell. His statistics show that attendance at

[1] Alice Mitchell, *Children and the Movies*, p. 18.

cinemas declines consistently with age. He says: "More than one-third of the motion picture audiences throughout the United States are composed of children and youth under the age of 21".[1]

Today the weekly attendance of juveniles in the U.S.A. is 11,000,000 out of a total attendance of 85,000,000 and a population of 130,000,000. That is, children constitute 12.9 per cent of the weekly attendance at the cinema. Of the 85,000,000, however, a great many are repeaters and even of the 11,000,000 children there are many who go even two or three times a week.[2]

From England a more or less similar story is reported. Investigation reveals that children in towns go more frequently than adults and that a very large proportion go at least once a week, unless restrained by censorship regulations. On the whole, boys go more frequently than girls. All told about 4,500,000 children go to the cinema weekly.[3]

Attendance of adults at cinemas in Great Britain and the U.S.A. far exceeds their attendance at any other form of amusement. In America, about 80,000,000 to 85,000,000 seats are sold every week. In Great Britain, some 25,000,000 seats a week are sold. These figures exclude the groups of very young and very old people who do not constitute an effective potential audience. Among these also there are many who attend the cinema more than once a week. Taking these facts into consideration it is estimated that about 50 per cent of the total population of both countries are regular cinema-goers.[4]

Amongst children, it was noted that boys attended more frequently than girls. Does the same difference exist between the sexes among the adults? The evidence is conflicting. In *New Survey of London, Life & Labour*, it is stated that 70 per cent of the weekly

[1] Edgar Dale, *The Contents of Motion Pictures & Children's Attendance at Motion Pictures*, p. 2.
[2] Roger Manvell, *The Film*, p. 163; M. F. Thorp, *America at the Movies*, pp. 15-16.
[3] Richard Ford, *Children and the Cinema*, pp. 32, 39; Roger Manvell, *The Film*, p. 163.
[4] Roger Manvell, *The Film*, p. 163; M. F. Thorp, *America at the Movies*, pp. 15-16.

audience consists of women and girls.¹ *The Mersey Side Survey* states: "Of the married, women go more often than their husbands".² On the other hand, the most comprehensive investigations made by Edgar Dale into this question reveal that even in the age groups of 21 years and more, men formed 59.3 per cent and women only 40.7 per cent.³

One might say that, after all, the former figures relate to Great Britain, while Dale's enquiry relates to the U.S.A., and as conditions are different, they cannot be taken as conflicting accounts. Dale's conclusions were, however, confirmed by investigations carried out in Great Britain in 1938. Answers to questions revealed that men attended pictures more regularly than women and therefore there was a greater average attendance on the part of the former than the latter. Besides, a greater percentage of women than men had never been to the cinema. These results are at great variance with the popular conception that women go to the cinema more frequently than men.

What social group or groups are most attracted to the pictures? Statistics reveal that in Western countries all strata of society attend the cinema. The question which arises, however, is whether members of some class go more frequently than those of others. Evidence comes from the U.S.A. for believing that typical members of professional classes go less frequently than people of lower social status.⁴

From Great Britain much the same evidence is obtained. The manual working classes attend cinema shows more frequently than clerks, shopkeepers and shop assistants. But clerks go more often and more regularly than any other white-collared group while the skilled workers and professional men go least of all.⁵

As the above investigations and enquiries relate to

¹ Sir Hubert Llewellyn Smith, *New Survey of London Life and Labour.* Vol. IX, p. 46.
² Henry Durant, *The Problem of Leisure,* p. 117.
³ Edgar Dale, *The Contents of Motion Pictures* & *Children's Attendance at Motion Pictures* p. 64.
⁴ Henry Durant, *The Problem of Leisure,* p. 122.
⁵ *Ibid,* p. 23.

conditions in the U.S.A. and Great Britain, their findings are not applicable to India. It may be said that on broad psychological trends, children and adults of Western countries are similar to people here, but the differences in education, social life, upbringing, environment and especially in national cinema habits and censorship make it impossible to apply the findings of those investigations to Indian conditions. There is a complete absence of any similar data, regarding the cinema-going habits of our people. So far nobody, with the exception of the Indian Cinematograph Committee, neither the Government nor any educational or social institution, has found it either interesting or practicable enough to make a detailed and thorough investigation into the composition of audiences at our cinemas, nor has an effort been made to classify and analyse the contents of our films.

In 1927, the Indian Cinematograph Committee found that the cinema in India was an urban entertainment. Even in towns and cities the composition of an average cinema audience varied according to the part of the country concerned, the specific locality in which the cinema house was situated and according to the films it showed—Indian or foreign.

As far as Bombay was concerned, in an answer to a questionnaire many witnesses gave their evidence and opinion to the Committee. Sifting through all the conflicting views to be had on this subject, the salient feature that strikes one is that, in Bombay City, children under the age of 14 generally attended the afternoon and before dinner shows but even then their number was very limited. They varied from 3 per cent onwards but did not exceed 15 per cent[1] of the entire cinema audience, and that too, they were brought by their parents because there was no one else to look after them.

The proportion of adolescents between the ages of 14 and 20, however, was fairly large. They constituted about 30 to 40 per cent[2] of the cinema audience.

[1] *Indian Cinematograph Committee,* 1927-28, *Evidence* Vol. I, pp. I, 23, 50, 239, 260, 322, 348, 377, 465, 471, 548, 549, 593.
[2] *Ibid.*

Amongst adults, Indian women rarely attended cinema shows, especially Muslim women. It was only when a religious or mythological film was shown that there was an appreciable attendance of women and these were mostly Hindus. On the other hand, the number of women in cinemas patronized by Europeans, Parsis and Christians was fairly large.

As regards the composition of an average audience, it would be difficult to generalize as it varied from locality to locality. In Bombay, the cinema houses in the Fort area which exhibited exclusively foreign films were patronized only by Europeans and educated Indians. In Girgaum, Sandhurst Road and Lamington Road the cinemas were patronized mostly by Indians of the lower middle class as well as by the uneducated classes, while those at Parel, Dadar and the northern end of the City were frequented mostly by people of the labouring class, especially millhands and factory workers. Generally speaking, all classes of people attended the cinema, but among the lower working class and the uneducated class the tendency was greater and was on the increase. They constituted about 65 per cent of the total cinemagoers while the educated class, both Indian and European constituted only 35 per cent.[1]

Since the Indian Cinematograph Committee made its enquiry, the cinema-going habit has become more widespread and the number of cinemas have also increased to cater to the growing needs of the people. Even then the average attendance at the cinema is very low. Out of a total population of 400,000,000 about 700,000 people daily go to the cinema, and the average attendance in a month is approximately 21,000,000. That is to say, only 5.25 per cent of the total population go to the cinema every month. Of these, there are a fairly large number of people who go twice or even thrice a week. Therefore, the actual number of people going would work out to about to 2 or 3 per cent of the total population. Generally speaking, the percentage of attendance in larger towns is higher while in villages it is

[1] *Ibid.*

nil. In Bombay Province, for example, the attendance per day is about 150,000 giving an approximate average attendance per month of 4,500,000. In Bombay City, it was found from the data collected from Government sources that the average weekly attendance (taken for the first week of May 1948) was 575,050. Of this, the attendance at cinemas showing foreign films was 94,119 and at cinemas showing Indian films, 480,931. Indian pictures are more paying than foreign ones and bring in the greater returns. In both foreign and Indian cinema houses the one rupee five anna seat brings in the largest income.

Today as in the past, the number of people attending a cinema is determined by such conditions as the locality in which the picture house is situated, the kind of picture showing, weather conditions and so on. In regard to the foreign picture houses in Bombay City, about 13,000 people attend the cinema daily and the average week's attendance is approximately 90,000. Some picture houses like Metro, Regal and Eros have a fixed clientele—people who go regularly no matter what picture is on. In these cinema houses the majority of the audience consists of lower and upper middle classes and professional men and women. Children and adolescents constitute about 20 per cent of the total audience, while among the adults 40 to 50 per cent consists of women. Of course much depends on the type of picture. For example, generally speaking a sentimental 'sob-stuff' picture attracts more women than men, while children and the lower class crowd to see pictures depicting action and adventure of the Tarzan variety.

Taking into consideration all the cinema houses in Bombay, it may be said that adults of the labour and lower middle classes and adolescents are those who attend the cinema most frequently. No exact data are to be had, but approximately 68 per cent adults of whom 10 per cent are women, 30 per cent adolescents and about 2 per cent children comprise the average cinema audience. From the viewpoint of social groups

40 per cent of the audience consists of labourers and working classes, 40 per cent of officers, military personnel, businessmen, professional men and 20 per cent of students.

As regards the cinema-going habits of the younger generation, especially the student population of Bombay, a questionnaire circulated amongst them elicited varied answers from which may be gathered that of girls between the ages of 14 and 20, 9.4 per cent go twice a week, 25.9 per cent go once a week, 24.5 per cent go once a fortnight, 25.2 per cent go once a month and the rest go irregularly. Of the girls over the age of 21, 11.1 per cent go twice a week, 14.8 per cent go once a week, 25.9 per cent go once a fortnight, 18.5 per cent go once a month, 22.4 per cent go irregularly and 7.4 per cent go rarely. Among the adolescent boys between the ages of 14 and 20, however, 4.1 per cent go three times a week or more, 9.8 per cent go twice a week, 26.8 per cent go once a week, 3.6 per cent go thrice a month, 16 per cent go twice a month, 25.8 per cent go once a month, 8.8 per cent go occasionally and 5.2 per cent go irregularly. Among the boys of 21 and over, the once and twice a week habit is more common, but they are balanced by boys who go either twice a month, once a month or irregularly, as the following figures show: 2 per cent go three to four times a week, 16.3 per cent go twice a week, 22.4 per cent go once a week, 19.4 per cent go twice a month, 17.3 per cent go once a month, while the rest go either irregularly or rarely.

In contrast to the cinema-going habits of boys and girls in Western countries, the cinema-going habit here is generally not contracted very early. When asked when they saw their first picture, 26.9 per cent and 20.8 per cent adolescent girls and boys respectively stated that they did not remember; of the rest, however, 13.8 per cent both of girls and boys said at the age of 7, 10 per cent girls and 15.3 per cent boys said at the age of 6, and 13 per cent girls and 11.7 per cent boys said at the age of 5, while the rest varied between the ages of two and ten years. Among the older age

group, 25.9 per cent  young women and  15 per cent
young men did not recollect; 18.5 per cent women and
22 per cent men gave the age of 10 and over.  18.5 per
cent women and 12 per cent men said at the age of 7; 14.8
per cent women and 15 per cent men said at the age of
8 and the rest saw their first film either very early at
about the age of two or three or as late as eight and nine.

Even though the students went to the cinema quite
frequently, their most favourite pastime was reading;
77.6 per cent girls between the ages of 14 and 20, 51.9
per cent girls over 21 years old, 55.1 per cent boys between 14 and 20 and 55.7 per cent boys over 21 years
gave their vote in favour of reading as an activity which
they indulged in most frequently during their spare
hours.   They went to the cinema also, but not as often
as one might have imagined.   Only 9.2 per cent younger
boys and 8.2 per cent older boys, 3 per cent young girls
and 7.4 per cent older girls said that going to the pictures was their most common leisure hour choice, while
the rest indulged in sports or other recreational activities.   While a negligible number of parents—0.4 per
cent—objected to their children going to the cinema,
47.6 per cent boys and girls had to take their parents'
permission before going to the cinema, while the remaining 52 per cent had merely to inform their parents
that they were going to the pictures.

Between the foreign and Indian films shown, the
foreign films were more popular among the educated
adolescents and young adults of Bombay City.   69.8
per cent of the younger generation voted in favour of
foreign films because of their all round superiority; 15.9
per cent said they preferred Indian films mostly because
of the songs and because they could follow them with
less effort, while 14.5 per cent liked both Indian and
foreign films.

Judging both from box-office receipts and from
students' likes and dislikes it was found that among
Indian films the types which were most popular were
social pictures like *Hamrahi;* love stories containing good
music like *Devdas, Doctor, Zindagi, Pyar ki Jeet, Andaz;*

mythological pictures like *Shakuntala* and *Ram Rajya;* historical and biographical like *Pukar, Shah Jehan, Ram Shastri, Tansen* and *Doctor Kotnis ki Amar Kahani, Shaheed, Ramjoshi;* and films with spectacular setting like *Chandralekha.* Many of these pictures had a run of over twenty-five weeks in some key centres and their success must be attributed to their story and music. Indian audiences have a peculiar fascination for simple but catchy tunes.

As regards the foreign films the types which have been very popular are love stories like, *Romeo and Juliet, Gone with the Wind, Rebecca, Valley of Decision, Random Harvest, All This and Heaven Too, For Whom the Bell Tolls;* psychological dramas like *Spellbound, Leave Her to Heaven, The Snake Pit;* fantasies like *Arabian Nights, Matter of Life & Death, Fantasia;* commedies like *Cluny Brown, Sitting Pretty;* musicals like *Bathing Beauty, Diamond Horse Shoe, The Jolson Story;* historical and biographical stories like *Life of Emile Zola, Juarez, Blossoms in the Dust, Madame Curie, Marie Antoinette;* religious pictures like *Song of Bernadette;* social themes like *The Lost Week-end, The Best Years of Our Lives, Gentlemen's Agreement;* and classics like *Oliver Twist* and *Hamlet.* Mystery and horror films do not generally rank among popular films, but one exception to the rule was the film *Gaslight* which was very popular with boys as well as girls. Boys usually favoured historical, psychological, crime and mystery pictures while girls favoured psychological dramas, love stories, comedies and musicals. The popularity of these films was due to their story, acting, direction and photography. The fact that quite a few of the above films were in technicolour added to their charm and success.

Millions go to the cinema every day, and over 300,000,000 people a week attend the cinema throughout the world. Why do they go? There are many more answers to that question than one might at first imagine. The cinema is very popular for the obvious reason that to the majority of town dwellers it is easily accessible, easy to follow being visual and, compared to others, a cheap form of entertainment.

Today, over fifty years since the invention of the
cinematograph, films have become the principal means
of satisfying the hunger of the human mind for diversion. But apart from its recreational value, there are
many reasons why people go to the pictures. Elizabeth
Bowen putting herself along with the common man,
woman and child says: "I go to the cinema for any
number of different reasons...at random, here are a
few of them: I go to be distracted;........I go when I
don't want to think; I go when I do want to think and
need stimulus; I go to see pretty people; I go when I want
to see life ginned up;........I go to laugh; I go to be
harrowed;......I go to see America, France, Russia;..
......I go because the screen is an oblong opening into
a world of fantasy for me; I go because I like a story
with suspense; I go because I like sitting in a packed
crowd in the dark, among hundreds riveted on the
same thing;......These reasons put down roughly seem
to fall under five headings: wish to escape, lassitude,
sense of lack in my nature or my surroundings, loneliness (however passing) and natural frivolity."[1]

Often the cinema forms a means of escape from a
drab home and humdrum life to coolness, semi-darkness
and music; in fact to a type of life as unlike the audiences' as possible. As Charles Davy says: "As a social
institution the local cinema represents to a section of the
population the peak of glamour. Warmth and colour
are to be had there; there are pleasurable distractions;
there are comfort, richness and variety. The cinema is
often the poor man's sole contact with luxury, the only
place where he is made to feel a sense of self-importance.
....Not only the film programme but the deep carpets,
the bright lights, the attention fit for a king are the
weekly delights of a majority of picture-goers."[2]

Milton Sills, a film star of the early twenties in a
lecture at the Harvard Business School in 1927 said:

[1] Charles Davy, *Footnotes to the Film*, p. 205.
[2] *Ibid*, p. 230.

"Just how does this form of amusement function as compensation to the drudging millions?  By providing a means of escape from the intolerable pressure and incidence of reality.  The motion picture enables the spectators to live vicariously the more brilliant, interesting, adventurous, romantic, successful or comic lives of the shadow pictures before them on the screen....The films offer them a Freudian journey into made-to-order reverie, reverie by experts.  Now reverie may be unwholesome—our psychological studies are still too immature to decide this question—but in our present form of culture it seems to be necessary.  In any case, reverie engendered by motion pictures is certainly more wholesome than that engendered by the corner saloon or the drab walls of a tenement house.  For an hour or two the spectator identifies himself with the hero or heroine; potential adventurer at heart, he becomes for the moment an actual imaginative adventurer in a splendid world where things seem to go right."[1]

Meyer Levin, a film critic, gives another angle of approach and speaks of the hypnotic powers of the screen.  He says: "....even in the most obnoxious picture, I can feel the basic, physical hypnosis of the medium.  I want to sit and let the thing roll on and on......Now I know I'm not alone in feeling this hypnotic habit-forming need for the movie.  Sociologists, through the activity of social service workers, have in the past few years secured a fairly wide acceptance of the idea that the motion picture is a necessity, rather than a luxury to the population....  We are all familiar with the escape mechanism theory as an explanation for this strange need.  Perhaps it is the complete and the proper explanation......I think there is something more involved than a simple escape....I think the need for congregation is there, the need to feel oneself in a room with other folks sharing a common experience; and also a kind of religious experience in confronting the unnatural together with other folks.  Something primitive, like what makes a bunch of savages

[1] William Ortan, "Motion Picture—Social Implications", *Encyclopedia of Social Sciences*, Vol. XI, p. 67.

gather together and watch a witch doctor."[1]

Maybe this is why people not only go so frequently to the pictures but, in Western countries, wish to sit in the theatre and see two pictures one after another instead of one and prefer dual programmes which roll along and never seem to come to an end.

No matter why one goes—for amusement, through mere force of habit, because one has nothing else to do or because one's favourite film star, book, director or type of picture is being shown at the local cinema—the fact that the cinema is a very potent factor in modern social life is too obvious to be reiterated. The influence of the film upon mankind can hardly be overestimated. However, before studying its effects, another very important factor which must be considered is: what does the average audience see when it goes to the cinema or what are the contents of motion pictures?

The motion picture is such a potent factor in the formation of the public mind that an understanding of the nature of motion picture content is necessary in order to set up adequate forms of social control. The crux of the problem is what do people see when they go to the pictures? If pictures are good, movies have a wholesome influence, if they are bad, the influence is of the opposite nature, necessitating control. Pictures, however, can seldom be classified as good or bad for most pictures have both qualities to a greater or lesser degree.

In 1930 Edgar Dale[2] made a detailed analysis of 1500 of the films produced in the U.S.A. during the years 1920 to 1930. Five hundred films of each of the three years 1920, 1925 and 1930 were taken. Forty of these films were examined in greater detail and he classified them according to their main theme.

The first problem that confronted him was one of definition. He had to define what was meant by a crime picture, a war picture and so on. Accordingly he worked out a scheme of classification after going

[1] Roger Manvell, *The Film*, pp. 156-158.
[2] Edgar Dale, *The Contents of Motion Picture and Attendance at Motion Pictures*, pp. 15-16.

8

through the reviews of 1,500 films. This classification was neither complete nor mutually exclusive, and if used with other type of data would have to be modified.

His classification of motion pictures was as follows: Crime films in which gun-fighting was the main interest and criminal activity was predominant; sex films; love stories, including character studies where love interest was present but not dominant; mystery films; war and spy films; films for children or in which children were the leading characters; historical films; travelogues and animal studies; comedies and musical extravaganzas; and social propaganda films.

On this basis he examined 1,500 films and found that the three types—crime, sex and love—constituted the bulk of the pictures shown during those years, being 81.6 per cent in 1920, 79.2 per cent in 1925 and 72 per cent in 1930. Comedies formed an increasing proportion of the entire total, and all the other types amounted to 12 per cent at their highest.[1]

Making a comprehensive and minute scrutiny, Edgar Dale found overwhelming evidence to draw the final conclusion that on the screen the following aspects and problems had often received excessive attention.

1 Life of the upper economic strata;
2 Problems of the unmarried and young;
3 Problems of love, sex and crime;
4 Motif of escape and entertainment;
5 Interest appeal to young adults;
6 Professional or commercial world;
7 Personal problems in a limited field;
8 Individual and personal goals;
9 Variety of crimes and crime technique;
10 Emphasis on romance and the unusual in friendship;
11 The 'lived happily ever after' idea following an unusual and romantic courtship.

On the other hand the following aspects and problems had received either scant or no attention.

1 Life of the middle and lower economic strata;

[1] *Ibid.*

2  Problems of the married, middle-aged and old;

3  Other problems of every day life;

4  Motif of education and social enlightenment;

5  Interest appeal to children and older adults;

6  Industrial and agricultural world;

7  Occupational and governmental problems;

8  Social goals;

9  Causes and cures of crime;

10  Emphasis on the undramatic and enduring in friendship;

11  Happy marriages shown as a result of companionship and careful planning.

Thus Edgar Dale's enquiry and findings form a valuable contribution to a sociological study of the film, but he also has his limitations. Towards the end of his opening chapter he summarizes the aim of his study as (i) "to devise a technique for analysing the content of motion picture", and (ii) "to discover by this technique what the content of motion picture has been."[1] To a reader in 1949, the words 'has been' will suggest a more serious doubt as to the continued applicability of Dale's findings than it did to the reader of 1935, when his book first appeared. Even in 1935 many features which characterized the typical screen successes of 1925-31 were fast disappearing and the whole tone of the cinema was in the course of transformation. Even today, while major themes of foreign films have undergone great changes the fundamentals as regards details of settings, age-groups of leading characters, their occupation and aim have remained more or less the same.

An interesting sidelight on contemporary film content is provided by E.W. and M.M. Robson in *The World Is My Cinema*. Here the authors show with a wealth of detail and scholarship that murders, destructions, self-pitying introspection, sexual profligacy and double-crossing in films (all symptoms of a sadistic-fascist mental complex) will, in course of time, break up civilization into warring chaos. The opposite qualities, however, of love, integrity, constancy will help to heal

[1] *Ibid.* p. 19.

the moral sickness from which the world is suffering. They say: "the film in America  has had a cohesive effect.   Whether it was so intended by the film magnates is beside the point.  Today there is a backward negative tendency.   In America, it shows itself in a loosening of the Hay's Code and a descent into sadism, and in Britain there is the  same  decline into sadism, plus a denigration of British name and of religious  feelings plus a mocking at marriage ties and family life."[1]   It is argued that if this tendency is allowed to run its course unchecked, it will result not only in the end of the film industry but the end of society and end of all hope of a decent and peaceful world.   Undoubtedly there is much truth in what these writers have to say but at times they stretch a point too far or over-emphasize a trivial point which may have been a mere coincidence.

A survey of contemporary film content shows that the proportion of any particular type of film to the total output is continually changing.  Moreover, the type of story that appeals most to a people at any given time depends upon the cultural level of society.   Blood and thunder melodramas were at one time very popular because that was the cultural level at which the industrial society had left the people  when the story film first came to the screen.

Edgar Dale's information and conclusions are based on a structure which prevailed in 1930-31.  It is, therefore, impossible to apply his findings to present-day film fare.   The most valuable part of his study, however, is the technique of research which he evolved.  This method for separating the ingredients of motion picture content is as valid today as when the book was first published, and can easily be used on the films of our own decade.   In fact his method has been adopted in the following analysis of contemporary films shown in India.

CLASSIFICATION OF INDIAN FEATURE FILMS

*I LOVE STORIES* — In which the love element is predominant, stories dealing with marital pro-

[1] E. W. & M. M. Robson, *The World Is My Cinema*, p. 36.

blems and difficulties—

(1) Character portrayal and psychological drama—where love element is present but not necessarily dominant;

(2) Parental love and devotion—including stories of filial love.

II SOCIAL — Films which tackle some Indian social problem such as untouchability, dowry system, other marriage problems of child widows, polygamy and divorce. Problems of prostitutes, drink evil, poverty and unemployment, rural uplift, slums, conflict between capital and labour, and so on. In these a large proportion of love element is present but the underlying idea is to expose some social ill; stories which teach a lesson, allegories, stories depicting Hindu-Muslim unity. Here it must be pointed out that in current film terminology, 'social' is used to describe all types of films which are modern in dress and setting as distinct from mythological and historical. Here, however, the term has been restricted only to those films which deal with some social problem.

III MYTHOLOGICAL AND FOLKLORE — Stories and legends from Hindu mythology.

IV DEVOTIONAL AND RELIGIOUS — Depicting lives of religious devotees—very often the character is more a mythological figure than a historical one; films emphasising faith in God; films which depict the higher values of life.

V HISTORICAL AND BIOGRAPHICAL — Including historical romances, historical in character and setting; lives of great people excluding those of saints.

VI STUNT AND ADVENTURE — Including action dramas, thrillers, jungle thrillers and fantasies.

VII CRIME — Including stories of blackmailing, bribery, feuds, corruption in business, of smugglers, thieves, murderers, pickpockets, kidnapping, intrigues, plots and counterplots.

*VIII MELODRAMA* — Romantic and sensational dramas with more or less equal proportion of love, crime, murder, revenge or other sensational elements. A picture with a strong emotional appeal of the popular kind.

*IX COMEDY* — Including satires and farces, the humour side being predominant; musical comedies.

*X WAR* — Including films about spies, saboteurs, enemy agents, scenes of warfare and war propaganda.

*XI MYSTERY AND HORROR* — Pictures with an eerie atmosphere and in which the weird and mysterious elements predominate.

*XII CHILDREN* — Pictures in which juvenile and child stars play the leading role.

CLASSIFICATION OF FOREIGN FEATURE FILMS

*I LOVE STORIES* — Against a background of adventure, thrills, suspense and melodrama, marital difficulties and problems, historical romances, operetta type with colourful scenes, musical romances—
  (i) character portrayals and psychological dramas where love element is present but not necessarily dominant;
  (ii) parental love and devotion.

*II CRIME* — Including blackmail, vendetta, bribery, corruption in business and politics, crook plays about gamblers, doings of gangsters, smugglers, pirates, outlaws, bandits, highwaymen, rustlers, 'western' type of hold-ups, prison life, underworld melodrama, pictures in which criminal activity is predominant or gun fighting is the main interest.

*III MYSTERY AND HORROR* — Murder mystery type with thrills and horrors, vampires and ghosts; eerie atmosphere and emphasis on weirdness.

*IV WAR* — About spies, enemy agents, saboteurs, life of soldiers, actual scenes of warfare; aftermath of war; war on the home front; war and its effects; war and anti-war propaganda; life in occupied countries; drama of women's war services, war documentaries and semi-documentaries.

*V HISTORICAL AND BIOGRAPHICAL* — The expansion of American settlers to the West of America; life of American pioneers; reconstruction after the American Civil War; period pieces, historical in character and setting; lives of famous men and women.

*VI COMEDY* — Humorous side is predominant, satires, farces, burlesques, low comedies of the custard-pie variety, musical comedies where plot is secondary to music and dancing.

*VII COMEDY DRAMA* — Including romantic comedies and comedy thrillers where there is an equal proportion of humour, love and crime or adventure.

*VIII SOCIAL* — Tackling social problems and exposing social evils like that of lack of education, drink evil, lynch law, prison evils, evils in medical profession and problem of labour and capital.

*IX TRAVEL — ANIMAL — SPORT — CHILDREN PICTURES* — Pictures about travel and explorations; where animals or children figure as central characters; pictures about prize-fights and other sports.

*X FANTASY* — Emphasizing the unreal and fantastic elements.

*XI RELIGIOUS AND PHILOSOPHICAL PICTURES* — Depiction of stories from the Bible, where spiritual factors and faith in God are emphasized, pictures with philosophical themes; mystical pictures.

*XII HUMAN DRAMAS* — Pictures which bring out forcefully the higher and true values of life, stories with morals, e.g. *Blue Bird* depicting the vain quest for happiness in physical things, *It is a Wonderful Life* teaching us that no man's life is useless if he has many friends and so on.

XIII *ADVENTURE THRILLERS AND JUNGLE MELODRAMAS* — Adventures in wild jungles, scenes of wild beasts, Tarzan pictures and action dramas.

On the basis of the above classification the reviews of 603 Indian films exhibited in Bombay from 1935 to 1946 (no censors' records prior to 1935 were available) were examined and classified according to their main themes. The Bombay Board of Film Censors had passed 1,243 films for exhibition since 1935 but as the reviews of only 603 or 48.3 per cent were available these were gone through and the opposite, table, worked out.

In interpreting the above data it must be remembered that none of the above divisions are exclusive. A certain amount of overlapping cannot be avoided, and the films have been classified according to their main theme. A number of crime pictures and social pictures have a large proportion of the love element in them or the reverse may be true, but when it is said that 46.1 per cent of the total number of films examined consisted of love stories or 4.8 per cent consisted of crime films it means that 46.1 per cent of pictures had love as their main theme and 4.8 per cent had crime as their major theme. Again, it must be borne in mind that this scheme of classification has been worked out on the basis of the data available which consisted entirely of reviews, and on any different data the classification might have to be modified.

From the above figures it is clear that love stories constitute the bulk of the total films studied from 1935 to 1946, varying from the lowest figure of 36.8 per cent in 1938 to 54.5 per cent in 1943 and 57.4 per cent in 1941. Histories and biographies and comedies come next with 8.4 per cent and 8.1 per cent respectively. Mythological stories only form 7.8 per cent of the total output. It is interesting to note what a small number they constitute and how far from facts is the popular conception that mythologies form a large portion of the

## CONTENTS OF INDIAN FEATURE FILMS, 1935-46

| Year | No. of films passed by the Board of Film Censors. No. | No. of films for which reviews were available. No. | Per cent | Love stories incl. psychological dramas & character portrayals. No. | Per cent | Histories and bio-graphies. No. | Per cent | Comedies and farces. No. | Per cent | Mythology and folklore. No. | Per cent | Socials, stories with morals, allegories. No. | Per cent | Stunt and adventure. No. | Per cent | Devotional and religious. No. | Per cent | Melo-dramas. No. | Per cent | Crime. No. | Per cent | War. No. | Per cent | Children. No. | Per cent |
|---|---|---|---|---|---|---|---|---|---|---|---|---|---|---|---|---|---|---|---|---|---|---|---|---|---|
| 1935 | 142 | 39 | 27.5 | 15 | 38.5 | 3 | 7.7 | 2 | 5.1 | 4 | 10.3 | 6 | 15.4 | 4 | 10.3 | 2 | 5.1 | .. | .. | 3 | 7.7 | .. | .. | .. | .. |
| 1936 | 120 | 51 | 42.5 | 21 | 41.2 | 4 | 7.8 | 3 | 5.9 | 1 | 2.0 | 6 | 12.0 | 7 | 13.7 | 3 | 5.9 | 1 | 2.0 | 5 | 9.8 | .. | .. | .. | .. |
| 1937 | 110 | 57 | 51.8 | 23 | 40.4 | 2 | 3.5 | 5 | 8.8 | 3 | 5.3 | 1 | 1.8 | 12 | 21.1 | 2 | 3.5 | 2 | 3.5 | 6 | 10.5 | .. | .. | .. | .. |
| 1938 | 105 | 57 | 54.3 | 21 | 36.8 | 5 | 8.8 | 3 | 5.3 | 10 | 17.5 | 6 | 10.5 | 6 | 10.5 | 1 | 1.8 | 2 | 3.5 | 3 | 5.3 | .. | .. | .. | .. |
| 1939 | 97 | 41 | 42.3 | 18 | 43.9 | 7 | 17.1 | 3 | 7.3 | 2 | 4.9 | 2 | 4.9 | 1 | 2.4 | 2 | 4.9 | 6 | 14.6 | .. | .. | .. | .. | .. | .. |
| 1940 | 98 | 46 | 46.9 | 17 | 37.0 | 1 | 2.2 | 5 | 10.9 | 4 | 8.7 | 2 | 4.3 | 2 | 4.3 | 6 | 13.0 | 6 | 13.0 | 3 | 6.5 | .. | .. | .. | .. |
| 1941 | 84 | 54 | 64.3 | 31 | 57.4 | 4 | 7.4 | 5 | 9.3 | 1 | 1.9 | 4 | 7.4 | 2 | 3.7 | 3 | 5.6 | 3 | 5.6 | 1 | 1.9 | .. | .. | .. | .. |
| 1942 | 109 | 61 | 56.0 | 33 | 54.1 | 2 | 3.3 | 10 | 16.4 | 2 | 3.3 | 4 | 6.6 | 2 | 3.3 | 4 | 6.6 | 4 | 6.6 | .. | .. | .. | .. | .. | .. |
| 1943 | 107 | 55 | 51.4 | 30 | 54.5 | 3 | 5.5 | 7 | 12.7 | 6 | 10.9 | 1 | 1.8 | .. | .. | 3 | 5.5 | 3 | 5.5 | 2 | 3.6 | .. | .. | .. | .. |
| 1944 | 89 | 54 | 60.7 | 30 | 55.6 | 6 | 11.3 | 5 | 9.3 | 2 | 3.7 | 1 | 1.9 | .. | .. | 3 | 5.6 | 4 | 7.4 | 1 | 1.9 | 2 | 3.7 | .. | .. |
| 1945 | 67 | 48 | 70.1 | 23 | 47.9 | 6 | 12.5 | 1 | 2.1 | 5 | 10.4 | 4 | 8.3 | .. | .. | 3 | 6.2 | 1 | 2.1 | 2 | 4.2 | 2 | 4.1 | 1 | 2.1 |
| 1946 (upto Sept.) | 115 | 40 | 34.8 | 16 | 40.0 | 8 | 20.0 | .. | .. | 8 | 20.0 | 3 | 7.5 | .. | .. | 1 | 2.5 | 1 | 2.5 | 1 | 2.5 | 1 | 2.5 | 1 | 2.5 |
| Total | 1243 | 603 | 48.3 | 278 | 46.1 | 51 | 8.5 | 49 | 8.1 | 47 | 7.8 | 40 | 6.6 | 36 | 5.9 | 33 | 5.5 | 34 | 5.6 | 29 | 4.8 | 5 | 0.8 | 2 | 0.3 |

bulk of Indian films. All the other kinds amount to only about 29.5 per cent of the  total number of films examined.

In the above classification two sub-divisions have been made under love stories, viz., psychological dramas and character portrayals where the love element is not necessarily dominant, and films showing parental or filial love.

Of the 278 love stories produced between 1935 and 1946 only thirteen dealt with the parental love theme, thirteen others were character portrayals and only one was a psychological drama.  All together these three categories constituted only 9.8 per cent of the total love stories.

As regards the foreign films exhibited in Bombay, 72.5 per cent or 2,084 reviews were available out of a total number of 2,873 films passed by the censors.

On examining the foreign films exhibited in Bombay it was found that 29.4 per cent were comedies, while love stories constituted 15.8 per cent of  the  total  number. war films ranked third with 7.1 per cent. There was a marked increase in war films in 1940. Prior to this, war films constituted only 2 to 4.4 per cent of the total number of films studied. With the outbreak of World War II, however, the figure rose immediately from 4.4 per cent to 14.6 per cent in 1940, reaching its climax of 26 per cent in 1943 and falling to 5.8 per cent after the cessation of hostilities.  Another striking feature noted was that crime pictures formed 6.9 per cent of the total percentage coming very close to war films. But while prior to the war, crime films formed 9 per cent to 14 per cent of the total, during the war years their number fell to an average of about 6 per cent of the total. After the termination of the war there was again a gradual increase in the number of crime films. This was probably due to the fact that war and crime films excited more or less similar emotions. All the other types of films formed not more than 21.4 per cent of the entire number of pictures reviewed.

Of the total number of 454 love stories, 3.08 per cent

consisted of psychological dramas, 9.03 per cent of character portrayals and 4.6 per cent dealt with themes of parental devotion, especially mother love.

Of the comedies, musical comedies were very popular and figured in large numbers. About 40.1 per cent of the 613 comedies were musical comedies and the fact that many of them were in colour added to their charm and popularity.

Proceeding to a more detailed analysis of forty popular (in the sense that they were box-office successes) films both Indian and foreign which were examined, it was found that out of the 20 foreign films the location of 45 per cent of the pictures was entirely in the U.S.A.; 35 per cent of the settings were partly in the U.S.A. and partly in some other foreign country; while 20 per cent were set in other foreign countries entirely. The fact that the majority of locales seen are in the U.S.A. is, however, not surprising  since the greater portion of the foreign films publicly exhibited here are of American origin. As regards the settings it was found that interior scenes were a little more frequently shown than exterior scenes, that 54.8 per cent of residences shown were usually houses, though a significant proportion, about 19.4 per cent, consisted of apartments or flats. These residences were decidedly of the upper economic strata, 53.8 per cent being the residence of the wealthy and ultra-wealthy, 34.6 per cent being moderate, while only 11.5 per cent depicted poor residential quarters.

As regards the twenty Indian films, 95 per cent of the locales were entirely in India  and  only 5 per cent showed any foreign country. Of the settings, 40 per cent were entirely urban, 35 per cent rural and 25 per cent partly urban and partly rural. About 70.6 per cent of the residences shown were houses, while only 5.9 per cent were huts; 53.3 per cent of the residences belonged to the well-to-do classes, 26.6 per cent to the poor and 20 per cent to the middle classes.

Probably one reason for this emphasis on wealthy locales may be due, as an English director observed, to the fact that if one tries to reproduce an average home it comes out on the screen looking just nondescript, while there is always a certain amount of risk in giving the audience humdrum truth.

What do these data reveal? What effects are likely to be produced by displaying to an audience which consists largely of adolescents and young adults, scenes of homes most of which are far above the economic level of the spectator? It may be argued that many spectators will have their tastes improved by seeing such scenes. To this it may be replied that much of what is seen is inapplicable to the homes of the vast majority of motion picture audiences. Thus it is not easy to determine the final effect of such settings on sober or impressionable minds. Edgar Dale[1] points out, however, that often dissatisfaction and envy are likely to follow from a consistent and extravagant display of wealth in cinemas, and the energy that might have been used for careful planning of methods for attaining one's ambitions might be dissipated in fanciful thinking and in crying for the moon. There is no proof of any such practical instance. Edgar Dale's argument can merely be put forth as a probable effect. Nevertheless, it cannot be denied that the settings of a major number of films do not offer a realistic study of actual conditions. There is an overemphasis on the wealthy and ultra-wealthy classes while the poor and the not-so-well-off have been either inadequately treated or neglected.

The next important point is what characters delighted and thrilled the vast audience which flocked daily to the cinema houses? What were they like? Were they rich or poor, old or young? Did they work for a living, if so, what was the nature of their occupation? Did they resemble the great majority of the audience, or were they different from them in interests and experience? Examining in detail twenty foreign films shown recently in Bombay, it was found that 75 per cent heroines were between the approximate ages of 18 and 25, 15 per cent were between the ages of 26 and 30, 10

---

[1] Edgar Dale, *The Contents of Motion Pictures and Children's Attendance at Motion Pictures*, p. 40.

per cent between 31 and 40, while not a single one of them was above the age of 40. The heroes, however, were slightly older. 70 per cent were between the ages of 20 and 30, 20 per cent between 31 and 40, next came the age group of 41 to 50 which accounted for 10 per cent while there were none above the age of 50. Only in one picture did a child play an important role and he was a lad of 13 or 14.

In the Indian films seen, 60 per cent heroines were between the ages of 15 and 20, 35 per cent were between 21 and 30 and 5 per cent between 31 and 40. Of the heroes 95 per cent were between 20 and 30 and 5 per cent between 31 and 40. Not a single hero or heroine was above the age of 40. Children as a rule did not appear to play prominent roles. They figured only in those stories where the early childhood of the hero or heroine was depicted, but here too their appearance was of secondary importance to the main theme of the picture.

The evidence here presented shows clearly that motion pictures are built around the lives of young men and women, and only secondarily include the portrayal of events in the lives of older persons or children. From this it seems that the producers in their endeavour to cater for the needs of the younger generation, who form a large proportion of the cinema audience, neglect the equally large proportion of the older members of the audience. Or, maybe, they look at the whole business from the point of easy presentability of their characters and so avoid the very young and the very old age groups.

Considering the occupation and economic status of the leading characters in foreign films it was found that 15 per cent heroes and 30 per cent heroines had no occupation, 40 per cent heroes and 30 per cent heroines were engaged in some profession either as doctors, engineers or artists, 20 per cent heroes were employed in business, 20 per cent heroines were doing some personal service like that of secretary, companion, waitress or domestic servant, while the remaining heroes and heroines were more or less equally distributed between military and naval occupations, public service, agricultural work, stage work and criminal occupation. As regards their economic status, 41.7 per cent heroes and 34.8 per cent heroines were wealthy, 8.3 per cent heroes and 26 per cent heroines were ultra-wealthy, 29.2 per cent heroes and 26 per cent heroines were moderately well off, while only 20.8 per cent heroes and 13 per cent heroines were poor.

Of the Indian heroes and heroines, 20 per cent and 70 per cent respectively had no occupation, 35 per cent heroes and 25 per cent heroines were in some profession and 5 per cent heroines were on the stage. The occupation of the remaining 45 per cent heroes in the order of importance was either criminal, agricultural, business, student, personal service, military or government service. As regards their economic status, 62 per cent heroes and 38.1 per cent heroines were wealthy, 23.8 per cent heroes and 33.3 per cent heroines were moderately well off, 9.5 per cent heroes and 19 per cent heroines were poor while 4.8 per cent heroes and 9.5 per cent heroines were ultra-wealthy.

From these figures it is clear that motion pictures concern themselves in far greater degree with the wealthy and the ultra-wealthy than the proportion of these classes in the general population would justify. Further, in foreign films there are many more heroines in the wealthy and ultra-wealthy classes than in the moderate and poor groups, while in the Indian films there are more heroes than heroines in these two grades.

Here, however, it is necessary to make clear what exactly is meant by ultra-wealthy, wealthy, moderate and poor, as these are relative terms. A character is regarded as ultra-wealthy when he or his surroundings depict unusual wealth such as servants to attend on him, an immense house, elaborately decorated and furnished; a character is considered wealthy when his circumstances show an income above the average; the moderate group includes persons not so well off but nevertheless comfortable and free from undue financial care; while the poor are those who show evidence of poverty such as ragged clothes, insufficient food, poor housing accommodation and who have, generally speaking, difficulties in making two ends meet.

Thus the films' preoccupation with the favoured social groups is obvious here as was also seen in the data on settings. This preoccupation may be explained by the argument that when one attends the cinema one is seeking to escape from reality. Hence, since the majority of the population has only a small or very small income, they want their films to depict the lives of people as unlike themselves as possible.

This view may be disputed by some, and it cannot be denied that while at times the audience needs a drug, too much stress has been placed on this function of the cinema.

Another important fact which emerged from this critical analysis of the forty films was about the circumstances of meeting of the leading characters, and the standard set by films for love, marriage and divorce. What patterns did the films set up for the younger generations as regards the ways in which they might meet persons whom they may later marry? Were the methods of acquaintance shown as chiefly accidental and under unusual circumstances or did they show that the choice of a life partner was conditioned by the people with whom a person ordinarily associates? Did the films look down upon chance acquaintanceships and depict harmful consequences arising through such acquaintanceships or did they show marriages resulting from such friendships as highly successful?

The analysis of the circumstances of meeting has been restricted to the hero and heroine and does not include the love relationship of the other characters.

Further, the leading characters have been divided into two groups—those who were previously acquainted, engaged or married before the picture opened, and those who were not previously acquainted. Under the second group the means employed for securing an acquaintance were classified either as accidental and unusual (in the sense that they are rarely encountered in real life) or usual and ordinary, with a formal introduction or without a formal introduction.

On examining the twenty foreign films it was found that 80 per cent of them showed the leading characters as not previously acquainted, while 20 per cent showed them as previously acquainted. Of the 16 instances in which the hero and the heroine were not acquainted 68.7 per cent were shown to meet under accidental circumstances without a formal introduction while 31.3 per cent showed the first meeting under ordinary circumstances with a formal introduction.

Similar evidence was found in the Indian films. 40 per cent of the heroes and heroines were previously acquainted, engaged or married while 60 per cent were not acquainted. Of those who were not previously acquainted 83.3 per cent had an accidental or unusual meeting without a formal introduction while 16.6 per cent had an ordinary or usual meeting with a formal introduction.

It is evident from these data that the films emphasize the unusual and that here also there is an essential lack of realism. Whether this is desirable or not, and what is its effect on immature youth, it is impossible to answer from the data available.

One may, however, enquire whether it is possible to build up motion picture drama without these unusual types of meeting which bulk so large in the current film fare. One is inclined to believe that the utilization of such out of the ordinary situations shows a lack of skill on the part of the scenario writers for it is more difficult to build up a dramatic situation where the characters lead a humdrum life and are known to each other than when they are unknown to each other and meet under extraordinary circumstances. The greatness of the scenario writer and the director lies in their ability to build up a powerful or moving drama out of the ordinary circumstances of everyday life.

As regards the degree of acquaintanceship of the hero and heroine involved in love relationships and the standard set for marriage and divorce in the foreign

SHAKUNTALA:
*Directed by V. Shantaram; featuring Jayashree; Rajkamal Kalamandir; 1943.*

THE COURT DANCER:

*Directed by Modhu Bose; featuring Sadhona Bose; Wadia Movietone; 1941.*

SINDOOR:    *Directed by Kishore Sahu; featuring*
            *Shamim and Kishore Sahu; Filmistan*
            *Ltd.; 1947.*

RAMJOSHI:   *Directed by V. Shantaram; featuring*
            *Hansa Wadkar and Jayaram Shiledar;*
            *Rajkamal Kalamandir; 1947.*

pictures, it was found that 65 per cent of the films showed love after a few meetings, 15 per cent showed love at first sight, while only 5 per cent showed love as a slow growth. 10 per cent of the films showed the hero and heroine either in love with each other or engaged to each other before the picture opened, while 25 per cent of the films were stories of married life. In 25 per cent of the films, divorce takes place or there is talk of its taking place; in 40 per cent of the films the leading characters are married only once, while in 45 per cent of them they are married more than once after divorce or after the death of the partner.

For the Indian films also a similar analysis was made. It was found that while 50 per cent showed either love at first sight or love after a few meetings, about 25 per cent—a fairly large proportion as compared to foreign films—showed love as a slow growth. 10 per cent of the leading characters were either in love or engaged before the picture opened. 15 per cent were stories of married life. 70 per cent of the characters were married only once while 25 per cent were married more than once.

As regards the marital status of the 20 foreign heroes and 20 heroines it was found that 15 per cent of heroes were married before the picture opened while 85 per cent were single at the beginning of the picture. Of them 7 or 41.2 per cent were married during the course of the picture, of whom one's wife died and he married again. Of the heroines 20 per cent were married before the picture opened while 80 per cent were single when the picture began. Of these, 11 or 68.9 per cent married during the course of the picture, 4 or 25 per cent of whom were either widowed or divorced and remarried. In the remaining number of 58.8 per cent single heroes and 31.3 per cent single heroines the picture ended with the implication that they finally got married.

What about the marital status of the leading characters in Indian pictures? In the twenty films examined 15 per cent of the heroes and heroines were married

9

before the picture opened, while 85 per cent of them were unmarried. Of the single ones 76.5 per cent heroes and 70.6 per cent heroines were married once during or at the end of the picture, 5.9 per cent heroes and 11.8 per cent were divorced or widowed and remarried, for 5.9 per cent heroes and 11.8 per cent heroines marriage was implied; while 11.5 per cent heroes and 5.9 per cent heroines did not marry for some reason or another.

Some people may not be inclined to look upon these data with any seriousness, for they may feel that after all these are merely patterns of behaviour established by the films and hence are not taken seriously by the spectator. However, when one takes into consideration the large number of adolescents and young adults who are influenced by what they see and are inclined to take these patterns and apply them to real life, one cannot but agree with Mrs. Walter Ferguson when she says: ". . . These romantic stories are very pretty so long as we regard them as entertainment, but once we believe that they are models after which life should be patterned, we are lost."[1]

In the data regarding the marital status of the leading characters it was found that the majority of the characters were single and the films dealt largely with their problems of romance. This might be due to the fact that some producers feel that the love problems of the unmarried appeal to all, whether married or unmarried. Probably this is true. Nevertheless, it is obvious that producers as a rule have not yet discovered how to make the romance of marriage as appealing and interesting on the screen as the romance of pre-marital life. It may also be argued that since the adolescents and young adults are the most frequent attenders at cinema shows it is to cater for their needs that the film fare deals largely with the doings and problems of the unmarried. If this is true then it indicates that the producers have neglected the interests of the not-so-young audience who also form a reasonable proportion of the audience. Or it may be that such plots offer the greatest opportunities for light fun.

[1] *Ibid*, p. 90.

Whatever the reason, it is obvious that on the screen there is almost an obsessional emphasis on romantic love. It is the be-all and end-all of existence. Making money, work, friendship, one's place in society, are all of secondary importance. No doubt love plays an important part in life, literature and art and is one of the major ways in which an individual relates himself to life. Yet it is not the only way. Work is another way. Yet, rarely in films is work and the satisfaction obtained from it, stressed. On the screen, the love object is all that matters and once that is lost, murder, suicide, insanity or alcoholism often follows. In real life people do lose the love object, but how often is it followed by insanity or suicide?

What was the aim behind the action of the leading characters of films? What goals do the hero and the heroine seek or what do they try to achieve? From an analysis it was revealed that there were three types of goals motivating the action of the leading characters—individual, personal and social. An individual goal was one in which the character was trying to achieve something for himself alone. Personal goal was one where he was trying to achieve something for the benefit not of himself alone, but also of a small group—like his family or friends—whom he knew intimately. While a social goal was one in which the benefit of the action of the character would not accrue to him or his family or friends, but to his country or humanity in general.

Analysis revealed that in foreign films about 61.4 per cent of the leading characters sought individual goals, 25 per cent sought personal goals while only 13.6 per cent sought social goals. Again, of the various kinds of individual goals, winning another's love was the most common. It was found to be the guiding force behind the action of 41.4 per cent of the leading characters. Next in order came professional success which was found in 20.7 per cent of the films, followed by personal happiness and security which was found in 10.3 per cent of the films. The rest (about 30 per cent) were made up of marriage for love, concealment of guilt, desire for money, desire for an easy life and so on.

Of the different types of personal goals the most common was family welfare and happiness. This was found in 63.6 per cent of the films. It was also found that a much larger proportion of heroines than heroes were guided by personal aims. Only 14.3 per cent heroes but 34.8 per cent heroines had the personal goal as their guiding force. Even here family welfare and happiness came first, followed by protection of a loved one and happiness and recovery of a loved one. Of the social goals the most common was welfare of mankind, which accounted for 50 per cent of the pictures, followed by performance of duty and apprehension of a criminal.

In the Indian films also 72 per cent of the leading characters were guided by individual motives, 16.3 per cent by personal and 11.6 per cent by social aims. Of the individual goals 38.7 per cent characters were concerned with winning someone's love, 29 per cent with marriage for love, 19.4 per cent with personal happiness and security, while the rest were concerned with such aims as professional success, obtaining money to lead a gay life, desire for an heir, or search for an ideal character. More heroines than heroes sought personal goals, such as family welfare or happiness and success of a loved one; while more heroes than heroines were guided by social goals such as welfare of mankind or country.

From the above facts it is clear that the goals emphasized in motion pictures are merely a reflection of the goals stressed in our modern world. If, however, the film has a social purpose and a social vision, those who are responsible for production should not be content merely with a reflection of the current weakness of the social environment. The screen must depict a better way of living than the average which we find outside the cinema house. The screen must portray more frequently the type of social goals which benefits the community at large, if the film is to fulfil its social mission.

Another important factor to which attention was paid in this analysis of 40 films was the depiction of crime in the movies as it is often argued that films encourage crime. Though, of the twenty foreign films examined not a single one was a crime picture according to the previous definition (9 were love stories, 3 were psychological dramas, 1 dealt with the mother love theme, 2 were historical and biographical, 1 was a comedy, 1 was a fantasy, 1 a human drama, 1 a philosophical or religious drama and 1 an espionage thriller or a war picture), in twelve or 60 per cent of them one or more crimes were either committed or attempted.

What were the crimes committed or attempted in these 20 films? It was found that murder headed the list with 40 per cent, followed by suicide in 30 per cent of the films, followed by individual instances of abetment of crime, espionage, petty thievery, hold-ups, blockading and underground political activities. If this was the position in the case of films other than crime pictures, it would be no exaggeration to say that taking crime films into consideration, the proportion of crimes shown on the screen is not only very large but that motion pictures present to their spectators almost every conceivable kind of crime.

It is a common criticism that films depict violent methods of settling disputes and deaths by violence are very frequent. On analysing the violent deaths, including suicide, committed and attempted by various screen characters in foreign films, it was found that 42.1 per cent of the violent deaths were committed or attempted by heroines, 26.3 per cent by heroes and the remainder by the other characters. Again, suicide was more common among heroines than heroes. Of the 9 cases of violent deaths committed by women characters, 4 were suicides and 5 were murders, while in the case of men characters, of the 5 violent deaths committed, 2 were suicides.

Techniques for the commission of crime were shown in many pictures, especially the technique of murder and suicide. On analysis it was found that the revolver was used in 36.8 per cent of the cases of committed or attempted murders and suicides. Next came drowning with 21 per cent, poisoning 10.5 per cent, pushing over a great height 10.5 per cent, stabbing 5.3 per cent and strangling 5.3 per cent.

Were these characters punished for their crimes? Analysis showed that in 15.8 per cent of cases there was no punishment, in 21 per cent of cases punishment was inferred, while only in 10.5 per cent of cases was legal punishment carried out.    15.8 per cent of the criminals eluded punishment through suicide, in 15.8 per cent cases personal revenge was wreaked on the criminal, in 15.8 per cent the crime committed being suicide there was no punishment, while in 5.3 per cent cases the criminal was arrested but later released.

As regards crime in Indian films, though none of the films examined was a crime picture according to the previous definition (8 were love stories, 5 socials, 1 biography, 1 historical, 2 comedies, 1 adventure picture, 1 fantasy and 1 semi-documentary), in 9 or 45 per cent of them crime of some variety or the other was shown.    Of the crimes committed or attempted, murder headed the list with 39.1 per cent followed by suicide with 21.7 per cent, petty burglary 8.7 per cent, hold-ups 8.7 per cent, blackmailing 8.7 per cent, forgery 8.7 per cent, and underground political activity 4.3 per cent.

In contrast to foreign films 38.5 per cent of violent deaths were committed or attempted by villains or other men and 30.8 per cent by villainesses or other women.    The remaining were committed or attempted by heroines and heroes.    Again suicide was as common among heroes as heroines.

As regards the technique of murder or suicide, revolvers and poison were used in 66.6 per cent cases; while in the remaining cases the method followed was either stabbing, drowning or jumping from a great height.    In 36.4 per  cent cases no punishment  was meted out, in 18.2 per cent the crime committed was suicide and hence there was no punishment and in the remaining cases punishment was incidental, or there was personal revenge, or the criminal was arrested but later released, or the criminal was arrested but escaped.

These data clearly show that the criminal is not always punished in the films. This, however, does not necessarily constitute a criticism of motion pictures. For, if the screen is to have the right to depict crime as a social aspect, it must have the right to tell the truth; and it cannot be denied that the criminal is apprehended much more frequently in films than he is in real life.

However, there may be some danger in permitting impressionable adolescents and young children in seeing the criminal 'getting away with it'. Yet they need only to be able to read to realize that he often does get away with it in real life. Therefore, instead of laying too much stress on this aspect of escape of punishment, the screen would do well to depict the consequences, other than those involving legal punishment, that follow crime, and to portray the causes and cures of crime, which it fails to do.

What is the total significance of all these data on the contents of motion pictures? The most important conclusion concerning these data is that, to a great extent, the characters, the problems and the settings are very remote from the lives of persons who view them. This remoteness is seen in the great stress that the screen places on the unusual in friendship, romantic love and on wealth and luxury. This analysis shows very clearly that while the screen pays constant attention to the life of the more favoured social groups, it deals inadequately or not at all with the life of the middle and lower economic strata; it emphasizes the problems of the single and the young, especially their problems of love and marriage, but ignores the everyday problems of the married, the middle-aged or the old. The screen portrays the professional and commercial world, but what about the agricultural and the industrial labourer's world? The film provides a motif of escape and entertainment and its product appeals to the adolescents and young adults, but it pays scant attention to the motif of education or social enlightenment and fails to appeal to the older generation. And finally the screen depicts a large proportion and practically

every variety of crime and crime technique, but does
not go to the root of the problem and give a social investigation into the causes and cures of crime.

The film fare of today provides an escape from our
social problems but our need is for an art which
vigorously handles social realities.   The criterion of
motion picture content ought not to be 'can one make
money from it?' but 'does it make life richer,   more
purposeful, more   enjoyable?'   No   human   problem
which is suitable for the motion picture medium ought
to be excluded from the screen.   The film should be a
parade of life and manners, and a study of conduct
honestly, dramatically and entertainingly presented.

These changing times have seen the contents of
films also change from those of the earlier decades.   As
compared to films of earlier years there is more realism
in the films of today but, as already seen, the treatment
of reality is often so inadequate as to make it remote
from the audience who view them.   This investigation
of the contents of films, especially Indian films, shows
very clearly that the standard of films and of film appreciation has to be raised considerably and this can
be done to a large extent by a sociological analysis and
appreciation of the film.   However, nothing has been
done in our country in this direction.   Film criticism
and analysis is left to the professional film reviewer who
reports either his personal preferences, or what the publicity department doles out to him.   No one has tried
to analyse the meaning of the film in relation to its
audience.   We have yet to develop a new point of view
regarding the place of the cinema in our scheme of life.
At present, films are made for personal profit with little
consideration for the needs of the people who go to see
them. The producers view them as so much amusement
fare with rarely any standard of high class entertainment.   They   have   hardly   realized   that the film can
become the most powerful agency   of education and
hence of social change.   They must be made to realize
this and the audience must be roused to demand films
the seeing of which can honestly be regarded as a
worthwhile leisure activity.

*6*

## THE SOCIAL SIGNIFICANCE OF FILM STARS

THE film firmament is studded with 'stars' and 'starlets' of greater and lesser magnitude and luminosity. Their position is important, for not only do they rule in their own realm but even influence the lives of those who see them in all their brilliance on the silver screen. They are very often the determining factors in the popularity and financial success of a film, luring audiences to the box-office with the much publicized aura of glamour and fascination surrounding their names.

Strange as it may sound to the star-conscious picture-goers of the day, in the early years of the cinematograph, film actors and actresses were anonymous beings as far as the public were concerned and identified by them either by their physical appearance or by association with the film company in whose films they appeared. Handbills and poster advertisements of pictures of the pioneering days did not bear the names of those who featured in them. It had not occurred to producers that patrons could be lured into those murky little electric theatres by announcing that a particular actor or actress was featured in the film.

It was the trade war between the Independent producers and the Motion Picture Patents Company of America over certain patent rights, that gave to the film world its first film star in March 1910, fourteen years after the inception of the cinematograph. This was a significant milestone in the annals of the motion picture.

Carl Laemmle, the far-sighted leader of the In-
dependents, boldy announced the names of his actors
and actresses and thus broke the magic circle of anony-
mity which had hitherto shrouded them.    Thereafter,
producers fell over themselves in their anxiety to cash
in on any and every name that could be said to have the
slightest box-office pull.

To develop the star policy most companies turned
to publicity.    They sold photographs and slides of
players.    Posters of favourites were placed in theatre
lobbies, film star postcards were distributed to in-
quirers, now called 'fans', who wrote the once-despised
'who' letters.    Now such letters were encouraged and
promptly answered, while ambitious film stars sent out
personally autographed photographs on their own
initiative.

The star policy was more securely established by
a new type of medium, the 'fan magazine', first started
by J. Stuart Blackton of Vitagraph.[1]   Other companies.
realizing the commercial possibilities of fan magazines,
followed its lead and the succeeding years bore a large
crop of these magazines which focussed attention upon
film personalities.   Gradually, they became well known
through colourful anecdotes and legends which though
interesting, were not always true.

At first producers obtained their actors and actresses from among stage celebrities.   Soon, however, they
discovered that it was not necessary to depend on established stage players for star material.   They could
groom favourite actors and actresses for stardom just
as they made pictures.   By shrewd training, strategy
and publicity it was possible to turn a pleasing personality into a 'star'.   The process followed was to
feature a player in film after film in certain roles, till
the audience became so familiar with him (or her)
that they enjoyed recognizing him and welcomed his
appearance; while clever publicity made it appear that
the audience knew the star, his habits, home life and
tastes intimately.   Salary figures given out by the pub-

[1] Lewis Jacobs, *The Rise of the American Film*, p. 89.

licity department ran into fabulous sums, for it was
believed that a star was great because he enjoyed a
stupendous salary. In fact, so inflated did the star
salaries become during the period of World War I and
after, that producers were afraid of being ruined by a
system for whose creation they themselves were responsible. Criticism soon became rampant in the press.
The star-system was castigated as "preposterous,
anarchistic, insidious, evil and disastrous."[1] Associations
condemned many of the highest paid stars as box-
office 'poison' and bemoaned the domination of film
production by the star-system. Little heed, however,
seems to have been paid to such criticism for the star-
system continued to develop, and now salaries are even
higher than ever, in fact they constitute the largest item
of expenditure in a producer's budget. From the centre
of public attention in the days before World War I, the
star-system today has become the pivot of production.

Little is known about the star-system as prevalent
in India. As regards its origin, there is no authentic
information to be had. It is, however, reported that for
about a decade or so after the birth of the Indian film,
the names of Indian actors and actresses were never
published or given any publicity. In fact, film acting
was considered so derogatory that Indian women from
higher classes and even men were not easily persuaded
to come before the camera. The pioneers of Indian
film were therefore put to no end of trouble in securing
a cast, and especially women characters, for their pictures. It is therefore not surprising that, sometimes,
foreign artistes were employed while men were often
called upon to play women's roles.

Gradually, however, following the example of the
West, Indian producers started announcing the names
of their actors, but even then, little interest was evinced
in them by the public, nor were others attracted to the
profession. The Indian Cinematograph Committee reported in 1927, that only the larger studios maintained
a permanent staff of actors and actresses whose salaries

[1] *Ibid*, p. 163.

ranged from Rs. 30 to Rs. 700 for a film star—a miserable pittance compared to the incredible salaries earned by the stars in Western countries. With the exception of Bengal, stars were not drawn from the higher social strata, while the actresses were mainly recruited from a class which did not have the best of reputations. While there was no dearth of talent in India, there was no training or organization and, generally speaking, people were not attracted to the profession of film acting because of the stigma attached to the industry which had to employ many women of questionable social standing.

It was in the middle and late thirties, with the evolution of 'social' themes in films, that Indian film stars began to acquire popularity and fame, the height of which was reached in 1936 with Sulochana's performance in *Bombai-ki-Billi* or *The Wild Cat of Bombay* a significant landmark in Indian film history.

Henceforth, Indian producers began to employ Hollywood methods of publicity and 'star manufacture', and names like Sulochana, Gohar, Patience Cooper, Zubeida, Nadia, Sabita Devi, Devika Rani, Durga Khote, Surendra, Billimoria, Jal Merchant and many more besides, became known to screen audiences all over the country.

Magazines also helped to acquaint film fans with intimate details and incidents in the lives of their favourites. Posters and booklets were displayed and sold to ardent enthusiasts eager to know more of their favourite film personalities. Other methods of American showmanship and publicity were copied, but compared to the achievements of the West our efforts seemed crude and trite. Nevertheless they served their purpose. For, from the limelight of public gaze in the mid-thirties, the years that followed were to see stars becoming the centre of production. They had become so popular and were so much in demand that by 1939 one star was often featuring in as many as six or seven films simultaneously. In proportion, their salaries also rose and even today they are the highest paid among the film producer's personnel. As such they figure not only as the most expensive item of a producer, but constitute the major factor of production.

What is the significance of this star-system? Why do producers spend so much time and money in building up stars and why do cinema patrons not merely favour certain stars but at times even indulge in star-worship? The attitude of the producers and that of the audience is inter-related. From the point of view of the producer, the primary aim behind the fostering of the star-system is monetary gain. To him stars are the greatest box-office asset. Even here, however, the producer has to run the risk of a let-down, due to the fickleness of public taste. While some known personalities are always favoured, the attraction of most others is by no means as great as the ballyhoo which accompanies them would suggest.

It may be argued that the value of the film star is generally over-estimated, that he or she has nothing much to do with the success of a picture as many people imagine; and that the lion's share of responsibility goes to the director, the man who thinks out all the elements of the unmade picture, develops and puts them together and to whom the greatest actor is no more than one of the component parts. Such critics undervalue the film star, for there have been many films which have been sucessful mainly because of their star appeal. It must, however, be admitted that slowly but surely the public is beginning to realize the importance of the director. Such people, however, are limited and with the majority of film audiences, stars are still the drawing factor. They judge their filmfare from the featuring stars. In the choice of their films they follow the stars. This is understandable to a certain extent because a number of films are based upon stories which have never been heard of before, and hence without any stars in them they would not attract the public.

Certain film stars have a larger following than others and, in proportion, their box-office attraction is naturally greater. Of course it is impossible to go into the reasons for the popularity or otherwise of individual stars for it often depends upon personal whims and idiosyncrasies.

Whatever the reason for individual likes and dislikes, the significance of stars lies in the fact that they become the objects of identification. Terry Ramsaye observes: "Stardom is a job of vicarious attainment for the customers. The starring player becomes the agent in advance for the box-office customer. The spectator tends to identify himself with the glamorous and triumphant player, just as the tense, weakling little ribbon clerk in the last run of seats clenches his fists and wins with the winner of the prize-fight."[1]

The stars are the link between the film industry and the audience. They are the focal point on which the critical faculties of the audience centre. The channel through which the stars maintain close contact with their audience is the fan mail and, more so, the fan magazine.

Fan magazines are stimulants of the most exhilarating kind. Everything is mentioned in superlatives and a special vocabulary is employed which, instead of jarring, rouses the fan-fare addicts, especially women, out of the most sodden lethargies.

These magazines seem to function solely as a channel for studio build-up of a new film or a new personality, the feature articles and the chatter columns both supplying the magic that is supposed to turn a chrysalis into a butterfly.

These magazines bathe almost every aspect of the stars' life in a glow of luxury or surround it with an aura of glamour. At the same time they point out that underneath all their glitter and glory, the stars are very like the ordinary person in the street.

It is through magazines that the fans feed their reveries. The magazines supply the type of information which the screen has no time to give. As M. F. Thorp remarks: "They make it possible for the worshipper to identify herself with the glamorous star as she can do with no other character in fiction. When you read a

<hr/>

[1] Terry Ramsaye, *Motion Picture Herald*, July 8, 1939.

book you know only what the author tells you about the heroine even though you follow her through sequel after sequel.  On the stage you may not see the same actress once in five years, but on the screen you watch her over and over again in different poses against scores of different backgrounds and then you can follow her into fan magazines.  They will fill in for you all the little intimate details that make a personality real, that make identification close and exciting."[1]

The means by which fan magazines build up intimacy is through their fashion and beauty sections which give hints on dressing as the film star does.  The food and home decorations, tastes in reading, music, art and hobbies of stars are given publicity for the fans to emulate.  However, the most subtle intimacy building device is the article on what the film star is really like beneath the glittering exterior she or he wears on the screen.

Analysing the contents of twelve Indian fan magazines of July-August 1948, published in English, it was found that the advertisements and pictures were largely devoted to actresses.  They were shown either as they appeared in films or in their homes under the most glamorous circumstances.  In fact, pictures of actresses constituted 60.9 per cent of the total, while those of actors and mixed groups, usually of couples, were only 19.1 per cent and 19.9 per cent respectively.  Pictures of foreign stars were also given.  Here as well, the actresses far exceeded the actors.  They formed about 74.4 per cent of the total while the pictures of actors and mixed groups formed 9.8 per cent and 15.9 per cent respectively.

Even on the cover page, pictures of actresses were predominant.  Of the 12 magazines, 9 carried photographs of actresses—one of whom was a foreign actress—and three others had advertisements of coming films, featuring the hero and the heroine.

It is not the aim of fan magazines to criticize the doings of the film stars or their acting.  What they eat,

[1] M. F. Thorp, *America at the Movies*, p. 62.

how they dress and live, are they married and to whom
—this is what the zealous want to know and read about
and it is to them that the fan magazines cater. Though
almost all the journals reviewed the current film fare,
with the exception of a few of them whose reviews were
outspoken, the rest either published the publicity
hand-outs or the story of the film. Generally speaking
only Indian films were reviewed.

Practically every magazine had its editor's mail
section where the editor answered a large number of
enquiries. The type of questions asked varied considerably. However, the majority of them related to the
stars, their screen and private activities and to other
aspects of the film industry. A few questions related to
the fan's private problems and ambitions like: "I want
to join the films", or "I want to become an actor, how
shall I proceed?"

The interview is another popular form of writing
used in fan magazines. The stars answer the usual
questions like "why and how did you take to a film
career?" by giving the typical answer that she had
"early ambitions to become a great singer and dancer
or maybe even a star" but had to struggle hard to
achieve her goal "as parents did not quite like the idea"
but ultimately managed to persuade "Mama and she
finally gave her consent."

Another feature on which emphasis is laid is their
dress and homes and all the wealth and luxury which
surround them. Descriptions like the following are
fairly common.

"I met her at her home on Malabar Hill . . .
dressed in a yellow and black printed sari with a
short black choli . . . loves cooking . . . particular
about make-up. . .favourite colours blue and gold-
en yellow. . . ."

". . .lives in Calcutta's Regent Park, most
fashionable locality . . . devoted mother . . . is educated and cultured, graceful and sophisticated. . . ."

". . . .The only star with a Rolls Royce who
in those days lived among Malabar Hill's exclusive

social set....Dressed in a simple cotton white sari, she arrived on the scene without any make-up to adorn her....There was nothing formal about her talk, nothing snobbish in her be-haviour...."

"Has a cosy flat on Marine Drive where she lives quietly....She is the only daughter but is not spoilt or pampered. She likes swimming, read-ing books, loves dogs and has a couple of them...."

For foreign stars also the stress is laid on their early struggles and home life, as:

"....started her career as a tap dancer...."

"She was one of the show girls....rose to film fame by way of the chorus...."

"....from adventurer to motion picture star ... idolizes his father ... quite shameless in boast-ing of his accomplishments ... married twice, divor-ced his first wife...."

To attract women, some journals have a ladies' section devoted to items of particular interest to them. Cosmetics and dress styles are discussed at length. Hollywood beauty secrets, pictures of hair-styles and dress-styles are here revealed to women fans interested in imitating their favourites on the screen.

Of these twelve magazines, *Filmindia* was selected for more detailed analysis because it is one of the best got up fan magazines, has been in existence probably the longest, and is read by a large number of people— it boasts of a monthly sale of about 32,000 copies. Be-sides being one of the few Indian fan magazines sold in Western countries, it gives, as an American writer ob-serves, "the foreign reader a fascinating and often very amusing picture of the little known Indian film."[1]

On analysing the contents of *Filmindia* over five years it was found that here also pictures of actresses were proportionately very large. They formed approxi-mately 52 per cent of all pictures while actors consti-tuted only a meagre 11 per cent.

[1] Arthur Rosenheimer Jr. "A Survey of Film Periodicals I: The United States and England", *Hollywood Quarterly* Vol. II, July 1942, Number 4, p. 351.

From 1945 onwards, a few pictures of foreign stars, producers and directors also appeared, but here also actresses formed about 52.6 per cent of the total number of pictures.

As regards the cover page, of the 58 pictures, 29 carried pictures of actresses, 3 of actors, 11 had both actors and actresses (but here again the actress was given greater prominence), 13 carried advertisements of films and 2 had miscellaneous advertisements.

A striking characteristic of *Filmindia's* picture reviews is that they are blunt and outspoken. The story, direction, technique and acting are all criticized. As Arthur Rosenheimer says, "For forthright criticism of pictures, producers, exhibitors and government interference in film production, there has never been a magazine quite like *Filmindia*—certainly never a fan magazine."[2]  It maintains that it reviews all pictures worth reviewing without fear or favour and whether they are advertised in the journal or not. On an average about 49 pictures are reviewed annually. Of these about 31 are classified as poor, 13 as indifferent and 5 as good. As a rule only Indian films are  reviewed. Following are some examples of the type of  verdicts passed on various films:

"*Ever Yours* becomes ever so boring. Poor show, poor direction and poor technical  work. Snehaprabha fails miserably."

"*Kismet* another  money-making  clap-trap. Ashok Kumar gives another good  performance. Good music sustains audience interest."

"*Apna Paraya* fails to appeal at Swastik. Sahu Modak gives another silly performance."

"*Tansen* becomes terrific box-office success."

"*Shakuntala* an emotional disappointment."

"*Raja* reaches great  psychological  heights, Kishore Sahu presents a motion picture triumph."

"*Shikari* good framing of poor theme."

"*Albeli* a boring gypsy yarn, Ramola's overacting becoming tiresome."

[2] *Ibid.*

"*Safar* all round poor production.  Silly story with ugly artistes."

"*Chandragupta* historically incorrect, but entertaining."

"*Vikramaditya* becomes excellent picture."

"*Hamrahi,* New Theatres' brilliant production."

"*Lakharani,* Prabhat's expensive tomfoolery."

"*Zid* gives incurable headache."

"*Dil* presents good emotional story.  Baby Zubeida steals the show."

"*Sindoor* draws crowds in Bombay.  Progressive theme well received."

"*Beete Din* good theme badly handled.  Vanmala gives excellent performance."

"*Shehnai* a consequential entertainer.  Music and dance attract popular attention."

"*Chhota Bhai* revives New Theatre's old glory."

"*Swayam Siddha* is a picture to see."

Probably the most interesting part of *Filmindia* is its editor's mail.  A host of queries—some anxious several trivial and frivolous—from all over the country besiege the editor every month.  Of these, a few selected ones are answered "in an informative and humourous strain and no offence is meant to anyone."

A variety of questions are asked from serious ones like, "Don't you think,....that people are losing faith in Bapu's ethics of non-violence, particularly in this atomic era wherein the very idea of non-violence has become ridiculous?" to frivolous ones like "If one sleeps with *Filmindia* under the pillow what will be the effect?"

Enquiries relating to stars—either about their screen or private life—constitute the largest individual category.  Yet, on an average, they do not form more than about 21.7 per cent of the total number of questions asked.

The rest of the questions in their order of numerical importance, relate to the film industry and its members: other than film stars, to *Filmindia* and its editor, to pic-

tures, to the problems and ambitions of fans and lastly
to a vast variety of miscellaneous topics, such as, politics, love, marriage, art and so on.   A few examples of
these questions are given below:

"Can any Indian picture compete with Hollywood productions?"

"Who makes better pictures, Prabhat or New
Theatres?"

"Who is the greatest director of the year?"

"Why don't Bombay Talkies produce historical
pictures?"

"How many good pictures can a producer produce?"

"Which is the best picture between *Pukar,
Sikander,* and *Prithvivallabh?*"

"When will *Draupadi* be released?"

"How much do you gain from *Filmindia?*"

"Do you like pets?  Have you any?"

"Why do people abuse you?"

"I have fallen in love with Vasanti.   What can
I do?"

"I know dancing and singing.   Can I join your
studio?"

"I want to be an actor".

"I want to be a producer, where shall I start?"

"More fans ask you about love than films.
Why?"

"How long does a romance usually last?"

"How far and how much should one sacrifice
for art?"

"Is beauty to be judged by objective or artistic
standards?"

"What is the definition of love?"

"Do politicians also need publicity like film
stars?"

As regards the screen life of stars the queries cover
almost every aspect of it, as for example, their acting,
singing and dancing abilities, their best role, their next
picture, their standard of acting  in different pictures,
comparison between two or more stars, their rise to star-

dom, their period of popularity, their frequent appearance on the screen and its repercussions on their popularity, and their retirement from the screen.

With reference to the stars' lives off the sets, the most numerous questions asked relate to their family affairs, marriage and divorce, their dress and appearance followed by their age and health, their salary, their habits and hobbies, their occupation before they joined the screen, requests for their addresses and photographs, and diverse other enquiries.  It is interesting to note that, contrary to the general belief and in strange contrast to foreign fans, requests for photographs of stars do not appear in large numbers.  This is probably due to the fact that many of our stars cannot afford the expensive luxury of this type of publicity and fans have off and on complained that their requests for photographs have not been complied with.

In the sixty issues of *Filmindia* that were examined there were not many interviews with film stars.  However, in the few that were there, importance was given in the case of actresses, to their modesty, their appearance and talent, their hobbies, their early struggle and their wealth as can be noted from the following typical examples:

"She is modest....is not a bragging sort."

"Strangely enough this popular vamp of the screen is a very modest girl in her private life..."

"Full of energy and optimism...versatile... charming at will, coy under necessity and firm without provocation."

"With beautifully streamlined figure...is naturally an attractive artist's model...standing 5' 4½" without her shoes, she provides a graceful figure before the mirror".

"She does not go to the races, does not smoke, does not drink...Her favourite hobby is thinking deeply...loves cats...She is also a linguist.. knows seven languages . . ."

"When not working she spends her time reading Ibsen, Johnson, Bernard Shaw...Is a perfect cook in European, French, Indian and Jewish dishes...."

"As a child fond of seeing pictures...got her first chance for acting in May 1932..Ambitious at all times..won her way up through hard work and perseverance...."

"...At 15 passed Inter..worked as a school teacher, then as an accountant in bank...not enough to keep home fires burning. Success of her cousin lured her to the screen... She earns nearly Rs. 3000 a month...."

In interviews with actors, while appearance is not disregarded, it comes second to their intellectual attainments. Their hobbies and early hardships, however, come in for as much publicity as in the case of actresses. The usual remarks are like this:

"Dressed in rather loud style he was at considerable pains to make a good impression...."

"Not at all over-dressed...inclined to be silent and grumpy...six feet tall and 13 stone in weight, his general appearance reminds one of the jungle. Hefty, thick with a bull's neck, a curly top and not at all bad looking...Impulsive, brutally frank, but very intelligent."

"He spends his little spare  time in reading books on motion picture technique...has an elaborate library which he has collected after long pain through years..." (sic).

"Had a college education...graduated...a scholar in Hindi, Urdu, Persian and English.... [his flat] is hardly a home of comforts. Just a house of books. Books here, books there and books all over. People give him up as a bad friend and call him just a book-worm...."

"An educated man...a voracious reader..."

".... Intensely fond of outdoor sports... never misses a boating chance..."

"....hates races...doesn't take intoxicating drinks...doesn't smoke cigarettes..."

"....at 18 left school...at 21 joined Urdu

stage on salary of Rs. 75 per month...worked as an extra...on Rs. 30 a month..knocked about, got his big chance in 1933..became a star overnight..."

"....a rebel...did not go the way of his father ..joined films..floated his own company..went into liquidation...after a year box-office success.."

" 'Had it not been for my film career, I would have begged in the streets'....failed twice in the Matric examination..in 1939 made his first appearance before the camera and made a face at the hero....that settled it, he became a professional actor..."

Considering the fact that a large number of questions asked by fans relate to the star's family affairs, marriage and divorce, these topics, though dealt with now and then in the interviews published, were not given as much prominence as one would have naturally expected. The few interviews which mentioned this aspect of a star's life summarily disposed of the matter in a few words like the following:

"...married at 15...has two sons...incidentally votes for the traditional warm and happy home..."

"...is a married man having...a pretty film star as his wife. Terribly in love with his wife..."

Though at times articles of a serious nature are published, the greater part of these fan periodicals are devoted to men and women of the industry, to film gossip from abroad, to studio news about pictures in the making, a readers' forum ventilating their grievances, photographs of young men, though rarely of women, eager to join the industry and, last but not the least, film advertisements.

These fan magazines provide the reader with a means of further identification with the screen's artistocracy of good looks, grace, talent and wealth.

The fan magazines thus go a long way in linking the fan to the star. In the sphere of fashion the magic force of films is felt, for stars are the virtual dictators in matters of hair styles, dress, ornaments and accessories.

The influence of stars in the world of Dame Fashion is more marked in Western countries, especially in the U.S.A., than in ours, for fashion itself is fundamentally a modern, occidental phenomenon or culture trait. Moreover, there the people are not only more star-conscious, but the star-system is highly organized and exploited. At first people scoffed at the idea that films had any influence on fashion. Today, however, they are convinced that films have influence on practically everything.

It is impossible to give particular instances of fashions started or styles established by individual Indian stars, but from general observation it can be said that our screen personalities do exercise a certain amount of influence on the trends of fashions. For example, in the stride of the smart college student or in the way he brushes his hair or in the swinging gait of girls, their dress and make-up, can be seen some touch of a favourite hero or heroine. However, we have not exploited this influence nor the names of our stars to the same degree as America has done, for few of our traders and merchants have learnt to incorporate the names of stars in their goods to enhance sales. Consequently this influence is less marked but it is there all the same.

In matters of dress the Indian screen stars have once again brought into vogue the old fashioned 'cholies'. Mythological and historical films started a new trend which has now become a fashionable style of dress among some sections of society. Various methods of draping the sari, and different kinds of Indian dresses have been popularized by the stars on and off the screen. Not that these are new modes created by the stars, but the important fact is that it is through the medium of the screen that they are given a widespread popularity.

As regards coiffures our stars have borrowed liberally from Ajanta and from ancient literature, thereby reviving bygone modes which are more suited to our culture and dress than the Western styles. For example, the beautiful but elaborate head dress of Sushila Rani in *Draupadi*, of Vanmala in *Kalidas*, of Shanta Apte in *Kadambari* and the simple hair style of Veena in *Samrat Ashok* are adaptations from Ajanta frescoes. But while the beauties of Ajanta were hidden from the common eye, the screen has revealed them to thousands.

What is true of dress and coiffures is also true of ornaments. Old designs and settings have been revived along with the more frequent use of flowers as accessories.

The most outstanding influence of the screen, however, is to be seen in the use of 'kumkum.' Originally a symbol of 'sohag' among the communities of Central, Eastern and Peninsular India, it has now become a mark of beauty to many who did not originally believe in its traditional significance. From a simple vermilion spot it has now become a fashion to design elaborate patterns on the forehead, and many Indian women have followed the lead of the stars in this matter. Manufacturers and traders taking advantage of the new trend have created kumkum sets which have made the tracing of designs a simpler and quicker process.

Film stars influence the trend of fashion in cosmetics and toilet articles. It is they who establish the mode towards artificial or natural lines, and here too they have the power of endorsement. A screen-queen famed for her lovely hair, complexion, teeth or mouth is a good argument for buying a certain brand of shampoo, hair oil, soap, tooth paste or lipstick. In fact traders exploit the names of stars in advertising their goods.

The fact that they are so well and so widely known makes them powerful agents for the propagation of certain behaviour ideals or ways of life, for good or for ill.

The star-system is not flawless. It is becoming a racket thus inviting the castigation of the more serious and thoughtful. In this respect, Hollywood in particular has come in for a great deal of criticism for it is there that this system is most highly organized and exploited.

Once producers awoke to the realization of the box-office attraction of film stars they exploited the star-system to the fullest possible extent, so much so that it earned for the cinema an unenviable reputation. No serious thinking persons saw anything in the vaunted aesthetic value of the cinema. It called forth denunciations and scathing criticisms, which according to Paul Rotha, it rightly merited for "the star-system was nothing more or less than a flagrant prostitution of creative intelligence and of good film material."[1]

In India, prior to the advent of the talkies, the star-system was unorganized and film acting was stilted and highly exaggerated. With the development of the star-system, there has been a slight change for the better. With spectators becoming more and more star-minded, and producers ever eager to cash the box-office value of film stars, their salaries are rising higher and higher. In view of their limited number and an increasing demand, the top rankers have become dictators, and producers tempted by their box-office allure are submitting to their demands. Moreover, the stellar strength is not expanding as it should with the addition of new talent. Undoubtedly, there have been a few newcomers and these have become film stars almost overnight. Stardom is too cheaply won here and film acting is still in a state of immaturity. New stars have little or no previous experience. In fact the way they achieve stardom is most revealing. A director or a producer happens to spot some young woman who is fairly good looking, and offers her a contract for a leading role almost immediately. She is starred in a full length role and no one seems to find anything odd about it. However, having no knowledge or experience of film acting she gives a feeble performance but the masses are so accustomed to a low standard of acting that she is accepted as a new star. She twinkles brightly for a few years and then she is forgotten by her worshippers who

[1] Paul Rotha, *The Film Till Now*, p. 74.

have by then found a new idol. Undoubtedly, some Indian stars have lasted a long while on the screen; but these are exceptions. The majority are like meteors who shoot past quickly into oblivion. Unlike their American counterparts, Indian film stars enjoy a very short span of celebrity. For one thing they do not get the same grooming and publicity as foreign stars do, and having risen by pure chance, shine only so long as their luck holds. Bad casting and excessive free-lancing also shorten their professional life.

The standard of film acting here is very low. An actor repeats the same intonation, the same trick of expression, the same gesture in every role. Change of expression or personality which signifies the essence of dramatic art is unknown to him. Many try to replace their lack of talent by their looks, but without lasting success.

Very rarely does the film star merge his or her personality into the role he or she is depicting. More often than not the film is only a frame in which the film star is presented. Great acting demands that the actor should lose his or her identity in the role depicted, so much so that the audience forgets the performer and thinks only of the performance.

Another drawback of the Indian star-system which attracts attention is the exploitation of the stars by featuring them in five or six films at a time. This is probably due to a dearth of good actors and actresses. Sometimes if one goes round the Indian picture houses in the city one comes across an actor or an actress starring in three or four pictures simultaneously. As most of these pictures happen to be love stories, the player is dressed in more or less similar outfit, goes through the same mannerisms and gestures and plays the same role in all the pictures. The blame for this falls both on the excessive free lancing done by some of the leading players and on the attitude of producers who, being out to make money, exploit a star's appeal. Very often the stars do not protest, thinking that if producers are out to make money they also should have their share.

Working for a number of pictures simultaneously is not only wearing but also makes the film star very cheap. Too frequent appearances dissipate popularity and a stage is reached when the public surfeited with an overdose automatically transfers its interest to a new personality.

Apart from exploitation, there is a great deal of miscasting in our films. Film stars are given roles whether they are suited for them or not. Both producers and film stars are responsible for this. Producers out to mint money want to feature in their films the popular actors who are sure to bring in the greatest returns, while the popular stars are ever demanding juvenile roles. They are afraid that their popularity will suffer if they are cast in elderly roles. Thus incongruities often appear on the screen like elderly women vainly trying to play the role of adolescent girls.

Another reason for the great deal of miscasting seen in our films is that since songs play an important part in our pictures, actors and actresses are often selected for their singing ability regardless of the fact that they are unsuited to the character they are expected to portray.

However, neither the star-system, nor the habit which many of us have formed of seeing a film because of its leading characters should be entirely condemned. For the film star occupies a significant place in production and in society. The star-system gives to the average cinema-goer who knows next to nothing about direction or technicalities a focal point of interest, a means by which he can link himself to the glamorous and fantastic screen world.

What is to be deplored is a misuse of this system. Though, no doubt, it would be foolish to ignore the value of film stars to the commercial success of a film, it would be more foolish still to sacrifice imagination, good taste and intelligence for box-office returns.

Modelled on the American pattern, the Indian star-system has taken on the good and bad points of its prototype. But instead of benefitting from Hollywood's mistakes and avoiding similar pitfalls, our different social system and our less advanced film industry have enhanced the evils of our unorganized system. Our meteors have a long way to go before they can acquire the stability or brilliance of a Dhruva, and yet with a little courage and foresight on their part and understanding and intelligence on the part of producers, they should be able to acquire that luminosity which is rightly theirs. Before closing this chapter on screen personalities and their impact on social life, a few words must be written about their position in our society.

Since its very inception the cinema has been looked down upon by the elite. Even as a profession, men and especially women of the higher classes were not attracted to it. Today, circumstances have changed in that many men and women from  respectable classes have taken to the film as a career. Yet the stigma attached to the profession of screen acting still persists. In  the eyes of the world once a man or a woman has joined the acting profession he or she becomes not 'quite nice'. How far this judgment is deserved it is hard to say. Certainly it is a prejudice which has existed for years.

Though it is now thirty-six years since the birth of the Indian film, it has not been in existence long enough for it to be accepted without suspicion by our society. When a young man or a woman suggests that he or she would like to become a film actor or actress hectic discussions arise in the family circle. Persuasion, vituperation and even force are tried, but if the individual is adamant the final outcome in some cases is that the family gives in. More often,  however, he or she is ostracized from the family circle and left to fend for himself or herself.

The general trend of the argument is that films are not a respectable profession; that the moral standards of studios are very low and that anyone wishing to join the profession is morally depraved.

It is at times suggested that Indian society ostracizes those, especially girls, who have joined the film industry. When questioned if this were so, the stars themselves have given a lie to this statement.  Society receives them with smiles and garlands and lavishly entertains them in homes, clubs and restaurants.  This surely does not suggest ostracism.  But may it not be, as one star herself said, that this is all mere show?  As members of the film world they are popular in social circles.  People like to be seen with them and take a pride in their acquaintance.  They are welcomed at marriages and other social functions simply because their presence serves a decorative purpose.  They command respect for the glitter and glamour that goes with them and for the money they represent.  As this star writes: "Really speaking we do not command real and sincere respect... [and] our social status.. [is] hollow".

As things stand today our film stars have not earned for themselves the best of reputations.  In many cases the blackening of the character of film artistes is probably undeserved.   At the same time it cannot be said that they are beyond reproach.  But while there are black sheep in every profession, is it fair or justifiable to condemn an entire profession because of the misdeeds and misbehaviour of a few?  What is necessary for the films to occupy a definite place in our social life, is broad-mindedness and toleration on the part of the public and better organization and leadership on the part of the profession; by merely abusing the industry and its artistes we shall not be achieving anything.  A more tolerant attitude may tempt better educated and more  intelligent people into the industry bringing about an all round improvement, so much so that in another generation we may even find a Greta Garbo in our midst.

# 7

## THE INFLUENCE OF FILMS

WITH all this evidence and data on the attendance at films, the contents of films and the social significance of screen personalities, the question that now arises is whether this moving panorama which the people of all countries and of all ages daily witness, plays any direct role in their lives. Is it not forgotten as soon as seen and dismissed for what it is—an unsubstantial dream? It is impossible to answer this highly controversial question in a few words. In Western countries the film has been the subject of much discussion. The pros and cons have been gone into, and it has been found that the film is not what it superficially appears to be—a mere commodity for entertainment. It is a medium with a vivid and wide appeal, exercising an influence on contemporary society which is enormous, though still largely unmeasured. This influence is, in all probability, stronger than that wielded by the press or the radio. The nature of this influence which is exerted on all classes—though there may exist significant differences in class reactions—is a moral one. Value patterns, actual behaviour and outlook on life generally are very often manifestly shaped by film influences. Most of our contemporary society, though not film made, is yet vastly influenced by films.

The film's appeal is primarily and deliberately emotional, and its intellectual quality is often negligible. It is addressed mainly to the unintelligent masses, whose mentality is estimated to be that of a fourteen year old child. The baser and not the higher emotions are played upon for profit. There are many who believe that the standards exploited in films, encourage the violation of every moral precept, induce a disregard for law and order and stimulate the commission of crime. This, however, is only one side of the question, for there are others who hold diametrically opposite views.

The film in India, both foreign and indigenous, is an accepted part of our social life. However, its reactions on our society have not been gauged. Unlike what has been done in the West, we have never tried to measure its impact on our way of life; nor have we explored to the full its vast potentialities. Moreover, while the urban theatre is fairly common, the rural cinema is still a rarity. Travelling units do tour the villages; but what a pitiful ratio these four or five hundred bear to the 500,000 villages. Hence much of the influence that the cinema can possibly exert in this land is of an urban nature. This influence cannot be under-estimated, even though the major proportion of India's teeming millions live in villages, for it is the urban, industral centres which are the springs of thought and action.

The problem of juveniles in the cinema has always been the subject of controversial discussion and enquiry. Probably the most exhaustive investigation into this question was carried out in the U.S.A. under the auspices of the Payne Fund. In 1928 a group of university psychologists, sociologists and educational experts were invited by the Motion Picture Research Council to find out the effects of motion pictures upon children, a subject on which many conflicting opinions, though few substantial facts, were in existence. The investigations extended from 1929 to 1932. Its results were published in a series of monographs by the Macmillan Company and summarized by Henry James Forman in his *Our Movie Made Children*.

In 1937 the findings of the Payne Fund were ruthlessly criticized by Dr. Mortimer Adler in his *Art & Prudence* which was condensed by Raymond Moley in his interesting account entitled *Are We Movie Made?*

Further light has been thrown on this subject by Paul Cressey writing in the *American Sociological Review*, August 1938, and by a series of articles on the effects of motion pictures published in the *Annals of the American Academy of Political and Social Science*, November 1947, a number devoted exclusively to the investigation of the motion picture industry and its problems.

It must be pointed out here, however, that the investigations carried out so far in Western countries have only touched the fringe of the problem. The material so far collected has been more or less in the nature of factual data with a few psychological factors touched upon here and there. The basic roots of the problem dealing with the many aspects of the psychological reactions of the audience to film content yet remain to be explored. For example, the likes and dislikes of the audience not only operate as a basis for selection of the pictures for which the people will pay to expose themselves but, at the same time, limit the effects which films may have. People's reactions to films are conditioned by their own experience and values. The influence of the screen undoubtedly is, both for the industry and the public, the most vital field for future research. The exact nature of the influence of films or the conditions under which films are effective are not known; the practical limits to the powers of the screen are as yet scientifically undetermined.

Though much use has been made of the findings of the Payne Fund, the fact that they apply entirely to children and conditions in the U.S.A. makes them to a certain extent useless for us. Dearth of similar material regarding Indian conditions, as well as the lack of facilities to compile like data, has made the task of social investigation into Indian conditions very difficult if not impossible.

The only investigation, and that too a very superficial one, so far made into this question was by the Indian Cinematograph Committee, 1927-28. According to it, children were less likely to suffer from seeing films of doubtful morality than from witnessing scenes of

11

violence and sensation, which were harmless to adolescents and adults. Hence it was suggested that films should be passed for 'universal exhibition' indicating that they contained nothing harmful for children; or for 'public exhibition' indicating that such films though suitable for an ordinary audience, may excite or distress children.

### JUVENILES AND THE CINEMA

Attendance statistics reveal that the life of juveniles today is being invaded by the cinema. A majority of children come in contact with the films once a week or at least once a month. Naturally any institution that touches the life of children with this persistent regularity becomes of great importance to their welfare.

Having analysed the contents of films, the next important question is whether children remember what they see and, if so, for how long. Richard Ford[1] in his discussion with organizers of children's matinees found that children have a remarkable memory for details of films, especially short films and cartoons, and they often protest if the same film is repeated. The Payne Fund[2] investigation also revealed that children of seven to ten remembered at the end of six weeks 91 per cent of what they knew on the day following the show, while high school children remembered 88 per cent. Girls and boys remembered equally well. Even very young children remembered about 60 per cent of the incidents in a film recalled by adults. It was found that children retained the strongest memory of the stars, sport scenes, crimes, acts of violence and other items of high emotional appeal.

Though children remember 60 per cent of what adults do, their reactions to and impressions of a film are totally unlike those of an adult, since their mental make-up and their conception of the world, judged by their needs and experiences, are entirely different. Because of his experience an adult understands make-

---

[1] Richard Ford, *Children in the Cinema*, pp. 50, 131-2.
[2] H. J. Forman, *Our Movie Made Children*, pp. 63-5.

believe. The child on the contrary does not take it to be mere make-believe. As W. W. Charter says: "Watching in the dark of the theatre, the young child sits in the presence of reality when he sees the actors perform and the plot of the drama unfold. He sees the action of people living in a real world—not of actors playing a make-believe role."[1] Psychologists have proved beyond doubt that children believe a large part of what they see on the screen and believe it to be genuine and correct. If the information given is correct it results in an increase of general knowledge. But unfortunately inaccurate information is often accepted as valid. This fact places a great responsibility on those who provide films for the entertainment of children.

Why is this so? Mainly because the story or the incident is depicted in visual terms, and so long as the emotion expressed is something with which the child is familiar he can identify himself completely with the character on the screen. This identification is of great importance. When, for example, he sees the hero in an action drama chasing the villain or villains, he not merely admires the hero but for the time being he is the hero performing those deeds.

Psychologists define such identification as *empathy* which means the emotional placing of the observer himself in the observed object, producing the feeling he would have in the position of the object. Films being visual, offer great facilities for identification and vicarious experience, and children, adolescents and even young adults tend to identify themselves, either consciously or unconsciously with some character on the screen. There is no doubt that such identification is frequent. Investigation among Bombay college students revealed that 18 per cent of adolescent girls between 14 and 20 years, 25.9 per cent of young women over 21, 34.2 per cent of young boys between 14 and 20 and 37 per cent of young men over 21 identified themselves with screen characters, especially the hero or the heroine, while probably many more, even if they did so,

[1] Richard Ford, *Children in the Cinema*, p. 47.

hesitated to acknowledge it.

The process of identification is not only important but is often translated into behaviour. The imitation of fashions, speech and manners from films is fairly common, and it is thus known that imitation does take place. What is not known, however, are the differences in imitation. For example, how will a young girl coming from a well-to-do family, who has no household responsibilities, differ in her imitation from a girl of the same age, who comes from a labouring class family, who works for her living and also helps her mother in household work? The girl from the working class will be obviously more mature than the former, and her imitation is bound to be different from that of the other girl. Thus the social status of adolescents must be taken into consideration before judging their attitude and their reaction to films. This is a limitation to any social investigation into the reactions of adolescents to the cinema.

### PHYSICAL EFFECTS ON CHILDREN AND ADOLESCENTS

So far as children and adolescents are concerned the Payne Fund studies investigated the influence of films on sleep, emotional responses to motion picture situations, creation of ideas, social attitudes, standards of morality and on conduct, especially in relation to crime and delinquency.

With reference to the physical effects on sleep, investigations revealed that though the variation of effects upon different individuals was considerable, boys after seeing a film showed an average increase of about 26 per cent and girls about 14 per cent greater hourly mobility than in normal sleep. So great were the variations in individual cases that 50 to 90 per cent of increase in restlessness was noted.[1] It was also found that effects varied with age. Younger children between the ages of six and ten were more affected than the older ones. Effects on nervous and unstable children and other physical effects such as increase of pulse and heart action

[1] H. J. Forman, *Our Movie Made Children*, pp. 74-5, 82.

were also noted and it was found that sometimes these were doubled under great excitement.

Moreover, late hours at cinema shows often resulted in sleep starvation, tired, pale-faced children who were drowsy in the morning, dull at lessons, half-hearted in their attempts at games and easily irritated, resulting in an average diminution of physical strength by one-fifth.[1]

It is sometimes complained that cinema-going has caused a decline in the general standard of eyesight. Sifting through all the evidence, the general conclusion that can be drawn is that in the late twenties, due to bad conditions of projection, a certain amount of eye strain did result. Nowadays, however, these old types of projectors have more or less disappeared and the film is generally clear and steady. Care is also taken to ensure that the relative position of the screen and the front row seats is such that it does not cause eye strain. Hence, lately, no evidence has been found to suggest that cinema-going causes a decline in the standard of eyesight.

Some critics have also commented on the harmful conditions of display. It is argued that the darkness of the cinema halls creates an unhealthy and dangerous atmosphere and is liable to develop bad habits in nervous children. Many young people went to the cinema, it was suggested, on account of the erotic excitement produced by the darkness which dulled their critical sense of the film shown.

## PSYCHOLOGICAL EFFECTS

From a psychological standpoint a study of the emotional responses of children to different motion picture situations showed that children under 12 responded more intensely to scenes of conflict, danger, tragedy than did those of 12 years and over. The older the age group, the less intense was the response. However, the age group above 16 gave the strongest response to scenes

[1] Richard Ford, *Children in the Cinema*, pp. 60-1, 67-8.

of love and sex suggestion.

It was further found that "the younger the child the more he appreciated and emotionally responded to the separate items in the films and the less he appreciated or even assimilated the continuity of the story to say nothing of the moral or ultimate outcome of the picture".[1] This point can hardly be over-emphasized. Because isolated episodes stand out in a child's or an adolescent's mind, are most frequently responded to, and the whole story has little or no effect, it is impossible to expect the juvenile to make the same synthesis of a film as an adult does. As W. S. Dysinger and C. A. Ruckmick have observed: "An exciting robbery, an ecstatic love scene, the behaviour of a drunkard and the like cannot be toned down by the moral situation at the end of the picture when the episode is justified in terms of the hand of the law or the retribution of an outraged Providence...The ultimate outcome of the story, the moral that honesty is the best policy, the assumption that the way of the sinner is bad, are adult generalizations . . . Even if the picture clearly depicts this outcome it very seldom strikes the attention of the younger generation with anything like the force that it does the adult mind."[2]

The next important factor in this study of the film as a sociological force is to ascertain the influence of motion pictures on conduct.

One way in which the cinema has influenced children is in determining the forms of their games. Children love to play make-believe roles, and from films they can obtain any amount of material which they can use in this way. Professor Blumer found on investigation[3] that out of 200 boys under the age of 12, 75 per cent admitted playing at impersonation of film stories, while of the 70 older boys between the ages of 12 and 14, 60 per cent made similar admissions. While boys preferred scenes of fighting, shooting, police arrests or escapes, girls tended to imitate love scenes.

Though these influences are confined to a child's

[1] J. P. Mayer, *Sociology of the Film*, p. 141.
[2] H. J. Forman, *Our Movie Made Children*, p. 119.
[3] *Ibid*, pp. 142-3; Richard Ford, *Children in the Cinema*, p. 65.

play the question that now arises is—what is the significance of play in the life of the child and in the formation of the adult. This is a debatable question and various theories have been propounded. It may be argued that play acting does not make a deep impression on the child's personality, since he is capable of changing from one role to another with the greatest ease, no matter how absorbed he may be in a particular one at any given time. On the other hand, it is likely that continual imitation of stereotyped film characters would produce somewhat standardized conceptions of life in the minds of the imitator, more so in the cases where information obtained from the cinema is not supplemented by other kinds of knowledge. As Margaret Lowenfeld observes, "Modern dynamic psychology, however, has suggested that certain elements of a child's nature and outlook do not change, in the process of growth, into adult versions of those elements, but persist unchanged in some part of the mind and form the ultimate background to all adult life."[1] The significance of this statement with reference to those children whose minds are filled with screen imagery and with little else, is obvious.

It has already been noted that in a child's play there is a great deal of make-believe and that the impersonation of a film character is an end in itself—a mere pastime which has no practical aim in the everyday affairs of life. When, however, we note the forms in which the influence of films manifests itself in adolescents, we are conscious of a deliberate use of film material as a means of furthering the designs of real life. It is difficult to distinguish between the fanciful dressing up of older children and the more deliberate imitation of clothes and hair styles by adolescent girls and young women. Nevertheless, there is a marked tendency for the adolescent to seek in the cinema, patterns of behaviour which he or she can incorporate in daily life.

One of the spheres in which this influence is most obvious is in the field of dress, jewellery, hair style and personal mannerism. Professor Blumer found that out

[1] J. P. Mayer, *Sociology of Film*, pp. 147-8.

of 458 high school students 62 per cent admitted such imitations.[1] He also found that the most striking way in which juveniles used films as guides to living was in their relations with the opposite sex.

However, while what Professor Blumer says may be true of Western countries especially the U.S.A., the same cannot be said of Indian adolescents. The American adolescent tends to attach greater importance at an early age, to his relations with the opposite sex, and is more sophisticated in his outlook than an average adolescent of 14 or 16 in this country, since our concept of life and morals and our social environment is entirely different. In matters of dress, make-up, hair style, jewellery, however, it can be said from general observation that our films do exert a powerful influence, especially in towns where the cinema is a common form of entertainment. Not only adolescents but even young adults imitate styles from the screen.

Again there is the effect on speech. Since the advent of the talkies, children and adolescents have picked up a new language with the words and phraseology of the screen. The use of American slang is very common. Even in India, this influence of foreign films has penetrated and can be noted in the case of boys and girls who frequent foreign films. They tend to use more and more American colloquialisms in their everyday language. This tendency is more marked among boys than girls, probably because they see more crime, 'western' and other adventure thrillers, where such Americanisms abound, than girls do.

Hitherto, the subject under consideration has been the external life of juveniles, but there are other ways in which the film affects the lives of individuals and that is in the material it provides for day-dreams and fantasies. Undoubtedly the tendency to build castles in the air is inherent in the mental make-up of certain types of individuals and this tendency is stimulated by books and music as well as by the cinema. The very nature of the

[1] H. J. Forman, *Our Movie Made Children*, pp. 144-52; J. P. Mayer, *Sociology of Film*, pp. 149-50.

film with its power to facilitate the identification of the spectator with the actor, its freedom from the restrictions of time and space, and its vivid depiction of reality, makes it a more potent inspirer of day-dreams than any other kind of art or entertainment.

Adolescents most frequently indulge in day-dreams. Frequently the dreamer imagines himself or herself in the place of the hero and heroine in a particular film. Sometimes the story of the film is re-enacted without any modifications while at times the screen material is only used as a starting point from which an entirely new phantasy is woven according to the individual's personal tastes and experience. This kind of phantasy is more subjective and therefore likely to play a more significant part in the individual's life.

The fact that even grown-up college boys and girls indulge in day-dreams about pictures and unattainable ideals is also proved by the large number of letters received by the editors of fan magazines from enthusiastic fans.

What is the function of day-dreams in life? Not enough is known for us to judge how far phantasies stimulated by films affect the conduct and outlook of the individual. Moreover, there are two points of view on this phenomenon. According to one set of psychologists, day-dreams serve a useful social function in that they act as safety valves for emotions and impulses which would be harmful if not allowed uninhibited expression or may even lead to neurotic conditions if entirely repressed. The other opinion on day-dreaming is that it is indulged in by people who cannot cope with the problems of reality and who turn to phantasy as to a drug. This at first makes them happy but ultimately makes them completely unfit to tackle the everyday problems of life. None of these two aspects have been proved; but the application of either of these theories to phantasies stimulated by pictures would be an interesting study.

Frequent indulgence in day-dreams encourages and often creates desires and inclinations which may be expressed in actual conduct should favourable opportunity arise. Examples are given of boys who indulged in escapades suggested by some of the films they had seen. In the case of girls it was found that the sentimental and romantic side of their nature drove them to launch into adventures of which they became the victims. Many such adventures ended in rape or prostitution.

Herbert Blumer also dealt with different aspects of a type of experience which he called "Emotional Possession". J. P. Mayer says: "This condition . . . . results when feelings which are usually restrained, are stimulated to such an extent that the individual undergoes some diminution of his power of self-control and behaves in a manner which is a departure from his normal conduct."[1] Such a state can be induced by intense absorption in a film. The mind becomes so obsessed with what it sees that for the time being it is swayed by emotions which ordinarily it would be able to master. The experience is usually a temporary one, but at times it may leave an indelible impression as in the case of fear or terror.

Every investigation into the effects of films on children, reveals some element of fright or fear. This aspect can be easily over-emphasized for the word 'fear' suggests nightmares and may be outstretched to mental derangements and even lunacy.

However, it must be remembered that any honest young adult can recollect an early instance of a fright produced by a picture seen, and though the memory is clear, the individual is none the worse for his experience. Hence, the influence of fear should be regarded as an almost inevitable occurrence among film-goers.

Professor Blumer's accounts reveal that children and young people are very often frightened by certain films or episodes from films. As he says:"The experience of fright, horror or agony as a result of witnessing certain kinds of motion pictures seems common from the accounts of children and of high school and college students. The experience is most conspicuous in the case of children. Its manifestations vary from shield-

[1] J. P. Mayer, *Sociology of Film*, p. 155.

ing the eyes at crucial scenes during the showing of pictures to nightmares and terrifying dreams including, sometimes, experience of distinct shock, almost of neurotic proportions."[1]

The effect of films on the nervous system was particularly noticeable among children and especially among young girls between the ages of 10 and 13, but it is not unusual among adolescents and young adults. On investigation among the students of Bombay City, it was found that among the adolescents 47.47 per cent girls and 28.5 per cent boys acknowledged that they had been frightened some time or the other on seeing certain films. While among the young adults 37 per cent girls and 15 per cent boys had experienced similar reactions.

This investigation also showed that the types of films which were particularly liable to induce terror and fright, were films belonging to the mystery and horror category where emphasis was placed on ghosts, vampires and eerie and weird elements. Among the films mentioned were *Dr. Jekyll and Mr. Hyde, The Mummy, Frankenstein, Ghost of Frankenstein, Son of Frankenstein, Wax Museum, Dracula, Invisible Man, Hound of the Baskervilles, Fear in the Night, Hunchback of Notre Dame, The Body Snatcher* and *The Picture of Dorian Gray.* Among the Indian films the only one that was given as an instance was *Kapal Kundala.* These findings are corroborated by J. P. Mayer's and Roger Manvell's investigations and the London County Council Report of 1932. The list of things which frightened children included ghosts, phantoms, gorillas, grabbing hands and claws, spiders, terrifying close-ups and grotesque faces.

The emotions expressed by children during the show included nail biting, grabbing one's neighbour, closing the eyes, screaming, jumping out of the seat and even at times getting under the seat. Richard Ford describes frightened children in the cinema thus: ". . . there is usually a tense hush when children are frightened

[1] *Ibid;* Richard Ford. *Children in the Cinema,* pp. 51-2.

during a film, and they hold their breath, emitting small restrained squeaks, while they grip the edge or arm of the seat. The noise of healthy screaming during a chase scene is entirely different."[1]

After the show many children ran home, avoided dark corners or streets, were frightened of shadows, wanted a light in the room at night while sleeping, had nightmares and frequently were afraid of sleeping alone.

Although in many cases the fear induced by films is temporary and the episode which gave rise to it is forgotten in a few days, cases are known where the effect is more lasting. Frequently too the child or adolescent or youth is aware of the absurdity of his fears but is unable to dispel them however hard he tries. It is this condition of emotional possession, when the ordinary commonsense of the person concerned is overpowered by an irrational and uncontrollable impulse which is the most important aspect of the experience of fear aroused by films.

What is the attitude of authorities towards fear? The element of fear is officially recognized as harmful and undesirable by the British Board of Film Censors who have invented a Horrific Category—'H'—to label certain films and to prohibit persons under 16 from seeing them.

Local authorities have also the power to supplement this ruling by prohibiting certain films altogether or increasing the strength from 'universal' to 'adult'. A film which caused much criticism and comment in this respect was Walt Disney's *Snow White and the Seven Dwarfs* which was originally given an 'A' certificate, since it contained enough horrific element to frighten children. Much criticism was aroused because many insisted on believing that this was a children's film. Disney has never pretended to be a film maker for children, though children have adopted him in spite of the horrific element symbolic of evil in his films and which is an essential part of Disney folklore.

In India there is no such separate category for hor-

[1] *Ibid*, p. 55.

ror films, though certain episodes like those mentioned below are regarded as objectionable by the Boards of Film Censors, and therefore likely to be deleted:

1 Cruelty to animals, young infants, torture of adults especially women.
2 Exhibition of profuse bleeding.
3 Realistic horrors of warfare.
4 Gruesome murders and strangulation scenes.
5 Executions.

An emotional condition with psychological features like those noted in the case of fear is often induced by pictures which portray overwhelming pathos. Everyone is familiar with people who weep at any sad or touchingly sentimental incident in a film. There are, however, others who make valiant efforts to control their emotion but are unable to do so, and these people may be said to be in a state of emotional possession. Their emotions have swept aside the restrictions imposed by commonsense and they have for the time being lost control over themselves. Pathetic pictures and incidents were found to be very powerful in exciting the emotions of pity, sympathy and tenderness.

As a general rule girls are more prone to this type of emotional possession than boys. On investigation in Bombay it was found that among adolescents 39 per cent boys were sometimes moved to tears, 18.8 per cent were moved but did not cry, while among girls 21.8 per cent nearly always cried, 57.1 per cent at times shed a few tears. Among young adults, 27.2 per cent boys and 25.9 per cent girls cried at times, 37 per cent girls cried often and 33.9 per cent boys though they did not cry, got a 'lump in the throat' or became sad and depressed.

The next important factor to be taken into consideration is the love element. It is commonly believed that the really harmful elements for children in films are the amorous episodes. Richard Ford's enquiry, however, showed that children are bored by love scenes on the screen. Often there is hissing, catcalls and loud exclamations of disapproval when such scenes come on

the screen.  The child regards such incidents as mere
waste of time.  *The Film in National Life* quotes a
Methodist minister, Dr. Soper as saying: ". . . . even the
sex film may do no harm, for the simple reason that a
child does not understand half of what is  being said.
Passionate kisses simply give them the giggles. . . ."[1]
W.W. Charters, summarizing the findings of the Payne
Fund, observes: "Few children at the age of 9 years
react to erotic scenes in films; this reaction occurs in increasing numbers of children until it reaches its climax
among the 16 to 18 year olds."[2]  These findings are
confirmed by other enquiries.  The element which the
adult would most deprecate to be put before children is
not only ignored by them but in fact bores them.

The case of adolescents, however, is entirely different.  J. P. Mayer's and Professor Blumer's investigations lead them to believe that love and passion are perhaps the most powerful forms of emotional possessions in
the case of adolescents.  Stimulating romantic sequences
on the screen may kindle desires in the minds of adolescents for similar experience in their own life.  In some
cases the relaxation of inhibitions  may be quite temporary but in others, where a film has made a more
lasting impression, it may even lead to a way of behaviour which the individual might not have  followed
had he or she not been emotionally  prepared by the
film.  Very often, however, the pleasure and thrill derived from films does not lead to any direct action, but
only to a vicarious enjoyment and this sort of pleasure
is derived more commonly by girls than boys.

As regards Indian conditions, lack of information
and investigation makes it impossible to form an opinion.  But witnesses giving evidence before the Indian
Cinematograph Committee in 1927-8 were of the opinion that foreign sex and love films (in 1925 and 1930
49.6 per cent and 44.6 per cent of films exhibited dealt
with sex or love as their main theme) had a demoralizing influence on the adolescents of the country.  More-

[1] *The Film in National Life,* Report of the Commission on Educational and
Cultural Films, 1932. p. 74.
[2] Richard Ford, *Children in the Cinema,* p. 63.

over, such scenes shown on the screen without the background of knowledge of Western ideas and institutions
gave a wrong impression about foreigners to the illiterate and ignorant masses in India.   The Committee's
opinion was that children were less likely to suffer from
seeing scenes of doubtful morality than scenes of
violence.

Another form of emotional  possession is that of
thrill and excitement.    This is more prevalent among
children than adolescents.   Children become intensely
absorbed in the film when it is a thriller or serial and
give vent to their feeling by shouts, cries and even physical movements like jumping in their seats.     Excitement is intense if the hero or heroine is in danger, especially when a fight is going on.   The villain is hissed,
and if he succeeds for the time there are groans, but if
the danger is passed, sighs of relief are heard.   This
type of reaction though common among children is not
unknown among adolescents and has even been noticed
among the less sophisticated adult audiences in Indian
cinema houses.

Judging from all the evidence quoted, it is impossible to refute the fact that films do create states of emotion which some people find difficult to control.  The
graphic and vivid presentation of reality, in which the
screen is a past master, captures the imagination of the
onlooker, and by stirring his impulses and weakening his
forces of self-discipline makes him more susceptible
to whatever tendencies of anti-social behaviour are
dominant in his particular case.   Generally this state
of feeling is shortlived and the mind goes  back to its
normal state, but at times the return is never quite complete and the impression left by the film may prove to
be indelible.

In cases of emotional possession the individual concerned is, as it were, at the mercy of the film because he
is so overpowered by what he is seeing that it is impossible for him to be critical or prevent himself from being carried away by the scene in progress. Such a
state of mind and its harmful effects could be avoided if

a more detached attitude towards films could be developed by picture-goers especially children and adolescents. The creation of this attitude is helped by open discussion of the pros and cons of various films, a greater knowledge of the technical aspects of screen production and through acquiring of real life experience which generally runs counter to what is shown on the screen. By these means the individual is less likely to be affected by what he sees in films.

Apart from wielding a very significant influence on the emotions and conduct of individuals the film may prove to be a determining factor in the creation of the individual's general outlook on life—his plans for the future, his ideas of the way in which people in different circumstances from his own live and behave, his conception of what kind of life is best and so on. Often he may be led to compare his life with what is shown in the film, to the detriment of the former. This may either result in unrest and dissatisfaction or ambition to do something better. Such schemes may either remain mere day-dreams or may even lead to direct action which, though praiseworthy at times, may also have the effect of making him liable to anti-social temptation if by such means he can achieve his ambitions and desires.

Films, at times, also give false impressions of other nations and nationalities, create conflicting attitudes towards certain social institutions or present a bewildering standard of values regarding certain ways of life by stressing one favourable feature of it. Thus the screen, by its constant depiction of the life of the rich and its preoccupation with luxury and enjoyment, provides the average youth with the justification to want the same for himself, but at the same time it stresses that there is more in life than mere pleasure and enjoyment. Is it not therefore inevitable that the conflicting standards of value presented on the screen should cause mental disturbance and bewilderment amongst the impressionable members of the audience?

The type of influence which any particular individual may receive from a particular film, depends to a

KALPANA: *Produced and directed by Uday Shankar; featuring Amla Shankar and Uday Shankar; 1948.*

CHHOTA BHAI:    *Directed by Kartic Chatterji; featuring*
*Shakoor; New Theatres Ltd.; 1949.*

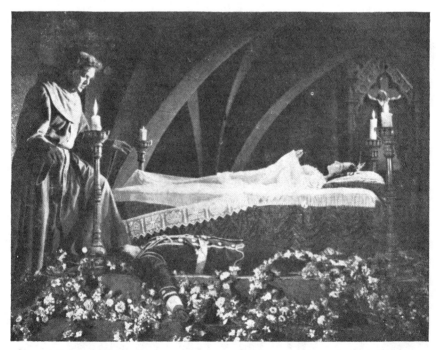

ROMEO AND      *Directed by Akhtar Hussein; featuring*
JULIET:        *Nargis and Sapru; Nargis Art Concern;*
               *1948.*

certain extent on his personal idiosyncrasies, his psychological make-up and general social experience. M. Wiess and S. Cole, studying the influence of commercial motion pictures on children's attitudes, found that the effect of a film was determined in a large degree by the social, economic and cultural origins of each individual. These factors governed in a large measure what a film meant to a particular person. Paul G. Cressey also came to the conclusion that motion picture experience is modified by the social background and personality of the individual concerned. He says: "At the cinema he [the individual] is physically but not psychologically detached from his own background and at least some of his responses are necessarily affected by his earlier associations, his present interests and his other contacts. What he perceives or fails to perceive upon the screen, what he feels or does not feel, what he remembers or fails to remember, or what he does or does not imitate are inevitably affected by his social background and personality as much or more than by the immediate motion picture situation. Likewise the ultimate meaning of the cinema experience cannot be determined without consideration of subsequent events which have reference to it. . . . While this approach does not disprove the finding that in certain cases the cinema's incidental 'contribution',....has seemed to be 'socially desirable' and in other cases definitely undesirable, it adds the significant conclusion that the types of conduct in which cinema influence is discernible appear to be determined largely, if not entirely, by the subject's previous experience and associations, his problems and interests at the time and by the pleasure or displeasure later associated with this conduct."[1]

This debatable question of juveniles in the cinema has been partly solved in Western countries, especially Great Britain, by organizing special shows and children's cinema clubs; by producing special films; by their

[1] Paul G. Cressey, "Motion Picture Experience as Modified by Social Background & Personality" *American Sociological Review*, August 1938, pp. 516-21; *Annals of the American Academy of Political and Social Science*, November, 1947.

system of censoring films for Universal exhibition, for
Adults only and by giving a special certificate for Horror films.  It is not necessary to go into the  pros and
cons of these methods.  As far as our country is concerned this problem has been relegated  to the background.  The great majority of us still look upon the
cinema as a mere money-making device and few have
realized its social potentialities.  When we have not investigated into the effects of films on adults who constitute the bulk of our audience it is not in the least surprising that nothing has been done about the needs of children and adolescents who constitute about 2 per cent and
30 per cent respectively of our average audience.   A
sorry state of affairs, it cannot be denied nor can it be
overlooked.  The  Indian  Parliament  realizing  that
something must be done amended the Cinematograph
Act, in May 1949.  This amendment which came into
force on September 1, 1949, prohibited the admittance
of children under 18 years of age to films given an 'A'
Certificate.  However, much water will flow under the
bridge before we in India can produce special films or
probe seriously into the important question of the effect
of entertainment films on juvenile minds.

### CINEMA AND CRIME

Another highly controversial topic  which comes
within the ambit of the influence of films is  whether
the cinema encourages delinquency and anti-social behaviour, especially among juveniles.

For many years the cinema has been made  the
scapegoat for the existence of crime in society.  Many
people believed that the 'blood and thunder' entertainment of the silent film days, exhibited for the benefit of
the lower classes, in ill-ventilated, unhealthy, flea-rid-
den halls was responsible for much of the anti-social behaviour among children.  This belief is still entrenched
in the minds of many people particularly conservative
people, who condemn the cinema for what they believe
to be its gravest fault.

Are films really responsible for crime?  The pros

and cons of the case are evenly balanced. It is impossible to go into details[1] about the conflicting opinion of learned men and women. Nevertheless, the opinion of Dr. Cyril Burt, an authority on child crime is reproduced from his standard work *The Young Delinquent* (1928), for he answers all questions readily and comprehensively. Although his observations apply to the old silent films, children concerned are very little altered, except perhaps in that they tend to copy mature ways of life, even at an earlier age. Dr. Burt admits that the cinema is branded with a false stigma. He says: "The cinema like the 'penny dreadful' before the advent of the film, has been freely censored and abused for stimulating the young adventurer to mischief, folly and even crime. Among those who criticize it on this ground, the most credible are teachers of wide experience and magistrates of high standing. . . . It is alleged that what is called the 'faculty of imitativeness' renders the child peculiarly prone to copy whatever he witnesses upon the screen. . . But how far, in point of fact, are children influenced in this way? On sifting the evidence adduced by those who express these fears, it is plain that both their influences and their psychological assumptions are by no means free from fallacy. Nor are their facts better founded. They have between them hardly one well-attested instance from their own first-hand knowledge.

"The direct reproduction of serious film crimes is, in my experience, exceedingly uncommon; and even then it is usually the criminal's method rather than the criminal's aim which is borrowed; the nefarious impulses themselves have been demonstrably in existence beforehand."

On the question as to whether the desire to go to cinemas encourages stealing, Dr. Burt says: "No doubt after the confectioner's shop, the place where pilfered pennies are most frequently spent is the pay-box of the picture house. But because they are spent at a cinema;. once they have been stolen, it does not follow that they

[1] For details vide Richard Ford, *Children in the Cinema*, pp. 70-89.

were stolen with that purpose consciously in view. The attraction of the cinema can be counted as a direct incentive (to stealing) only where the child has acquired an overpowering habit, an inveterate taste and craving for that particular form of diversion."

As to whether film-going does more good than harm, Dr. Burt states: "It is clear that in comparison with the incalculable number of films, the offences resulting are infinitesimally few. The victims are almost wholly those who temperamentally or otherwise, are, already, disposed to anti-social conduct. For the others—the steady and healthy-minded—the picture house supplies an alternative, not a provocative to mischievous amusement. I could, I think, cite more than one credible instance where the opening of a cinema had reduced hooliganism among boys, withdrawn young men from the public house, and supplied girls a safer substitute, for lounging with their friends in the alleys or the parks."[1]

In regard to conditions in India, some journalists, propagandists, men of learning, critics and even some institutions have been drawing the attention of the Boards of Film Censors to what they believe to be a fact, that Indian films are increasingly glorifying crime.

Some witnesses giving evidence before the Indian Cinematograph Committee 1927, were of the opinion that due to the cinema there had not only been some increase in the number of crimes committed, but the way in which they had been done showed greater skill.

At the Indian Film Journalists Conference on April 30, 1939, on the occasion of the silver jubilee of the Indian film industry, the following resolution was passed:

"This Conference views with alarm the general increase in crime throughout the country, in number and variety of methods and is convinced that the said increase is largely due to the effect of the crime pictures which have been shown in India for the last so many years. In view of the far-reaching influence of the

[1] *Ibid*, pp. 85-7.

screen on the public mind and especially on the juvenile mind, it is essential for films shown in India, whether Indian or foreign, to conform to a rigorous code of morality and to avoid stories that exploit or teach different and ingenious methods of crime or any other acts of delinquency or other scenes which make punishment merely incidental. This Conference further urges upon the Government to take immediate and stringent steps either by censoring or by completely banning crime pictures, Indian or foreign, which exploit crime in one way or the other."[1]

Another critic, Baburao Patel, editor of *Filmindia,* gives a few instances where a crime committed resembled in its technique some screen episode, or when parents blamed the cinema for the criminal activity of their boys. He goes on to say: "Thousands of instances can be quoted in support of the argument that films with crime themes are having a disastrous effect on the growing minds of the youth of the country."[2]

On the release of the Bombay Talkies' *Kismet* in January 1943, produced by S. Mukherji, directed by Gyan Mukerji and starring Ashok Kumar and Mumtaz Shanti, a picture which glorified crime and the criminal and was inspired by the American film *Trans-Atlantic Merry-Go-Round,* an investigation was conducted by *Filmindia* into crime pictures and their influence on juveniles. The opinions of experienced and learned men and women and well-known public personalities were collected and published from time to time. These views are reproduced below.

Dr. Miss K. H. Cama, Presidency Magistrate, Juvenile Court, Bombay, intimately connected with the young offenders, on being interviewed said: "Crime pictures can do immense harm to the young. They may twist the tender minds of children and ruin them for life. The sooner our producers and others interested in the film industry and, above all, the parents realized this, the better for all concerned..."[1]

She was of the opinion that the cinema was becoming more and more an evil influence and that the fact that it was more powerful than any other educational device known to man in impressing and moulding the child mind, made it a potential danger of a magnitude which could not be easily grasped. The cinemas, according to her, if uncontrolled by public opinion, could degenerate any day into a nation-wide school for turning out young criminals, a school which has had no parallel in criminal history.

Thousands of delinquent children laid bare their inmost thoughts before Dr. Cama, and from such confessions she observed that a large number of them traced their criminal tendencies to the crime pictures that had impressed them most. Almost 40 per cent of them appeared to her to have been led into mischief, more or less, by the films they had seen. There were other factors too which influenced them, but the cinema predominated.

According to her, the tendency towards waywardness and rebellion in the young and the habit of stealing were specially attributable to crime pictures. "Cinemagoing children see their favourite heroes swaggering about on the screen with a devil-may-care air about them, committing robberies with astounding ease and shooting down people and defying the guardians of law with strange nonchalance. The children are spellbound, and it is no wonder that as soon as they go home they try to imitate their heroes and start defying their parents. This is but the beginning of the downward path to delinquency."[2] She also said that Court records revealed that a considerable number of stealing cases could be attributed to the desire on the part of the child to secure money to attend cinema shows. Several delinquent children when questioned as to what part they would like to play in a drama or a film, readily replied that they would love to be villains. When asked why,

[1] *Filmindia,* July 1943 p. 49.
[2] *Ibid,* p. 53.

they said that their screen favourite had played the villain in some particular picture and they had liked him immensely in that role.

Thus, while even the slightest emphasis on crime was in itself bad, its glorification in a subtle way was worse, and as for the argument about the moral at the end of the story about crime meeting with just punishment, she was of the opinion that it had little value, for the child, in the first place, was not capable of taking in and assessing the picture as a whole, and secondly, was unable to discriminate between good and bad as an adult would do.

Dr. J. M. Kumarappa, Director of the Tata Institute of Social Sciences, and a social worker who took keen interest in juvenile problems, was of the opinion that the danger did not lie so much in the presentation of crime as a natural and normal concomitant of life as in the deliberate attempt made by the producers to appeal to the baser instincts of man by embellishing and exaggerating crime from purely commercial motives. In his opinion, Indian producers were not as great sinners in this respect as Western producers and he was specially opposed to American gangster pictures which specialized in sensational robberies and hold-ups, which gave an impressionable child an entirely wrong outlook on life. To combat this evil, Dr. Kumarappa suggested that a responsible Committee should be set up to classify new films as they came and to publish periodically a list of such pictures as could be safely seen by children.

Mrs. Tara Ali Baig, one time member of the Bombay Board of Film Censors, observed: "Crime and sex are part of life, no doubt, but it depends on how the producers present them on the screen. Crime can be made dangerously fascinating or subtly seductive as some unscrupulous producers do. That is definitely harmful to children. If on the other hand crime is shown honestly with the drabness and misery that go with it, it should have a moral of its own..."[1]

Mrs. Lilavati Munshi as Chairman of the Children's

[1] *Ibid,* August 1943, p. 41.

Aid Society which looked after delinquent children had
ample opportunity of studying the causes which lead to
juvenile crime, and she was of the opinion that "Crime
pictures are undoubtedly most harmful to the growing
minds of children."[1]  She felt that the problem should
be tackled not by prohibiting children from attending
certain films, but by providing equally interesting films
as substitutes.

Mrs. Hansa Mehta, was of the opinion that "Villainy
of any type should not be gilded or overdrawn on the
screen to pander to the tastes of the mob...It may have
serious consequences on the nation as a whole and on
children in particular."[2]

Sir Sitaram Patkar, one time Judge of the Bombay
High Court felt that "Society is entitled to expect that
the pictures do not exercise an unwholesome and dele-
terious influence on impressionable minds of young persons.  It is therefore essential that pictures depicting
episodes of sex, love and crime should be carefully
scrutinized by the censor board or any other competent
authority with a view to prevent their evil influence on
children and young people."[3]

Dr. Mrs. Malini Sukthanker when interviewed, expressed her opinion that producers were too preoccupied
with crime, sex and other baser aspects of human life
and children who saw such pictures, especially those
which reeked with crime, could not but be influenced
in the wrong way.  The campaign against crime pictures must be carried on relentlessly and parents must
be roused from their present apathy and ignorance regarding the influence of pictures on children's minds.

Mrs. S. Tyabji, Honorary Magistrate of the Children's Court, Bombay, was definite that crime pictures
were very bad for children and unless this canker of
crime and immorality in films was eradicated, the moral
health of the entire younger generation might be jeo-
pardized.  This could best be done by producing educa-

[1] *Ibid*, p. 45.
[2] *Ibid*, p. 55.
[3] *Ibid*, p. 83.

tional pictures in large numbers so as to wean children away from unhealthy films.

When Dr. K. R. Masani, a well-known psychiatrist of Bombay, was asked whether crime pictures were good for children, he said: "Certainly not. Who can deny that crime pictures are definitely bad for children? But the whole question hinges on the point, how crime is presented in the picture. If the psychological background of crime is given and the process of criminality scintifically traced in such a way as to discourage crime and not to encourage it in any way, then such a picture can't be bad. But if crime is presented in glorious colours and the criminal made into a hero or depicted as an unrepentant wrong-doer, nothing could be more dangerous to the sensitive and impressionable child mind..."[1] Dr. Masani was definitely against crime films and opined that any attempt of Indian producers to copy from American gangster films was to be strongly condemned.

Crime on the screen is good neither for children nor for adults unless the picture is produced in a scientific spirit to show people the cause of crime, to analyse its motives and suggest remedies. Crime pictures should be condemned and boycotted, was the opinion of Mrs. Alva.

Madame Sophia Wadia warned against crime pictures and said: "Children, especially, must be given only clean fun and instruction in the most artistic way possible. Statistics have proved that the gangster and sex-ridden films have very badly affected the mental activity and the behaviour of children and young people in Chicago and elsewhere."[2]

There are more or less as many critics to defend the position of cinema in India as there are to blame it.

While some witnesses before the Indian Cinematograph Committee (1927-28) blamed the cinema, there were as many others who did not believe that films encouraged crime. The Committee observed that the

[1] *Ibid*, October 1943, pp. 41-3.
[2] *Ibid*, February 1944, p. 47.

effect on crime was negligible. "Every responsible police officer in every province assured us that in their judgment the cinema had had no effect whatever on crime and its methods. A person with criminal propensities might, they admitted, occasionally get an idea from a film, but, given those propensities, his natural abilities or observations would be much more likely to be a source of action. There is little doubt that sometimes prisoners untruthfully plead the influence of the cinema as an extenuating circumstance in this country as in others, and this makes a good headline for the more sensational press. A Bombay trade witness actually showed us a headline in a local paper attributing a crime to cinema influence although the body of the report contained nothing whatever to justify such an attribution. ....The fact that the police believe with such unanimity that the cinema does not incite crime is proof [enough]. ....The police evidence is to our minds conclusive..."[1]

The film industry defending the charge of producing films which glorified crime observed: "That this has never been so has elsewhere (vide Motion Picture Magazine September 1939) been proved with the aid of Government statistics of crime in India, none of which have even so much as hinted at the motion picture as the influence that prompted and promoted crime..."[2] "All those Indian critics who have so far taken evident pleasure, bordering on jealousy in criticizing Indian films as so much incitement to juvenile delinquency without supporting themselves with incontrovertible facts, have again and again been proved to have blundered..."[3]

Lastly, the Bombay enquiry revealed that while 27.6 per cent young girls, 23.5 per cent young boys, 31.0 per cent young women and 26.2 per cent young men occasionally felt sorry for the criminal if he was like Jesse James or Robin Hood, or was the victim of circumstances, and though 8.9 per cent girls, 15.5 per cent boys and 11.9 per cent young men wanted to behave as Robin Hood or Jesse James, the greater number—37.8 per cent

[1] Report of the Indian Cinematograph Committee, 1927-28, pp. 113-4.
[2] Journal of the Film Industry, July 1941, pp. 10-3.
[3] Ibid, September 1941, pp. 10-3.

adolescent boys and an equal percentage of girls, 34.5 per cent young women and 28.6 per cent young men felt that every criminal should be punished while the rest either sympathized with the victims, were indifferent or did not see such films. Though some sympathized with certain kinds of offenders, there is no evidence to prove that they imitated the behaviour of criminals or violated the law. Hence this enquiry gave no proof, nor are other accurate and reliable data available to prove that films encouraged crime.

In concluding, it can be said that it is well nigh impossible to deduce one way or the other from all that has been said and written. Is the weight of condemnation comparable with the weight of opinions which absolve cinemas from blame? Government authorities, experienced psychologists and psychiatrists, learned men and women assert that films do not cause crime, while there are others who hold the cinema responsible. On which side does the balance weigh? Enough has been written for the reader to form his or her own judgment.

## ADULTS AND THE CINEMA

So far we have been dealing specifically with the film and the younger people who, being more malleable, were most liable to be influenced. The cinema, however, is not an entertainment restricted only to the youth of a country. It has become the staple entertainment of an average family—a collective entertainment which has no barrier of age or sex. In many households, cinema-going is a family affair. The typical audience is not highbrow, nor is it critical in the sense that it analyses its impressions, but it certainly knows what it likes and it is with the influence on these people that we are here mainly concerned.

Shows of any kind have always had a profound appeal for the masses. The spectacle provided by the cinema with its vivid representation and often feverish action staged on an immense screen in garish light while the spectators are plunged in semi-darkness and silence,

an atmosphere reminiscent of seances and other occult
experiences, produces a kind of hallucination.  Hence
the actors in the drama, their emotions and their actions,
carry greater conviction than any other form of entertainment.  However, it cannot be denied that the impression made by this medium is very often superficial
compared with the influence of certain books especially
sacred books.  But it is a striking fact, that "Only the
Bible and the Koran have an indisputably larger circulation than the latest film from Los Angeles."[1]  Even
though the impression of the best of films is as shortlived as it is immense, the production of films, taken as
a whole, exercises a constant influence, as the mass of
the public has a veritable passion for the cinema.

Laymen and experts have tried to explain the influence of films on the behaviour and attitudes of the
people in a variety of ways.  Some believe that films
are 'pure entertainment' providing a means of escape
from the world of reality.  An opposite view is that
films, far from being mere entertainment,  definitely
have a bad effect on the people.  Between these two
extremes there are those who believe that the impact
of films on human behaviour is based on a variety of
assumptions about human nature and how man reacts
in different social situations.  None of these views,
however, are comprehensive, for even in Western countries very little systematic research has been done to
guage the type of influence exerted by the films.  In
spite of the incompleteness of these studies, it is obvious,
from the little that has been done, that any film, regardless of its type and main theme, has some effect on the
attitudes of those who see it, provided some means for
measuring it could be devised.

From a study of all the research work done in this
line, Franklin Fearing comes to the conclusion that films
"Afford an opportunity for the expression of the basic
meanings inherent in the relationships of human beings
to each other, to their environment and to the society
of which they are a part.  This is not limited to a passive

[1] W. M. Seabury, *Motion Picture Problems: The Cinema and the League
of Nations*, p. 236.

reflection of those meanings but may be a dynamic and creative interpretation... [the picture-goer whatever his level of sophistication] finds affirmations for his doubts, alternative solutions for his problems and the opportunity to experience, vicariously, ways of behaving beyond the horizons of his personal world."[1]

## FILMS AS INSTRUMENTS OF CULTURE

The cinema is primarily an instrument of entertainment which has enriched the lives of millions by bringing within their reach its stimulating fare. Depending for its existence on a mass market, a mass appeal and a mass audience, it exercises a widespread influence. In fact the film is, relatively speaking, less significant as an economic institution than as a social institution functioning with varying degrees of effectiveness in the transmission of artistic ideas, the portrayal of human character and emotions, the depiction of the culture patterns of diverse social groups, the dissemination of current information and the interpretation of individual and social experience. In the uniqueness of the power that it wields, and in the fact that it is related to the older arts of drama, dance, music and painting, lies the success of the motion picture as the most powerful instrument of culture.

In regard to India, a very significant factor to be taken into consideration is the influence of foreign films on our people, their social thought and practices. The motion picture came to India as a result of the impact of the West, and the foreign film remains to this day the most vivid and lucid portrayal of the West to the average Indian. The Indian public is more informed about the West through their feature films of the last five decades than it has ever been before, or ever could be through the press or the radio. Even taking into account the quantitative limitations of foreign films in India and the language barrier, the average Indian today seems to be quite familiar with Western customs, mannerisms and habits. Contact alone cannot account for

[1] *American Academy of Political and Social Sciences*, November 1947, p. 79.

such familiarity, and to the cinema must be attributed
this intimate knowledge of the West that our people, especially the educated, possess.   Their family life, their
social arrangements, their scheme of values—in fact a
thousand and one details of behaviour, habits and ideas
are unfolded before us in an unending stream.

Geographical facts, historical personalities and
events, scientific ingenuity, industrial and agricultural
pursuits, music—classical, jazz or swing—and dance,
both ballet and ballroom, a panorama of Western life
and manners are brought before our eyes.   From the
grim struggle for life in the depths of the glacial North
through fields of golden corn to gorgeously colourful
South America and the luxuriant tropics, men and methods are brought to our very doors, and we are launched upon a magnificent travel that few of us could hope
to undertake in reality.

Information,   wider experience and better understanding are the  direct  results of foreign films upon
Indian thought and social life.   Many of those who have
had an English education have learned to incorporate
many Western ideas and suggestions into the daily
routine of their life, thus bringing about a closer contact
between East and West.   At times, however, Western
ideals and mannerisms are thoughtlessly aped and this
has led more to the deterioration of Indian culture than
anything else.   The fault, however, is ours for it is up
to us to select and incorporate the best and leave out the
unsuitable aspects of an alien culture.

It must be here pointed out, however, that since the
vast majority of foreign films shown in India, in fact
everywhere, are American, it is the impact of American
films, American ideas and products which is most significant.

Before the advent of the cinema, drama was almost
exclusively the property of a small privileged class all
over the world.   Great artists whose names had become
more or less legendary in their own sphere, undoubtedly performed before their audience of thousands, but
almost always in large urban areas.   Lack of means and

difficulties of transport made it impossible for those living far from large urban areas to enjoy the performances of the great figures of the day. In the same way it was economically impossible for the best artists to go to these out-of-the-way places and cater for the needs of a few hundred or thousands, though a few small theatrical companies did tour the interior.

The celluloid ribbon, however, has changed the face of things. With it the finest of acting is available to most people. The silver screen has not only multiplied the renowned figures of the day, but has made them and their times immortal.

No less important are the achievements of motion pictures in the re-creation of history. The lives of personalities of the past, of kings and of queens, statesmen and generals, scientists and artists, Henry V, Henry VIII, Akbar, Ashok, Victoria, Cleopatra, Lincoln, Disraeli, Napolean, Alexander, Pasteur, Curie, Beethoven, Zola —the list can be unending—have been ransacked and brought to the public view, after months and even years of laborious work.

Not only the lives of great men but even the works of well-known writers have been liberally explored and produced. Shakespeare, Kalidas, Tagore, Dickens, Dumas, Stevenson and the Brontes to mention only a few, and even folklore and legends from ancient mythology have been picturized and their characters taken out of the dark covers of the book into the light of a world especially created for them.

The most significant feature of picturizing and, incidentally, popularizing the ancient classics has been the stimulation of demand for the original book. Hundreds of people are induced to read or re-read a book on which a film is based. Booksellers and librarians have found a sudden demand for some particular book which could only be explained by the fact that a picture based on that particular book had been released. The incentive which the film supplies to the reading of 'good books' is an undeniable contribution of motion pictures to culture.

Another aspect of equal importance is the film's influence on writing. Since so many 'best sellers' are screened, modern books especially novels, plays and biographies are written with a view to adapting them to motion picture purposes if and when an opportunity occurs.

What is true of books is true of music and dance also. The cinema has inculcated in many a taste for classical music, and incidentally increased the sale of some records. No doubt the radio has also played a very important part in stimulating interest in good music, but just to hear is not as interesting as to hear and see at the same time. Through the instrumentality of the cinema leading exponents of famous musical compositions of the East and the West and classical Western and Indian music, have played to an audience of millions, something which they had never done before.

The classical grace of ballet and the rural simplicity of folk dances have revealed their beauty to hundreds of thousands of patrons of the cinema.

The film has given to the renaissance of India's dance art an additional fillip. Dance recitals on the stage, though very realistic and picturesque are, after all, limited to a certain number of people living in a restricted number of towns. On the other hand, films released in cities and towns and even taken to the villages can reach a far greater and cosmopolitan public.

The films can do a great deal in spreading the art of dance. In the West, for example, some beautiful 'shorts' and documentaries showing the dances of the world in their natural and authentic setting have been produced, and they have played a significant part in popularizing the dances of the various countries.

Through films, much of the provincial taste in dancing has been spread far and wide. The exquisite statuesque dance of Tanjore, Bharata Natyam, known and appreciated throughout South India has, through the films, been greatly appreciated by thousands in other parts of the country. This is also true of the Manipuri with its soft lyric grace, a dance originally hailing from the far-off mountain region of Manipur in Assam. Presented artistically, danced with emotion, bodily grace and rhythm, the various dances of India have, through the films, acquired widespread popularity.

The numerous seasonal festivals of India have inspired beautiful folk-dances. In some films of village life, these dances have been realistically portrayed in all their picturesque surroundings.

It is also possible to study the art of dancing, on the screen. With the aid of various angles, close-ups and sound any dance can be picturized and projected for detailed study of foot work, body movements, hand gestures, facial expressions and correct timing.

While some believe that the films have done and can still do a great deal to spread the art of dance in India, there are others who hold the opinion that the dance, as depicted in Indian films, is an insult to the dance art with its rich traditions and perfected technique. As G. Venkatachalam says: "....And now see what the gentlemen and ladies of the shadow world have done to it [the dance art]. They have prostituted it as no other art or aspect of Indian life has been prostituted before. It may sound a cruel indictment, an exaggerated denunciation. I honestly wish it was; but the facts are otherwise."[1]

It is argued that while the dance may be exploited on the screen, it must be done with understanding and taste and not indiscriminately, violating the traditions of the art and the beauty of the dance itself. On the contrary the policy of the majority of producers has been just the reverse. They believe that the greater the number of dances, the more money will a film fetch and so they "catch hold of any girl or girls...and train them to shake their hips, jerk their necks, to blink their eyes and to jump to the drum beat [they] don't mind if the dance is in any particular style, or in no style or in all styles...money is the thing."[2]

[1] G. Venkatachalam, *Dance in India*, p. 70.
[2] *Ibid*, p. 71.

13

That, to put it crudely, is the policy of the producers who not only make a jumble of styles and technique but at the same time make it cheap and vulgar, so that it appeals to the lowest of tastes and makes the film 'a stupendous masterpiece of the age' and a box-office success.

Not only has the dance itself been misrepresented and vulgarized, but so far no Indian director has succeeded in putting across a really first class dance film. Here and there a director has managed to take a few interesting shots but such cases are rare. Even *Kalpana,* though a unique dance-fantasy, was not an unqualified success.

The Film Congress of 1939 paid a tribute to the cinema as a substantial factor in the evolution of Hindustani as a national language of India. With the advent of sound, the Indian film industry had to choose a language understood by all; and it fixed upon Hindustani as the lingua franca of filmdom. The Film Congress claimed that one of the beneficial things achieved by the film industry was that it had proved to be a potent "purveyor of the knowledge of the Hindustani language"[1] for the largest number of films were produced in this language.

Besides, the studio, where the majority of people speak Hindustani, forms a nucleus from which have spread the outward branches of this language to the remotest corners of India, so much so that in many cities Hindustani is understood by even the most ignorant. In fact the cultural future of India lies not with Macaulay's English or with any provincial language but with Hindi or Hindustani as the accepted common medium of expression.

The motion picture, it is suggested, has contributed largely to the breaking down of the cramping boundaries of provincialism and communalism. For example, it is claimed that cinemas have had a great influence in reducing group prejudice like that prevalent against the Jews, or the American Negroes, and this problem is being increasingly tackled on the American screen.

[1] Resolution forwarded by the Subjects Committee of the Film Journalists Conference to the Open Conference, April 30, 1939, p. 6.

Even in this country it is argued that the most out-standing influence of the cinema is one of synthesis. It is supposed to have brought the extremes together and bred tolerance and understanding and has become one of the most potent factors in nation building today.

It cannot be denied that the Indian film has made an outstanding effort to cement Hindu-Muslim unity by not only making indirect references towards communal harmony in many films, but also through special films based on this theme. In this respect *Padosi*, produced in 1941, was a remarkable effort.

However, in the light of the events before and after the Partition one is inclined to be sceptical as to the success of the Indian film in doing away with communal prejudice and hatred which have tarnished the fair name of this land.

It may be argued by some critics that if films are capable of contributing to culture, why is not greater attention paid to this factor? Why are so many cheap and trivial pictures produced and why do film moguls cater to the lowest tastes? It cannot be denied that this is often true, but then the main purpose of films is not always cultural. The producers' viewpoint is to make money and supply entertainment and relaxation amid all the hustle and bustle of modern life, and in this respect the film ranks high among the enriching forces of life.

From national to world-wide spheres and influences is the next step. The influence of the film is by no means limited to an effect upon commercial relations; it extends to the whole national outlook of the people of one nation towards the peoples of other nations of the world. As Herbert Hoover once remarked: "The motion picture is not solely a commercial venture; it is not solely an agency of amusement and recreation; it is not solely a means through which the world has gained a new and striking dramatic art; nor is it solely a real and effective means of popular education. Beyond all this it is a potent purveyor between nations of intellectual ideas and national ideals. But it can also transfer the worst within us as well as the best.... herein lies a heavy obligation upon this industry . . ."[1]  In this connection it must be borne in mind that Hollywood is the single centre of production dominating film-making all over the world and coupled with this is an American estimate that there are 70,000 cinemas in the world at which 235,000,000[2] attendances are recorded each week. These attendances are at shows made up largely of Hollywood films.  Moreover, America produces today about 85 to 90 per cent of the world's total film output and as such is the only national film which is yet international.  The American film has thus invaded every nook and corner of the earth and its influence on the nations of the world is very significant.  American ways of thought, American customs, American history, American ideas on music, dance, clothes, housing, American standards of material comforts and hygiene, of physical fitness and beauty, the rough and ready moral standards of American 'westerns', have all gripped and fascinated the imagination of millions the wide world over.

It is well nigh impossible to measure the indirect effect of American films on the sale of American products.  In a number of films a great many American goods are not only displayed but their practicability is demonstrated, as it were.  The influence of such depiction of luxuries is to create a desire for them, thus incidentally increasing the sale of American products. Trade no longer follows the flag but the film, is the slogan of the modern world dominated by the American film which has proved to be the most effective salesman for American goods.

It might be argued that the depiction of such conveniences, luxuries and high standards of living might induce envy and even despair in some areas.  But the more common result is not jealousy or bitterness: it is the desire to emulate, as is evident from the constant and increasing demand for American goods.

It is a matter of common observation that American

[1] W. M. Seabury, *Motion Picture Problems, Cinema and the League of Nations*, p. 27.
[2] Sinclair Road, 'The Influence of the Film,' *Penguin Film Review* I, p. 59.

films have largely influenced the views and ideas of peoples throughout the world as regards the United States and its people. The extreme care exercised by national censors shows how keenly they appreciate the power of the cinema over the people. *The Los Angeles Examiner* dated April 4, 1937, says: "It is undoubtedly true that from Hollywood emanates one of the strongest influences on the thoughts, opinions, speech and manners of this and other nations."

In an interesting article entitled '120,000 American Ambassadors' published in *Foreign Affairs,* October 1939, Walter Wanger, a Hollywood producer, pointed out that since about 600 pictures are sent abroad from the U.S.A. every year, and each film has on an average about 200 prints, the result is that there are 120,000 American ambassadors sent to foreign countries annually. They enable the masses of other countries who neither hear the American radio nor read American papers, who in fact have very little knowledge of America and its people, to get in close and intimate touch with a foreign country and an alien culture.

Very often, of course, the sensationalism, commercialism and misrepresentation of foreigners in American pictures have proved a hindrance to the establishment of amicable relationships between different nations, and at the same time, given foreign audiences the false and unfavourable impression that America is 'a land of bandits, bootleggers and social high-flyers'.

While the impact of the American film is immense, equally great is its responsibility for not disseminating misinformation, distorting facts of history or otherwise circulating ideas which create a wrong impression or are injurious to the world audience.

In the international sphere, the most outstanding problem is that of war and peace. It has already been seen that if properly and effectively handled, the cinema can contribute largely towards the breaking down of group and communal prejudice within a nation. We have, however, yet to realize that motion pictures can also break down barriers of misunderstanding

among nations and thus help towards the elimination of
war and the foundation of world peace.

Any machinery set up to aid the preservation of
international peace must include appropriate control of
the means by which war is or may be stimulated or induced.   This must, therefore, include particularly an
adequate national and international treatment of motion
pictures as well as other media of mass communication.
Our disregard of this in the past has made us pay dearly.
We have seen how war propaganda, carried on unchecked through this means of communication played, and can
still play havoc with world civilization.  In modern
days, propaganda in times of peace has become increasingly important, and the first of the instruments to be
organized for this purpose should be the cinema.    Real
international co-operation in the making and distributing of motion pictures depicting the interchange of men
and ideas, could be a magic instrument in cultural
understanding, and consequently in preserving world
peace.

While on the one hand thoughtful persons are considering the possibilities of distribution and exchange of
worth-while films of genuine international significance,
the screen fare offered by film leaders in the past and
at present has, qualitatively and quantitatively,  over-
emphasized the whole question of war as Edgar Dale's
analysis of the contents of films shows.

The cinema being a powerful instrument for the
dissemination of ideas  and  for the  stirring of human
emotions, the very foundations of a future world civilization depend upon whether we understand this
medium and make it work for our good.   The film, if
properly handled, can create far greater understanding
between nations, at the same time being capable of
causing widespread trouble if it is allowed to become
the  plaything of self-interested  and  self-seeking producers.

It is obvious that the influence of the film is varied
and widespread.  Old and young,  men and women of
every class, creed and profession come under its spell

and are influenced by it. As far as children are concerned the general conclusion arrived at is that for the vast majority of them the cinema is beneficial rather than harmful provided care is taken in the selection of films shown to them. It increases their store of knowledge, broadens their outlook and makes them more alert. The depiction of unaccustomed scenes and modes of living, the provision of wholesome amusement and the quickening of the spirit of adventure are certainly not an unworthy service to childhood.

As regards adolescents and young adults, all the evidence cited goes to show that motion pictures may affect their conception of life and course of conduct, because the cinema presents an extensive range of experience much of which is new and fascinating material to the average film-goer. While the available data show that the influence of films is strong even among the sophisticated and cultured class, it is plain that in the much larger class of film-goers who are less self-conscious, less sophisticated, less well-informed and hence easily impressed or moved, the effects must be still more marked. In trying to estimate how far and in what ways a particular film will affect a particular person or group of persons, it is necessary to know something of the general background, social code and degree of experience of the person or group concerned. Though the type and intensity of influence may vary from country to country, class to class, age group to age group, in men and women, yet in one way or another films do a great deal to provide patterns of behaviour, to stimulate the imagination, to determine the conception of life and even to initiate action. The contribution of the film to culture is immense, and in the international field it can wield an influence mightier than the sword. All told therefore, it is a much more important factor in the contemporary social scene than is implied by those who regard it merely as a means of temporary escape from the harsh or drab reality of daily existence.

*8*

## THE FACTUAL FILM

THE aspects of the motion picture hitherto considered were those mostly confined to entertainment films. This chapter deals with the use of the
film for purposes other than entertainment; for spreading information and news, for teaching, for training and
for research. Thus it includes within its scope the
documentary film, the newsreel and the use of film in
education.

The cinema, as already noted, is a powerful instrument of social significance today, and the documentary
film represents the first real attempt to use the cinema
in this respect.

What is a documentary film? These two words
cover such a multitude of activities and approaches,
that various answers could be given to this question. It
could be defined as a short film, as a travelogue, as a
description of how things are made, as an instructional
film, as an aid to teaching, as an artistic interpretation of
reality. It is, however, much more than this. The
term 'documentary' was coined by John Grierson in
February 1926 in a review, written for the *New York
Sun*, of Robert Flaherty's *Moana*, a film of the South Sea
islanders and their daily life. It is derived from the
French 'documentaire' used by them to denote travel
pictures.[1] Grierson used it not to describe a particular
group of short films or a technique of film making but a
new idea, for he later defined it as the "creative interpretation of actuality" or "the drama of the door step."[2]

[1] *The Factual Film. A Survey by the Arts Enquiry*, p. 43; Forsyth Hardy,
*Grierson on Documentary*, p. 11.
[2] *The Factual Film, A Survey By The Arts Enquiry*, p. 46.

'Actuality' has been explained by Paul Rotha thus: "Our very familiarity with everyday surroundings prohibits us from forming a true estimate of them. That is why the documentary film has an important purpose to fulfil in bringing to life familiar things and people, so that their place in the scheme of things which we call society may be honestly assessed. The world of documentary is a world of commerce and industry and agriculture, of public services and communications, of hygiene and housing. It is a world of men and women, at work and leisure; of their responsibilities and commitments to the society in which they live."[1] What was meant by 'creative' treatment was further elucidated by an analogy. "The documentalist goes to nature or actuality for his visual and aural imagery in the same way that a writer goes to a dictionary for the proper sense and spelling of a word. But just as a dictionary is not a great work of literature, neither is a series of photographic views (however lovely in themselves), nor a chain of recorded sounds of natural objects and persons projected on a screen and through a loud speaker, a documentary film. It is the reason underlying the choice of natural material, and the purpose which is in mind for bringing it to life on the screen—that really constitute film creation."[2]

A documentary film does not, therefore, mean a short film of ten or twenty minutes. It may be anything from a three minute instructional for schools to a full-length fully dramatized feature. In the course of years it has been accepted as describing a particular type of film production used for social analysis.

According to Paul Rotha the task of the documentalist is to find a means of persuasively bringing before the eyes of the people their problems, labour and services. "His job is of presenting one-half of the populace to the other, of bringing a deeper and more intelligent social analysis to bear upon the whole cross-section of modern society; exploring its weaknesses, reporting its events, dramatizing its experiences and suggesting a wider and

[1] Paul Rotha, *Documentary Film*, p. 17.
[2] *The Factual Film, A Survey By the Arts Enquiry*, p. 46.

more sympathetic understanding among the prevailing classes of society."[1]

His sphere of action is in the homes, streets, factories and the workshops of the people, but mere observation and pictorial descriptions of things, people or places of interest are not enough. Nor is it the purpose of the documentalist to give a superficial portrayal of actuality. It is the meaning behind the thing and the significance underlying the person that are his chief concern.

The documentary mirrors present day realities and problems. It can, and does at times, draw on the past, but only for comparison, to lay stress on the modern argument. By no means is a documentary a historical reconstruction, it deals only with contemporary facts and events in relation to human associations.

For many years before John Grierson started the documentary movement there had been all kinds of short films—travel talks, country scenes, nature studies and glimpses of interesting odds and ends—and all such factual films made from natural material are often classed as documentary films. They all represent different qualities of observation and different intentions in observation. These lecture films, newsreels, nature studies and travelogues, often interesting and brilliantly done within their own limits, do not dramatize nor analyse an episode, and hence, according to some, fall short of the basic documentary requirements. This criticism, however, does not detract from the craftsmanship of such films, or their claim to be documentaries. It merely shows that interpretations of the documentary method and choice of style may vary and different intentions may underlie the viewpoints of observations. It shows that while some documentalists may find their theme among the primitive races, others find their material in the factories and workshops; while some prefer an attitude of romanticism, others build from a materialistic basis. It is all a question of personal character and inclination, artistic fancy and subject matter. As Grierson

---

[1] Paul Rotha, *Documentary Film*, p. 130.

observed: "The documentary idea, after all, demands no more than that the affairs of our time shall be brought to the screen in any fashion which strikes the imagination and makes observation a little richer than it was. At one level the vision may be journalistic; at another, it may rise to poetry and drama. At another level again, it's aesthetic quality may lie in the mere lucidity of its exposition."[1] For example, there was the lyrical beauty of Basil Wright's *The Song of Ceylon,* the dynamic impression of Paul Rotha's *Shipyard,* the realistic approach of Ray Elton's and Edgar Anstey's *Housing Problem,* or the analytical presentation of Edgar Anstey's *Enough to Eat.*

## FACTUAL FILMS OF BRITAIN

The documentary is Britain's outstanding contribution to the film, for there it originated and persisted; whereas similar movements in other countries, except Russia, were failures. Produced by John Grierson under official patronage, the first documentary was *Drifters,* a film about the everyday work of the Scottish herring fleet. A landmark in the documentary world, this film laid the foundation, established the principles and set the technical standard for future documentaries. Developed under Government and industrial auspices, the documentary movement expanded rapidly in England and rendered admirable service to the nation during and after World War II.

The documentary film could be described as 'the higher journalism of the screen'. It analyses and interprets society from the viewpoint of an individual or school of thought. It is educational in character but its aim is allied more to propaganda than to simple instruction. The educational, instructional or training films proper, though they may be regarded as sub-divisions of the documentary, differ from the documentary in that they are not necessarily dramatically related but present straightforward facts in as lucid and interesting a manner as possible. They are not analytical in their

[1] *The Factual Film, A Survey By The Arts Enquiry,* p. 48.

approach, but serve the purpose of a moving, visual text book.

The attributes of a good teaching film according to Marion Evans writing in *The Journal of the Society of Motion Picture Engineers* are the following. The subject matter of the film should appeal to native human interests. It should contain sufficient mental stimulus to be thought-provoking, problem-raising or problem-solving. It should have a definite social value and an emotional appeal to make it elevating and inspiring. Its titles should be brief and simple. Its continuity should be good with the main points of the lesson clearly defined. Its presentation of the subject should be unified and balanced. Its photography should be clear and artistic. And on the whole it should conform to the range of comprehension and attention of one of the five grade levels viz. kindergarten, primary, elementary, secondary and adult.[1]

The advantages of using film in education have long been realized. It can vividly illustrate what the teacher is explaining, while at the same time it can bring into the classroom, information and knowledge beyond the range of the teacher. It can illustrate movement and growth unlike other visual aids. It is capable of conveying a great deal of information in a short space of time, and being visual it makes a more lasting impression than verbal or written explanation. As observed at the National Education Association in 1914: "The motion picture multiplies the advantages of the ordinary picture a thousandfold. Its benefits are incalculable. It may be regarded as a great educational lever whereby the very great portion of our present-day schoolroom work may be lifted out of the shadows of the valley of the abstract into the clear sunlight of human interest."[2]

It may be argued that with the use of the film in education, teachers will have to face severe competition and probably unemployment. But no good teacher

[1] *Journal of the Motion Picture Society of India,* January, 1936, p. 26.
[2] *Annals of the American Academy of Political and Social Science,* November 1947, p. 103.

need fear competition from the film, for he is the chairman of his group's discussion, and the film can only promote but not substitute that discussion.  The teacher is necessary to fill the gap between the class and the film.  The material of the film, however, should be selected and arranged keeping in mind the age-range and mental ability of the audience, so as to encourage mental effort, for one of the greatest drawbacks of all mechanical aids is that they may induce an attitude of passivity.

The presentation of news is an important function of the cinema.  The newsreel itself started with the first films of the Lumiere Brothers in 1895, but the weekly issue of newsreels was started by Charles Pathe in 1910.  These films were of commercial origin, and newsreels remain so to this day.

The contents of the average British newsreel before the war were trivial.  It dealt mostly with events which had a popular appeal but avoided controversial subjects.

As the newsreel presents the real everyday world, why is it not a documentary in the real sense of the term?  Primarily because it presents no analysis of the subject.  It merely gives glimpses, impressions, headlines, whereas a documentary deals as exhaustively as possible with one particular subject.  As Andrew Buchanan says: "The newsreel is more or less superficial.  The documentary film is fundamental."[1]

In contrast to the usual newsreel is the American *March of Time* inaugurated in 1934.  A significant milestone in factual film, the *March of Time* is more akin to a documentary than a newsreel in its approach and treatment.  A recent *March of Time* is a film on India entitled *Asia's New Voice* covering the Partition and its aftermath.  Reported to be very well produced though too brief for so vast a subject, it has impressed its audience wherever shown.

The *March of Time* films are documentary films as well as the most advanced form of newsreels we have today—the kind of longer, comprehensive newsreels which one would like to see replacing the very brief

[1] Andrew Buchanan, *Going to the Cinema*, p. 100.

superficial ones of the present day.   It is factors such
as lack of sufficient programme space and certain commercial considerations which have resulted in the short
newsreels of today.   If the audience becomes increasingly critical towards newsreels, and if newsreels are given
more programme space in the future,  the longer and
more analytical newsreel may eventually appear, the
purpose of which should be to increase our knowledge
of current affairs, widen our sympathies and  increase
our understanding of the other nations of the world.

## Factual Films in India

Now, what about the factual films of India?

The Indian film industry is over three and a half
decades old and during the course of that time has developed into one of our major industries.   Since 1931,
India has produced over 3,000 feature films, and today,
quantitatively speaking, she stands second only to the
U.S.A. in the field of entertainment film  production.
But while the production of feature films has
been prolific, another vital aspect of this mass medium
has been neglected.

In the sphere of factual  films, India is far behind
other countries. Prior to World War II, little or no
attention was paid to these films.   At the time of the
silver jubilee celebrations in 1939, one of the important
subjects which the Motion Picture Congress considered
was the production of short, educational, information
films and newsreels.

Attempts had been made by Prabhat Film Company, the Wadia Movietone and a few  other independent producers to make documentaries and newsreels.
A few films were made on industries such as steel, sugar
and cotton; but in the absence of enthusiastic support
from exhibitors and Government, these attempts were
unsuccessful.  Further efforts in this direction were not
made till the outbreak of World War II.

During the course of the war, when the Government of India realized that every instrument in the

armoury of national resources had to be mobilized to achieve victory, the importance of the film, especially the factual film, was brought home. Following the lead of Western countries, the Indian Government decided to harness this medium of publicity not only to build up its war effort but also to educate the country's teeming millions.

The establishment of the Film Advisory Board (F.A.B.) in June 1940, not only heralded a new era for factual films but was a landmark in the annals of the Indian film. On it were represented both Indian and foreign film industries including importers of British and American films. Its headquarters were at Bombay. The Board produced and distributed its own shorts as well as foreign films with commentaries in Indian languages. An auxiliary of the Board was constituted in 1941, at Calcutta. Government purchased its own equipment and also secured premises for the film producing unit. In 1941, the services of an expert in the production of documentaries were obtained from the United Kingdom. This, however, was only for the initial period, and later the work of the Board was left in Indian hands.

As the activities of the Board gradually expanded to cover a wide field, the Government thought it proper to appoint a person at the head of the establishment who would be responsible to it. The organization was, therefore, taken over by the Government on February 1, 1943 with the designation of Information Films of India (I.F.I.).

Between June 1940 and April 1946 the F.A.B. and the I.F.I. between them produced and released about 170 films excluding newsreels.

A few of these films were also produced by private individuals and concerns and by the industry. They were purchased by the I.F.I. if they were found suitable. The industry, however, was never very enthusiastic about the production of such factual films as it was an unprofitable undertaking. Besides, having little experience in the method of presentation of factual material, a high standard was seldom achieved. Arrangements were also made to exhibit interesting, foreign, factual films in India.  These films provided a very  welcome variety including as they did films produced by the British Ministry of Information, films made in other countries of the British Empire, Russian newsreels, as well as documentaries from America produced both by the United States Office of War Information and by commercial producers.  One of the documentaries released under this arrangement was Walt Disney's Technicolor cartoon on malaria.  This was the first time a Disney cartoon was exhibited here with  commentaries in the main Indian languages.

As regards distribution, the Government  tapped both  theatrical  and  non-theatrical  channels.  These films were released in five languages—English, Hindustani, Tamil, Telugu and Bengali.  They were distributed to the English and Indian cinema houses every week. A rental ranging from Rs. 2/8 to Rs. 10 was charged depending on the box-office collection of  the  picture house.

As these factual films were never very popular with the audience, the exhibitors were not willing to exhibit them.  However, the Government felt that its propaganda should reach the maximum number of people. Moreover, under the Lease-Lend arrangement, raw film could be obtained from the U.S.A. only on condition that it would be used to promote the war effort.  For these reasons, on September 15, 1943, the Government of India issued an order under rule 44A of the Defence of India Rules whereby exhibitors were  compelled to include, in every one of their programmes, a minimum of 2,000 feet of film approved by the Government. This order led to the compulsory exhibition of the I.F.I. films, and was responsible for much of its adverse criticism.

In addition to the permanent cinema houses, the Information films were released to cover a hundred touring cinemas and a large number of regimental and camp cinemas.  Educational institutions in different parts of India were also screening these films.  While numerous requests for films from social welfare, public health and

municipal organizations and other similar bodies were
successfully met, arrangements were also made to screen
information films in Indian languages at several industrial centres. The rural areas were covered by mobile
vans. The success of this non-commercial screening
prompted I.F.I. to open film libraries in Bombay, Calcutta, Madras, Lahore and Lucknow, from where the
supply of films for non-theatrical purposes could be regularly and systematically maintained.

Extensive as their internal coverage was, the Information films were regularly despatched abroad. Selected
films on India's culture, industries, arts and craft were
sent to many parts of the British Empire and also to
Allied countries. Not only were these films popular in
countries with a large Indian population or close cultural
affinities, like South Africa, East Africa and the Middle
East, but they were found suitable for exhibition even
as far afield as China, Russia, Great Britain and the
U.S.A.[1]

As the factual film came to India in the midst of a
global war, its object was mainly to promote the
country's war effort. A review of the films produced
and released by the F.A.B. and I.F.I. shows that a large
proportion of them were war propaganda films. The
Government did not distinguish between the war propaganda film and documentary film proper, but on
examining a list of all the films and their synopsis it was
found that out of the total of 170 films produced and released, 38 were films on India's war effort; 14 dealt with
wartime problems; 4 were war instructional shorts; 4
were wartime topicals; 25 were other war propaganda
films; 21 were films on agriculture, rural life and rural
problems; 22 were films on Indian industries; 8 were
films on Indian art and culture; 11 films were on India's
means of communications; 3 films were about public
health and hygiene; 3 were on socio-economic problems
and the remaining 17 were miscellaneous factual films.
Even the films which were not directly war propaganda
films, had a wartime bias.

[1] *Information Films of India Annual,* 1945, pp. 6-7.

14

With the cessation of hostilities the grave emergency period also terminated and the Indian Assembly, looking upon the I.F.I. as a mere waste of money, drastically cut down the grant to the Information Department, thereby compelling it to cease production. The assets of the I.F.I. were purchased by a private concern —the Central Cine Corporation—which intended to continue the production of newsreels and short films on educational and other topics. Nothing substantial, however, was done and till the present day the factual film has not been taken seriously.

In December 1947 the Standing Finance Committee of the Government of India, approved of a scheme for the revival of the I.F.I. and the Indian News Parade. Government has, therefore, revived its film organization. It is designated 'Films Division' with headquarters at Bombay. The old names, Information Films of India and Indian News Parade, have been replaced by the names, Documentary Films of India and Indian News Review.

The Films Division, in its initial stages, will have six units for the producton of short films and a newsreel organization with ten cameramen posted at important centres for the production of newsreels. The target of production of factual films by the six units is 36 documentaries annually and 52 newsreels to be released alternately every week. These films will be produced on educational, cultural and social subjects, will be made with commentaries in English, Hindustani , Bengali, Tamil and Telugu and in 35 mm. and 16 mm. sizes. Approximately 16 suitable documentaries produced by the trade will be purchased and distributed by the Government.

Foreign factual films will also be accepted if they are found suitable for distribution in India. The foreign films will be mainly from Great Britain, the U.S.A., Canada and Australia.

For purposes of distribution, five centres have been established, in Bombay, Madras, Calcutta, Lucknow and Nagpur, from where films are distributed to exhibitors at equitable rates. For purposes of non-commercial distribution, film libraries will be maintained at these regional offices from where schools, colleges, public institutions and other interested parties can borrow films at nominal cost. Provincial (now State) Governments will be supplied with films in standard and substandard sizes to be circulated through mobile vans. For overseas distribution, 16 mm. size versions of these films are being supplied to India's representatives abroad.

Between June 3, 1949, when Films Division started the commercial distribution of its films, and December 30, 1949, it had produced and/or released 30 documentaries, of which 4 were foreign films released with commentaries in Indian languages. Of the remaining 26, 3 were on Indian art, 4 were on Kashmir, 4 were on public health and hygiene of which one, *The War that Never Ends*, was in cartoon form, 4 were on Indian industries including two popular I.F.I. films which were revived, 2 on Indian agriculture, 1 on a socio-economic problem, 1 on India's means of communication, 1 on food, 1 on hydro-electricity, and the remaining 5 on miscellaneous topics of general interest.

Factual films have been revived in spite of the fact that the first efforts in this field were unpopular with the industry and the public.

*Filmindia*, commenting on the Information Films, observed: ". . . I.F.I. output seems to be cordially disliked by all in the country. Though the I.F.I. stuff is imposed on the public with the help of Defence Rules, no one seems to be willing to see it. All over the country people choose to leave the theatre when I.F.I. films are being shown and to make it easier, newspapers advertise the exact timing of the main features for the benefit of their patrons. . . the odd timing mentioned therein [in *The Evening News of India*, a Bombay paper] have a grim story to tell about the popularity of the I.F.I. shorts'.[1] Though no doubt a part of the cinema audience entered the auditorium only when the feature

[1] *Filmindia*, May 1945, p. 9.

film began, it is, perhaps, not too much to presume that the exhibitors were trying to build up a case against the I.F.I. Galled by the thought of being compelled to show a fixed footage of propaganda films for which they had to pay what they termed arbitrary rates, the exhibitors probably hoped with the advertisement of exact timings not merely to accommodate a section of their patrons, but at the same time to make out that the Information Films were very unpopular and hence should be withdrawn from circulation.

In spite of their many shortcomings much can be said to the credit of the I.F.I. Some of the most interesting experimental work of the I.F.I. was done in the field of agriculture, industry, public health, medicine, art and culture.

These short films represented a valuable medium through which various aspects of agriculture, industry and public service could be brought to the notice of the people throughout the country. Films on agriculture were produced with the aim of creating interest in agricultural problems and teaching practical methods of rural reconstruction. Films like *Winged Menace, Soil Erosion, Tube Wells, School for Farmers, Need of the Moment* (on soil fertilization) and *The Land of the Five Rivers* revealed not only the best way of tackling locusts, floods, droughts and other periodical threats, but of solving some of the basic problems of Indian agriculture.

The I.F.I. also brought on the screen India's major industries. Coal, cement, hydro-electricity, ship-building, sericulture and other small scale and cottage industries all figured in this category and stressed the rapid rate of industrialization in India.

The immense popularity of I.F.I.'s first cultural film *Our Heritage*, on Indian architecture, prompted Government to take up the production of more cultural films, on topics like Indian dance classics and musical instruments. The production of these films marked the first serious attempt to make authentic film records of some of India's most important traditional art-forms.

Banking, commercial art, public health and medical problems were among the other subjects of general interest on which short films were produced. Films like *Malaria, Victory over Blindness, Life in Storage* or *Blood Bank, Industry Behind Surgery* and similar others depict the quick development of scientific research in India and its practical application in varied fields.

The technique of conveying information about the problems of the day in brief and effective form was tried out in the shape of two to three minute films, popularly known as 'Quickies' on transport shortage, wartime scarcity and price control, saving, rationing and other problems of daily life under wartime conditions.

Factual films have thus brought on the screen the kaleidoscopic national life of this country—its problems and achievements, its varied dress, customs and festivals and its scenic beauties.

Some of the I.F.I. films received praise even in America. This was the first time that any Indian film was favourably received and reviewed in the American press. In the opinion of *Box Office*, one of the American journals, the Government of India's films were considered good enough to merit superlatives. It observed:

*"Handicrafts of South India*—excellent, possibly because it portrays manners and customs dissimilar to ours, this one reeler seems particularly exotic and interesting.

*"In Rural Maharashtra*—colourful. This short, one of the 28 produced by the Government of India's Information Services for showing in that country's 700,000 villages, is of superior quality throughout....

*"The Land of Five Rivers*—Interesting. This one reeler, entertaining and educational, is one of many the Government of India is showing....Documentary yet diverting, the film shows the beautiful Punjab, once a desert, now blossoming like a rose, thanks to India's artificial irrigation system....

*"Tree of Wealth*—Absorbing. Beautifully photographed against idyllic backgrounds, the picture shows the graceful trees leaning over the canals in Travancore,

as well as India's cottage industries."

The last named documentary had earned many tributes. Walt Disney singled it out along with two others on Indian dance classics and Indian musical instruments for praise, from a host of other films. He observed: "These films are tremendously interesting. I think you will find that the people of this country are most keenly interested in knowing the people of other countries. It is films like these that create a better understanding and stimulate interest in the culture and way of other nations."[1]

In fact, it redounds much to the credit of the I.F.I that for the first time an Indian documentary— *Tree of Wealth*—was among those considered for the coveted annual award for the best production in this field given by the Academy of Motion Pictures Arts and Sciences, U.S.A. This pictorially beautiful film which deals with the varied uses of the coconut palm in an instructive and informative manner was among the few selected from the hundred submitted by the United States producers and those of many other countries. Though it did not win the final award it was highly appreciated both in the U.S.A. and Great Britain. Besides, this film along with another, *Dance of India,* was among the numerous documentaries exhibited during the second International Film Festival sponsored by Washington World Affairs Centre on May 25, 1949. It was also awarded the appreciation prize for giving an inspiring theme for the best utilization of an item of natural wealth at the International Film Festival, Czechoslovakia, in August 1949.

It would, however, be a grave mistake to be simply carried away by the praise bestowed on some of these films into the belief that the documentary method was well advanced here and that the I.F.I. was needlessly maligned by the industry. The I.F.I. productions were intended both for the urban and rural population. This inevitably resulted in a fiasco. The educated townspeople were soon bored by slow-moving, tedious, over-

[1] *The Motion Picture Magazine,* March 1946, p. 84.

emphasized instructional and propaganda films; while
for the rural audience the films were often unsuitable or
inadequately treated. Though the I.F.I. did achieve
something, it cannot be denied that a large majority of its
films were indifferent productions, and, with the exception of a very few, could hardly be termed documentaries. They were either directly war propaganda films
or indirectly geared to the war effort. Barring a few,
the other so-called documentary films of the I.F.I. will
perhaps never again be projected on the screen unless
the approach to and treatment of the subject are
modified.

Other efforts in the realm of Indian documentary
are the work of some independent film producers such
as the Documentary Unit of India, Educational Films of
India Ltd., Motwane Ltd., Ama Ltd., D.R.D. Productions
and Film Group of India Ltd., The National Education
and Information Films Ltd., Hindustan Information
Films Ltd., and others many of whom have organized
themselves into a Short Film Guild. Here special reference must be made to the Documentary Unit of India,
probably the most energetic amongst them all, which
under the direction of Paul Zils, released for preview in
April 1948 three documentaries which were studies in
social welfare work in an Indian village in Satara District, Bombay. They had been sponsored by the United
Nations Organization for release in India and in all
member countries with the primary aim of boosting re-
cruitment into social welfare work and for training social welfare workers in India. They were planned with
the assistance of Miss Marion Dix, UNO's representative
in India on themes worked out with the help and co-
operation of three experts, Dr. K. S. Mhaskar, Dr. J. M.
Kumarappa and Dr. Miss Sujata Chaudhari.

These three documentaries enjoy the unique distinction of being first in a world series that have been
planned by the UNO. India and China were given priority but, so far, it is reported that nothing has been done
in China. The films entitled *Mother, Child* and *Community* deal with maternity welfare, child welfare and

community welfare respectively.

Undoubtedly these films, especially *Mother* and *Child*, are among some of the better documentaries produced here. Their themes are simple but interestingly tackled and well presented while the photography is picturesque and beautiful. Though technically very good, their subject matter and presentation have aroused a great deal of controversy with the result that these films have not so far been released for public exhibition in India.

Among the other documentaries produced by this Unit may be mentioned *Know Your Neighbour*, a film on bad driving sponsored by India Tyres and Rubber Company (India) Ltd., *White Magic* dealing with the problem of nutrition, *Kuruvandi Road* sponsored by Ciba Pharma Ltd., and *A Tiny Thing Brings Death*, a film on malaria sponsored by Imperial Chemical Industries (India) Ltd. Some of the other important documentaries made by independent producers include *Indian Shipbuilding* and *Mahatma the Immortal* both produced by Motwane Ltd., *Storm Over Kashmir* produced by B. D. Garga, *Our Nehru* produced by M and T Films Ltd., *Apni Panchayat* produced by Cine Unit of India, Ltd., and *Dance of the Golden Harvest* and *Magnificent Memories* produced by D.R.D. Productions.

At the Documentary Film Festival held at Edinburgh during August-September 1949, India was well represented. Among the Indian documentaries shown there were: *Story of Sindri, Saga in Stone, Ladakh Diary,* all produced by the Films Division, Government of India, *Country Crafts, Tree of Wealth, Handicrafts of Travancore and South India* and *Bharat Natyam*, four old films of I.F.I. These seven Indian films were highly praised both in the British Press and by film makers from many European countries. One of the subjects chosen concerned Indian dancing which evoked considerable interest.[1]

There is tremendous scope for documentaries in this country. It is with their help that India can nur-

[1] *The Times of India,* September 14, 1949.

ture the growth of social reform among her people. They are absolutely necessary for the spread of education and social welfare. Fully realizing this, India is now giving serious consideration to this aspect of the motion picture, and everyone interested is waiting to see how Government's new, large scale undertaking is going to work in the future.

## THE INDIAN EDUCATIONAL FILM

The fate of educational films in India has been no better than that of documentaries. While Western countries have been forging ahead with ambitious but practical plans for the use of films in the classroom, India, with its illiterate millions, has been indifferent to the immense possibilities of this medium for the purpose of mass enlightenment.

Conferences have been held, innumerable committees have been formed and the question of educational and instructional films has been made the topic of heated discussion. But to what purpose? The percentage of Indian literacy has not made a substantial advance, the great majority of Indian schools and colleges have no projectors and the position of educational films today is where it was ten years ago.

Nevertheless the attempts so far made may be briefly noted.

The pioneering work in this direction was undertaken by the Motion Picture Society of India over a decade ago. The Educational Committee of the Society distributed the educational films at its disposal through its members in different parts of the country. At first the scheme was successful and very popular. Soon, however, lack of funds, difficulties of obtaining projectors, trained men and suitable films in large numbers, the difficulty of overcoming deep-rooted social prejudice and the outbreak of World War II brought all plans to a standstill.

In the meantime, the industry had tried to enlist the help of the Government of India for making the

exhibition of Indian educational films compulsory. At
the second All-India Motion Picture Convention held in
December 1936, a resolution was passed urging the Government to make the exhibition of Indian educational
shorts and Indian newsreels in every cinema programme
compulsory by legislation, thus creating a new avenue
for the industry.[1] The Government of India, however,
summarily disposed of the matter by saying, "The subject matter of the resolution falls within the provincial
field and the Government of India are no longer empowered to take legislative and executive action in these
matters."[2] The Central Government shifted the responsibility on to provincial shoulders but the Provincial
Governments, with the exception of the Government of
C.P. and Berar, were equally indifferent. The C.P. and
Berar Government appointed a Visual Education Committee, in December 1937, with the object of working out
a practical scheme for popularizing the use of films in
education. But the outbreak of World War II upset all
plans.

This, however, was recompensed by the establishment of the Film Advisory Board in 1940 and the use of
films by Government for training men and women for
active service, as was done by the Combined Kinematograph Services Training and Film Production Centre of
the Directorate of Military Training.

At the same   time, the Government of Bombay
whose Visual Instruction Department possessed about
30 imported 16 mm. films on educational subjects
and whose Labour Welfare Department had 84 foreign
16 mm. and 8 Indian films (16 and 35 mm.) for exhi·
bition in schools and welfare centres respectively,
launched an important scheme of visual education and
publicity at the village of Turumbha near Thana.

According to this scheme the Government was to
have purchased a hundred projectors to be distributed
among the various districts on a population basis. Each
projector was to be passed on from village to village in

[1] K. S. Hirlekar, *Newsreels and Educational Shorts, What Provincial Governments Can Do*, p. 3.
[2] *Ibid.*

a given area, so that it would be in constant use. Every fortnight, a completely new 45 minute programme of films comprising a newsreel and two other features was to be prepared and distributed by the Director of Information. Thus the villages throughout the province would receive an endless chain of programmes with a new show each fortnight. The features were to have a definite educational value, many of them dealing with such subjects as health, sanitation, agriculture and social welfare. They were to be silent, with commentaries provided in the regional language. The distinctive feature of this scheme was its circuit system which aimed at being extensive but inexpensive.

In the wake of this, in December 1945, came another plan, this time put forth by the Government of India. Its object was to inaugurate rural propaganda with 224 mobile cinema units, one for each civil district in India, and increase the number to 1,000 in the course of three years. These mobile units were intended regularly to carry to the village gates, visual education and the latest information on subjects like farming, soil preservation, co-operative societies, forest conservation, public health and prevention of epidemic diseases. These mobile units were to be fed partly by the Information Films of India and partly by foreign documentaries and cartoons.

Along with this, I.F.I. together with the Motion Picture Society of India and the Bombay Head Masters' Association, made arrangements to show to students in Bombay a series of educational shorts on consecutive Sundays. It was proposed to exhibit these educational films in different localities first in the city, and then gradually to extend them to the suburbs and different centres in the province. But all these schemes remained only on paper.

The problem of educational films, however, is only now, after World War II, receiving serious consideration. The Government of India have recently set up a Committee of Visual Education. Its terms of reference are to investigate the use of films in primary, secondary, university and adult education; to organize the Government's Central Film Library which is to have local branch offices, and to advise on the buying of films from abroad.

The Government of India also intend to have, as a part of its Central Institute of Education, a Department of Audio-Visual Education. Various Provincial Governments have a visual education board to advise on matters relating to the planning and development of educational films. At present there are a few film libraries, and films are sometimes used in adult literacy centres and, occasionally, in factories. The films used are mostly imported for there are no organizations making educational films. One or two private organizations had undertaken such production but have abandoned them and are awaiting a lead from Government.

The story of the educational film movement in India is a record of lost opportunities and wasted efforts. There has been a great deal of talking, a lot of ink has been spilled and reams of paper have been used, but no material benefit has resulted. The haphazard and sporadic attempts so far made have not contributed to the real advancement of the educational film, nor has the problem of mass illiteracy and education been effectively solved.

The stupendous problem of mass ignorance and illiteracy which is facing this country today and hindering its forward march, can best and most effectively be solved by the film. It is not necessary to plead here the case for film as a medium of education or to dilate on the causes that have prevented its application in our educational system in an era when so many countries of the West have made an extensive use of it for instruction.

Education through films is pre-eminently suited to Indian conditions. To enlighten and to instruct the rural and urban population scattered throughout the length and breadth of India is a Herculean task for which no better means could be found than the non-theatrical film. Visual imagery makes not only a more lasting impression but has a special significance in a country like ours where the vast majority are ignorant and illiterate and where words, whether written or spoken, often falter and fail.

The experience of Western countries has shown that it is impossible to depend entirely on commercial or amateur producers to supply the manifold requirements of educational films. If the varied needs of the teaching profession are to be satisfied and a high technical and educational standard achieved, the Government must sponsor the production and distribution of educational films and, at the same time, make it possible to obtain sound projectors at a reasonable price. Moreover, to make an efficient use of film in education, it would be necessary to organize a Film Institute which would be the centre of information on all matters relating to the educational film. It would provide critical and intelligent review of suitable films, initiate and finance research in the use of film in education, publish information on educational films and encourage schemes for training teachers in the use of the film in schools, colleges and universities.

At the same time, Government must enlist the support and co-operation of all its other departments. And by exempting film producers from import duty on raw films and materials used for educational purposes, it can persuade the industry to co-operate in this venture.

For the distribution and exhibition of these films, both commercial and non-commercial means must be developed. For theatrical distribution, Government must work in co-operation with the industry. Educational and other factual films, if they are to be exhibited in local cinema houses, must be distributed either free of charge or at a nominal price for, being unprofitable, they are never popular with the trade, and compulsory exhibition only makes them all the more galling.

On the non-theatrical side, the first essential step would be to establish a National Film Library where factual films of foreign countries should be kept along with indigenous productions, so as to cope with the demand. The Library should have its own auditorium and projector for giving special shows to the local public. Since the great majority of the masses live in villages and cannot have direct access to the Library, mobile units should tour the villages from time to time. Travelling vans should also visit factories, mills and workshops so as to cater to the largest percentage of the audience possible. Our educational institutions also must have access to the facilities offered by the Library. But before this can come to pass, our schools and colleges and training centres must be provided with projectors and trained men and women to handle the films. The great majority of schools, however, are not in a position to install projectors or use educational films, and, unless the Government extends a helping hand, there can be no rapid progress. Once projectors are provided, educational films could be borrowed from the Library at a nominal cost.

It is, however, in rural India that there is the widest possible scope for the development of the educational film. Any propaganda for rural uplift to have a lasting effect must rouse the interest of the villagers, and for this purpose the 16 mm. mobile unit is the best instrument. If the film could by practical demonstration, bring to life valuable suggestions, the interest of the villager would be roused, and the instruction would be given in so pleasant a manner that village apathy and conversation might be attacked with at least some hope of success. For, as Sarojini Naidu once said: "The peasant is the unit of India's progress—the backbone of India's political, social, cultural and economic freedom, and unless the two stumbling blocks in the way of his betterment, namely, colossal ignorance and grinding poverty, are removed, there is little hope for the future of this country."[1]

Undoubtedly, the film as a medium of village uplift and rural reconstruction is bound to involve heavy expenditure on the part of the Government; but it can

[1] *Journal of the Motion Picture Society of India,* December 1936, p. 11.

be said, without the least hesitation, that neither the initial outlay nor the recurring expenditure would be too much considering the magnitude of the task and the pace at which it is to be achieved.

The screen thus offers great possibilities as a supplement to oral teaching in classrooms. It discloses a new world for observation and study, bringing the miracles of nature realistically to the student and revealing many of the long hidden secrets of Mother Earth. Through the pictorial screen, geography becomes 'the great, wide, beautiful, wonderful world' with its varied peoples, their customs and activities. History is revived so that pupils cross the arid snowy mountain ranges with the hordes of early invaders, or follow an aerial flight encircling the globe today. In the science laboratories, microscopic photography makes visible minute objects that are invisible to the naked eye. Slow-motion depicts movements and growth that the eye does not ordinarily observe and, within a few moments, reveals processes that would take days, weeks and even months.

Besides being an effective aid in the classroom, the film is of inestimable value in imparting instruction on subjects of general interest, for training and guiding young men and women in their choice of vocation and for helping in the betterment of the peasant population, in fact proving itself, all round, to be one of the most vital forces given to the educational field today.

### The Indian Newsreel

As India marches forward on the road to progress, the need for a really efficient Indian newsreel is urgently felt. While the advanced countries of the West were quick to grasp the significance of a topical newsreel, India, as usual, was loath to undertake production of any kind other than the story film. Newsreels along with the other types of factual films were left severely alone, so much so that it was only with the cataclysmic upheaval of World War II that it was realized what an important role the film could play in war or peace.

The story of the Indian newsreel is a sorry tale of spasmodic and unco-ordinated effort. In 1927-28, when the Indian Cinematograph Committee made its enquiry, with the exception of Madan Ltd., no Indian producer had undertaken newsreel production, it being an unprofitable venture. J. F. Madan, however, produced a few, both for home consumption and export, and found them paying on account of the facilities he had for exhibition in his larger circuit of theatres.

In the early thirties a few efforts were made by a couple of enterprising concerns to produce news films. Their attempts, however, failed through lack of support on the part of the exhibitors and the public, and indifference on the part of Government and other authorities.

In 1939, at the silver jubilee celebration of the film industry, delegates urged the necessity for an Indian newsreel and sought Government's co-operation. The Government of India, however, did not think it worthwhile troubling itself about something which, though interesting, was primarily a matter of private enterprise.

Forthcoming events, however, altered its attitude. In July, 1940, it entered into an arrangement with 20th Century-Fox Corporation (India) Ltd., by which the latter undertook the production of Indian language versions of British Movietone newsreels. However, it was soon felt that there should be a purely Indian newsreel, and, in 1942, 20th Century-Fox commenced producing Indian newsreels entitled *Indian Movietone News* and made about 25 newsreels. These were taken over by Government in September 1943 under the title of *Indian News Parade*. The *Indian News Parade* films were released in the same five languages as the short films. They portrayed all the important events happening in India—social, economic or political. Most of them, however, related to the war effort of the country. Politically, they were quite unbiased and dispassionate. For some time, 400 feet of the *Indian News Parade* material were included in the foreign newsreels released in India. In 1944, however, this arrangement was discontinued and a complete issue of the *Indian News Parade* was distributed to all cinemas showing Indian films; but in the case of houses

SAGA IN STONE: *Directed by M. Bhavnani; Films Division, Government of India; 1949.*

LADAKH DIARY: *Directed by M. Bhavnani; Films Division, Government of India; 1949.*

KURUVANDI     *Directed by Paul Zils; Documentary Unit*
ROAD:     *India; 1948.*

MOTHER:     *Directed by Paul Zils; Documentary Unit*
*India; 1948.*

showing foreign films, other newsreels were used along
with the *Indian News Parade*. Though Government
made valiant efforts to bring forth entirely Indian newsreels its efforts were not popular and, compared to the
number of news films imported from abroad, its figures
were meagre as the following table shows.[1]

| Year | Number of *Indian News Parade* produced | Total number of news-reels produced in Indian languages | Number of foreign newsreels imported |
|---|---|---|---|
| 1934 | .. | .. | 260 |
| 1935 | .. | .. | 261 |
| 1936 | .. | .. | 247 |
| 1937 | .. | .. | 163 |
| 1938 | .. | 3 | 137 |
| 1939 | .. | .. | 185 |
| 1940 | .. | .. | 217 |
| 1941 | .. | .. | 564 |
| 1942 | .. | 36 | 539 |
| 1943 | 29 | 166 | 404 |
| 1944 | 54 | 332 | 433 |
| 1945 | 56 | 285 | 310 |
| 1946 (till Sept.) | .. | 182 | 132 |

With the close down of the I.F.I., the *Indian News
Parade* was taken over by the Central Cine Corporation.
It continued the production of newsreels till the end of
1946. With the revival of the Government's Films
Division, newsreels have been taken over by it, and, till
the end of December 1949, 63 newsreels were released.

The Indian newsreels so far produced have not been
very popular either with the spectators or the exhibitors.
In times of war, the propaganda reels were tedious and
uninteresting to an audience fatigued with the day's

[1] Ministry of Information and Broadcasting, Government of India, New
Delhi.

15

work and looking forward to some entertainment. Even after the war, Indian newsreels made no attempt to be Indian in character or outlook and failed to appeal. In the initial stages, even the newsreels produced by the Government's new film unit were failures. They betrayed a sad lack of news sense. The newsreels job, as has been aptly described, is to present in simple descriptive terms and within the minimum of time, the events of the day in itemised form without bias or special viewpoint. But the *Indian News Reviews* were so preoccupied in picturizing the activities and tours of ministers that they had little chance to do anything else. Besides, events were shown on the screen long after they had lost their topical interest and nothing can be more stale than 'yesterday's news'. The standard and output of the *Indian News Review* have improved considerably of late, and, in a few cases, have even scored film scoops. There is, however, considerable scope for improvement, technically, in their subject matter and presentation.

The factual film in India has a vast and bright future before it and there is an imperative need for it to be recognized and used as the most potent form of visual education for our country. A nation of many millions, ignorant and illiterate millions, we have to make up for years of backwardness and enlighten our people in the short space of a generation. No art or instrument can do this as effectively and speedily as the factual film, and it is up to us not merely to recognize it but to use it to solve the manifold and complex problems of our national life.

The factual film, planned and devised so as to illustrate the moot points of every argument, scripted and commented so that it touches the core of every problem, produced by expert directors and technicians so that it unfolds before our eyes the new angles of our ordinary experience and enlarges our inner vision, that is the imperative need of our country and of the world today.

## CINEMA AND CENSORSHIP

THE cinema, though its prime function is to provide entertainment and relaxation, influences, as repeatedly stressed, the minds of millions. It is because of this very power inherent in the film, and the fact that it can be misused by self-interested and self-seeking producers, that society has insisted on exercising control over the fare offered for mass consumption.

In the early days, social leaders and responsible men and women looked upon the film as a cheap innovation of no consequence, a mere passing novelty, and for years it was not considered intellectual to acknowledge, much less discuss the film! During these years the nascent motion picture, bereft of all guidance from educationists, sociologists or public men, developed on its own. Naturally it was unaware of its heavy responsibilities towards the public, and often unintentionally offended the very people it wanted to please and entertain. Gradually, however, as the feature film gained popular favour, public and social leaders became interested in the effect of motion pictures on the public mind, and with the introduction of the spoken word in 1926, the problem of the social significance of the film became magnified in extent and in degree. The period after World War I, was one of harassment for the motion picture industry. Box-office receipts were falling steadily, and intense competition resulted in morally objectionable output. Soon the industry was assailed by complaints from all sides about the content and tone of pictures. Out of such public and private dissension and random agitation gradually emerged the legal censorship of films. In the decade following 1912, a large number of censorship laws were enacted, some with state-wide and some with municipal application.

These early laws were often vague and confusing. Consequently, despotic powers rested with the enforcement officers who, as time went on, never failed to give evidence of wilfulness and caprice. Probably at no time did these laws meet with public approval. On the other hand they were severely castigated.

The film producers, on their part, regarded these laws as a menace or as a petty annoyance, depending on how seriously they interfered with their line of production. The producers looked upon themselves as manufacturers of a commodity, and saw no reason why their particular commodity should rouse the zealous attention of troublesome, even if well meaning, busybodies. Thus their general reaction was either one of defiance, if that was expedient, if not, then one of reluctant compromise.

Though legal censorship remedied the situation partially, the test applied by the censors was inadequate to meet the needs of a rapidly growing industry and fast changing social circumstances. Protests from the public became frequent, and in the interest of the business it was impossible to disregard the danger signals.

### CENSORSHIP IN AMERICA

In the U.S.A., by 1921, many producers and distributors realized that there was need for a trade association to further and protect their interests, so they formed themselves into the Motion Picture Producers and Distributors of America (MPPDA) now termed 'Motion Picture Association of America', under the Presidentship of Will H. Hays till 1945 and since under Eric Johnston.

This organization made many attempts to raise the standard of film fare and generally guide the production of films. But it was not always easy to control individual movie creators. There was no precedent to follow. This policy of self-controlling a mass art industry was something entirely new, and it took the MPPDA or the Hays Office, as it was also known, almost a decade to evolve a machinery of self-regulation.

After many series of 'Don't' and 'Be Careful' instructions to producers, in 1930 Father Daniel A. Lord, a Catholic priest, in collaboration with Martin Quigley, a distinguished Catholic layman, and Will H. Hays, drafted a Code of Motion Picture Production for the industry to follow.[1] This Code was adopted in March 1930 and became binding on all member producers.

Though the Code was based on moral principles and represented ideals of the highest type, there was no effective provision for its interpretation and enforcement till, in July 1934, as a result of a threat of public boycott, a new department called 'Production Code Administration' (PCA) was established to control film contents through self-regulation.

The Motion Picture Production Code, formulated by Father Daniel Lord, is a moral document. Terry Ramsaye, the movie historian, has called it "the motion picture industry's Magna Charta of official decency."[2] It enunciates the general principles of production, the basic rules governing the portrayal of various subjects and the reasons for such provisions.

The Code only sets out broad outlines and it is left to the discretion of the PCA to interpret and enforce it, for which purpose every member producer is obliged to submit all scripts before shooting a film, and all finished films must get the seal of approval before general release. There is, however, no distinction made between release for children and for adults. Independent producers have also the privilege of the service of the PCA but only if they so desire. Independent producers generally take the approval of the PCA with the result that about 98 per cent[3] of American production is

---

[1] Just who wrote the Code is a point of dispute but the preponderant evidence points to Father Daniel A. Lord. Says Ruth Inglis: "Martin Quigley interested him in the project, discussed the form of the Code with him and through Hays, arranged to present the idea to the producers." Ruth Inglis, *Freedom of the Movies*, p. 117.

[2] *Ibid*, p. 128.

[3] *Ibid*, p. 143.

submitted to and approved by the Motion Picture Association of America.

The Association also acts as a liaison between the industry and the public. It encourages the production of the best and the cleanest in American life. When its Code first came into existence, people were apprehensive that the screen would be stripped of all realism. Years of successful working have shown that this is not the case. Compared to the output of earlier years, the content of the contemporary American film is better and in good taste. The moral standard of films has been raised, and it is reported that there are a lesser number of protests from the public. The PCA records also reveal that there is a steady decline each year in the matter of deletions by censor boards. The PCA is not infallible, but it has achieved what it set out to do, and both the industry and the public are satisfied.

CENSORSHIP IN GREAT BRITAIN

The story of censorship in Great Britain is different. The Cinematograph Act of 1909, enacted primarily to safeguard the audience against the hazards of film fires, provides for the censorship of films. This Act empowers the Government to make provision for regulating public shows for which inflammable film is used. Public cinema shows can only be given in premises licensed for the purpose. Thus the local licensing authority exercises great control over the films exhibited in its area.

Profuse public criticism brought into being the British Board of Film Censors in 1912. This body was set up and financed by the industry, though it claims to be independent in its decisions. The President of the Board is generally a man prominent in public life. His appointment, however, must be approved by the Home Office. There are five examiners on the Board and every film meant for public exhibition is viewed by two of them. The Board charges a fee for viewing the films. The submission of films to the Board for examination is purely voluntary, but since 1933 no distributor ordinarily rents out uncertified films. The Board gives three types of certificates to the films examined—U certificate for universal exhibition; A certificate for exhibition to adults only, no child under 16 being admitted unless accompanied by a parent or bona fide guardian; and H certificate for horror films meant for exhibition only to persons over sixteen.

Though the Board's certificates have no legal sanction they are usually accepted by local authorities. The Board sends to licensing authorities a statement of the films it has passed and the certificates given. In addition, the licensee may be required to submit a synopsis of the picture and even to show the film to the licensing authority. At times, local authorities have given permission for the exhibition of films which have been refused a certificate by the Board.

Unlike the American Hays Office, the British Board is not guided by a written code but purely by precedents and commonsense.

The general policy of the Board seems to be to avoid controversy, hence films dealing with sociological problems are, as a rule, prohibited. Even short films on controversial topics are not exempt from the censor's ban. The only films exempt from the censor's ban are the substandard films as they are non-inflammable.

Though the British Board is an independent body, it is susceptible to Government influence. It has often been admitted by the Board itself that the wishes of the Government are ascertained on a number of subjects before it comes to a decision. The Government thus enjoys the unique position of hving its wishes not merely considered but often enforced without accepting responsibility for them.

Though the Board has been successfully working since 1912, it has often come in for criticism and its competence to judge matters of serious social and cultural importance has at times been doubted, due to the apparent absence of any one with special qualifications on the Board. Its policy of giving A and U certificates has also been criticized for it has been found that not only has children's curiosity been excited, but often ingenious methods are devised to gain entrance into a cinema when A films are being shown. To add to it, young girls under 16 incurred moral danger when they sought the company of unacquainted young boys of 17 or 18 to go to adult shows. Besides, the age of 16 was an arbitrary choice because psychologists have established that adolescence continues till 17 in girls and 18 in boys and hence it was in the middle of the normal process of growth. Again, the fact that the Government does influence the Board's decision without taking any responsibility for it, has led some to suggest that there should be a State censorship system. But while this would clearly indicate on whom the responsibility lies, it would involve the risk of direct political influence on the screen by the Government.

### CENSORSHIP IN INDIA

The present system of censorship in India was first evolved by the Indian Cinematograph Act, 1918. Prior to it there was some form of control exercised by voluntary boards but little information is to be had about them. An important milestone in the Indian motion picture history, the object of this Act was to provide for the safety of audiences and to prevent the exhibition of objectionable films. Like its British counterpart, it provided that no cinema show could be held except in a place specially licensed for it. These licences were granted either by the District Magistrate, the Commissioner of Police or any other authority appointed by the Provincial Government. Under this Act no film could be exhibited unless it had been certified by a proper authority as suitable for public exhibition. The power of appointing such an authority was vested in the Governor-General who could, and generally did, delegate his power to the Provincial Governments. If the authority so appointed to examine and certify films consisted of two or more persons, it was provided that not more than half of them were to be persons in the service of Government. In accordance with the provisions of this Act, Boards of Censors were constituted at Bombay,

Madras, Calcutta and Rangoon in 1920 and in Lahore in 1927. Thus, unlike the British Board of Censors, which is organized and financed by the industry itself, the Indian Boards were, and still are, Governmental organizations in whose policy the industry hardly has a voice. Each of these Boards is empowered to grant a certificate valid for the whole of India, but it is open to a Provincial Government to ban a film which it deems unsuitable for public exhibition within its jurisdiction. A Board can re-examine any film which has been certified and suspend the certificate in the area subject to its jurisdiction.

The constitutions of the Boards varied slightly from province to province. In 1927-28 when the Indian Cinematograph Committee made its enquiry the Bombay Board consisted of 6 members. They were:

1   The Commissioner of Police who was the ex-officio President.
2   The Collector of Customs.
3   A member of the Indian Educational Service.
4   A prominent Hindu citizen of Bombay.
5   A prominent Muslim citizen of Bombay.
6   A prominent Parsi citizen of Bombay.

The work of the Board was done by a Secretary and two Inspectors. The Board has been enlarged since then. The membership has increased from 6 to 17 of which one represents the industry. Originally the Commissioner of Police and then the Collector of Customs was the President. Today the Director of Publicity is the President of the Board.

Every film, before it can be released to the public, must be examined and certified by the Board. The Secretary and the Inspectors examine the film and report to the Board the nature of the film and whether it is suitable for public exhibition. The final decision rests with the Board whether or not to allow a film for public exhibition. The Board can also order a film to be re-examined by a Committee if the examiners disagree, before it takes its final decision.

Each film is judged on its own merits and nothing is approved which the Board believes is calculated to demoralize an audience or any section of it. No rigid rules of censorship have been laid down, but following the lead of the British Board of Censors, the Indian Board goes by precedents. The following kinds[1] of films are disapproved;

1 Films which extenuate crime or which familiarize young people with crime so as to make them conclude that theft, robbery, crimes of violence are normal incidents of ordinary life and not to be reprobated; or which exhibit the actual methods by which criminals carry out their purposes and make the methods of crime the main theme; or in which crime is the dominant feature of the picture and not merely an episode in the story.

2 Films which undermine the teachings of morality by showing vice in an attractive form even though retribution follows; or cast a halo of glory or success round the heads of the vicious; or suggest that a person is morally justified in succumbing to temptation in order to escape from bad circumstances or uncongenial work; or bring into contempt the institution of marriage; or suggest abnormal sexual relations; or lower the sacredness of family ties.

3 Films which exhibit indecorous dress or absolute nudity of the living (except infants and small children) or nude statues or figures in suggestive positions.

4 Films which bring into contempt public characters, e.g. soldiers wearing His Majesty's uniform, Ministers of Religion, Ministers of the Crown, Ambassadors and official representatives of foreign nations, the police, the judges or civil servants of Government.

5 Films likely to wound the susceptibilities of foreign nations or of members of any religion.

6 Films which are calculated or intended to foment social unrest and discontent.

[1] *Report of the Indian Cinematograph Committee*, 1927-28, p. 214.

7 Films which are likely to promote disaffection or resistance to Government or to promote a breach of law and order.

Among the scenes, incidents and dialogues likely to meet with objection[1] are the following:

1 Indecorous, ambiguous and irreverent titles and sub-titles.
2 The irreverent treatment of sacred subjects.
3 Materialization of the conventional figure of any founder of any religion.
4 Excessively passionate love scenes.
5 Indelicate sexual situations.
6 Scenes suggestive of immorality.
7 Men and women in bed together.
8 Situations accentuating delicate marital relations.
9 'First Night' scenes.
10 Confinements.
11 Subjects dealing with the premeditated seduction of girls.
12 Scenes depicting the effect of venereal disease, inherited or acquired.
13 Subjects dealing with White Slave Traffic.
14 Scenes laid in brothels.
15 Prostitution and procuration.
16 Illicit sexual relationships.
17 Incidents suggestive of incestuous relations.
18 Themes and references to race suicide.
19 Incidents and scenes showing the actual perpetration of criminal assaults on women.
20 Nude figures.
21 Unnecessary exhibition of feminine underclothing.
22 Bathing scenes passing the limits of propriety.
23 Indecorous dancing.
24 Offensive vulgarity and impropriety in conduct or dress.
25 Vulgar accessories in the staging.
26 Cruelty to young infants, and excessive cruelty

[1] *Ibid*, p. 215.

and torture of adults, especially women.

27  Cruelty to animals.
28  Gruesome murders and strangulation scenes.
29  Executions.
30  The modus operandi of criminals.
31  Drunken scenes carried to an excess.
32  The drug habit.
33  References to controversial politics.
34  Relations of capital and labour.
35  Scenes tending to disparage public characters and institutions.
36  Scenes holding up the King's uniform to contempt and ridicule.
37  Subjects dealing with India in which British or Indian officers are seen in an odious light; or otherwise attempting to suggest the disloyalty of Native States or bringing into disrepute British prestige in the Empire.
38  The exhibition of profuse bleedings.
39  Realistic horrors of warfare.
40  Scenes and incidents calculated in time of war to afford information to the enemy.
41  The exploitation of tragic incidents of war.
42  Incidents tending to disparage other nations.
43  Brutal fighting.
44  References to illegal operations and birth control.
45  Blackmail associated with immorality.
46  Companionate marriage and free love.
47  Unrelieved sordid themes.
48  Unpleasant details of medical operations.
49  Intimate biological studies unsuitable for general exhibition.
50  Gross travesties of the administration of justice.

No one can dispute that the general principles of censorship set forth above are good in themselves and reasonable from the point of view of those anxious to promote public interest. The difficulty, however, arises in their impartial interpretation and administration. As the Cinematograph Committee observed: "The object of censorship is strictly limited, namely, to preclude that which is definitely undesirable or unsuitable for public exhibition. Rules and principles may be laid down for the guidance of the censor, but it is in the application of these rules and principles to particular cases that the difficulty arises; and therefore much must be left to the discretion of the censor. Ultimately, the criterion to be adopted by the censor must be based on what he conceives to be the enlightened public opinion on the subject."[1]

Consequently it is not surprising that within a few years of its inception, the Indian system of censorship came in for much criticism both at home and in England.

In 1921, W. Evans, a cinema expert making a survey of the Indian film industry, observed in his report that the Boards of Censors were "weak and inexperienced" and suggested that the Government of India persuade the Provincial Governments to "stiffen up and raise to reasonable efficiency the present censorship, which is largely nominal."[2] Letters and articles appeared in the British press stating that much harm was done in India by the widespread exhibition of Western films, especially "cheap American films". In fact a well known Bishop intimately acquainted with India is reported to have stated at a conference in England in 1925: "The majority of the films which are chiefly from America are of sensational and daring murders, crimes and divorces and, on the whole, degrade the white women in the eyes of the Indians."[3] The problem was even discussed in the British Parliament and in the Council of State in India in 1925 and 1927 respectively. In fact, such violent criticism was aroused both from the industry which complained of the strictness of the censors and of bad organization, and from the public and Government which complained of laxity, that on September 15, 1927, the Council of State passed a resolution which ran as follows: "This Council recommends to the

[1] *Ibid*, p. 1.
[2] *Ibid*, p. 3.
[3] *Ibid*.

Governor-General-in-Council that he be pleased to appoint a Committee to examine and report on the system of censorship of Cinematograph films in India and to consider whether it is desirable that any step should be taken to encourage the exhibition of films produced within the British Empire generally and the production and exhibition of Indian films in particular."[1] Accordingly the Indian Cinematograph Committee was appointed on October 6, 1927, to make an enquiry.

When the Committee began its investigation, some of its members were inclined to believe that much of the criticism levelled against censorship, which permitted the circulation of cheap and demoralizing films, was well founded.  On investigation, however, it was found that such criticism was almost invariably expressed in general terms and all attempts to obtain definite instances of objectionable films failed.  While many who said that the cinema had a demoralizing influence, admitted, on examination, that they had seldom visited cinemas for the very reason that they believed them to be harmful, inartistic or boring. Moreover, almost every witness examined agreed—a few pleaded for more liberal censorship—that the canons of censorship adopted by the Boards were in every way adequate, provided they were intelligently and consistently applied, and the Committee concurred with this view.

Among the charges levelled against the Indian censorship system the three most important were:

1  The charge by the British Social Hygiene Council, incorporated in 1926, that a number of films which "had been rejected by large cities in England were, or had recently been, in circulation in India and Burma."[2]

2  The charge that the moral standards of the different Boards varied and that what was passed by one, was often banned by another.

3  The charge that too much indulgence was shown to communal, racial, political and even colour considerations.

[1] *Ibid*, p. xi.
[2] *Ibid*, p. 117.

In regard to the first, the Committee made many attempts to get the particulars about such films but without success. The British Social Hygiene Council was given every opportunity of supporting its allegations but it declined to do so. Thus, the conclusion to be drawn was that this charge, for which no evidence was given, was made without any attempt at a serious enquiry and partly through prejudice.

As regards the second charge, the Committee found that the standard of censorship followed by the various Boards was very similar, if not identical, and their enforcement seldom differed. There were, no doubt, differences of opinion which led to the release of a particular film in one province and its banning in another. But as this was not fair to the producers or the importers of foreign films, the Committee suggested the formation of a Central Board of Censors for the whole of British India, whose certificate should be valid throughout the country.

The third charge was not altogether unfounded. In India, as elsewhere, people went to the cinema to be entertained and not to learn political or any other lessons. Objectionable scenes, no doubt, had to be cut, but the Committee deprecated the idea that a film should be banned "merely on the general ground that the subject matter may, by over-subtle analogy, be interpreted as having a possible reference to current questions."[1] The Censors were right in not permitting themes or scenes which might deeply wound the susceptibilities of large sections of the public, but if films were banned on the ground that the Muslim community would object to the depiction of Nur Jehan without a veil, or the Hindus would object to the discountenancing of child marriage, then the Indian producers would be hopelessly handicapped and no progress or depiction of social themes would be possible.

Generally speaking, the Cinematograph Committee found that, on the whole, the Indian Boards of Censors were carrying out their arduous and responsible duties

[1] *Ibid*, p. 119.

conscientiously, efficiently and with general success.

One may be tempted to ask, how was it that if censorship was functioning properly, there was such criticism of it? The Cinematograph Committee on going through all the charges levelled, found that much of the criticism was ill-informed. To add to it, there was a great deal of trade rivalry and propaganda on the part of Indian and British producers with the object of discrediting American production which was almost monopolizing the home market. A part of this propaganda was to run down the Censors Boards for permitting the exhibition of so many 'objectionable' American films. That this was one of the reasons for criticism was felt not merely by the Committee but by the Indian press, as is substantiated by the following example. In 1926 the Federation of British Industries urged that American films were "detrimental to British prestige and prejudicial to the interests of the Empire, especially in the Dominions which contain large coloured populations."[1] *The Times of India* dated April 21, 1926, and *The Indian Daily Mail* of April 22, 1926, ridiculed this idea. *The Times of India's* comment on this was: "American films should certainly be fought by business competition, but to try to suppress them by a hypocritical plea for Imperial welfare, is merely ridiculous."[2] Again, a careful study of facts revealed that much of this criticism originated outside India and from persons who were either not conversant with Indian conditions or who had certain prejudices about this country.

No doubt, a few inferior films were in circulation but this was due to the fact that prior to the inauguration of statutory censorship, a number of films were in circulation throughout the country, and it was impracticable and impossible to call all these films back for detailed examination. The Boards retained the power to examine them and in some cases did examine them. The majority, however, were given certificates as a matter of course on payment of a nominal fee of Re. 1. Many of these films were very old and had they been re-

[1] *Ibid*, pp. 3, 116.
[2] *Ibid.*

examined it is doubtful whether they would have passed the new test, for before the days of legal censorship,
lack of experience permitted doubtful films and scenes
to slip through. These films, however, were gradually
falling into disfavour, as the public preferred indigenous
films, but to accuse the Boards of moral laxity on the
basis of their existence was unjustifiable.

The Committee also debated the problem of children in the cinema but did not approve of the suggestion
that certain films should be certified 'for adults only';
because not only would it be impossible to follow up the
suggestion but such a certificate would excite the curiosity of children. The Committee, however, suggested a
U certificate for universal exhibition and a P certificate
for public exhibition which would indicate that, while
the former was harmless, the latter might excite or distress children, and, therefore, parents should use their
discretion in sending children to see such films.

Even though the censorship system was working
quite satisfactorily, the Committee recommended the
establishment of a Central Board of Censors, whose
certificate would be valid throughout India and would
thus overcome the difficulty arising due to a film certified by one Board being banned by another. Such a
Board would achieve uniformity which was lacking in
the prevalent system of censorship. The Board was to
consist of 7 to 9[1] members, a majority of them being
non-officials, and was to be located at Bombay but pay
a half-yearly visit to Calcutta. The Central Board was
to lay down the general principles and keep complete
record of all films certified either by itself or any other
authority.

Unfortunately, however, this recommendation, like
all the other recommendations of the Committee, was
shelved, and no outstanding changes have been made
thereafter. No doubt a few minor alterations in the
constitution of the Boards or their methods were made,
but the general policy remained the same. Now and
again criticisms appeared in the press regarding the

[1] *Ibid,* p. 122.

16

vagaries of the censors. They arbitrarily deleted scenes
and dialogues and it was complained that they were apt
to see more than was shown to them. But no heed was
paid to such criticism. The volcano, however, had been
smouldering and, with the accession of the popular
ministry in 1946 and the adoption of a more stringent
policy by the Government, it erupted giving rise to a
heated controversy.

What was the Government's new attitude and the
industry's reaction to it?

With a view to rid the Indian screen of its demoralizing aspects and encourage a higher educational, moral
and all round general standard in films, the Government
adopted a stricter code of censorship. The Home Minister of Bombay complained that "there is too much frivolity" in current Indian films which was to be avoided if
the industry was to justify its claim as a medium of enlightenment and education.

With the formulation of this policy, the censors'
work increased. The footage cut from films varied
from $2\frac{1}{2}$ to 400 feet.[1] Obscenity, vulgarity, and immoral suggestions were the main ground on which cuts
were made. No doubt, previously also such scenes
were censored, but from now on no laxity was permitted.

The next step taken by the Government was the
banning of scenes showing drinking of liquor in view of
its policy of prohibition.

Clarifying as to what constituted a 'drinking scene',
the Government of Bombay explained the position as
follows:

"There are films which are avowedly meant to
propagate the idea of abstinence. In such films, drinking scenes being meant to condemn drink, will not be
cut out.

"If the scenes are meant to ridicule drink, to hold
it in abhorrence, to show it as poisonous, to paint the
drinking habit as ungentlemanly, unhealthy and anti-
social, or to condemn it in various other ways, then such

[1] *Journal of the Film Industry,* March 1947, p. 8.

scenes, though they show drinking, will be allowed.

"If the scenes are meant, on the other hand, to make fun of the idea of prohibition, to ridicule Government who have decided on the programme of prohibition, to induce people to become indifferent to such a programme, or to encourage them to break prohibition laws or to glorify drink, to show it as a fashion or to describe it as a social custom about which there is nothing wrong, to make it popular, to paint it as healthy, honourable or respectable and to make it appear as religious, then such scenes are objectionable and will be removed from the films."[1]

No discrimination is to be made between foreign and Indian films in regard to drinking scenes.

The Bombay Government started this policy of reform, and the cue was soon taken up by Madras. Drinking and other objectionable scenes were eliminated and cuts in films soon became a matter of routine, so much so, that during the year 1947-48, out of the 195 Indian pictures passed by the censors in Bombay, 82 were passed with endorsements, while in Madras out of the 37 Indian pictures censored, 18 were passed with endorsement. The footage excised varied from 10 to 800 feet. Moreover, 13 foreign films and 3 Indian films were totally banned throughout Bombay Province.[2] Among the scenes deleted were the following as stated by the censors themselves: drinking scenes; speeches and songs having vulgar suggestions; dialogues between prostitutes, their agents and customers; brothel scenes; songs and dances accompanied by vulgar gestures; nude suggestions and bathing scenes; school girls reciting love songs; 'sati' and 'johar' scenes; whipping scenes; jokes at the expense of priests and public servants; dead bodies kept hanging; mutilation of hands, feet, tongue; stabbing with dagger; women in labour; talks referring to abortion; workers revolt against millowners; gambling and 'satta'.

Conferences were held between the Board of Censors and representatives of the industry to discuss the

1 *Ibid*, June 1947, p. 11.
2 *Ibid*, February 1948, p. 11.

methods to be adopted with a view to minimizing the difficulties and the loss that might be caused to producers. The industry suggested the drawing up of a production code for the guidance of the producers, and a sub-committee of the Board of Film Censors, Madras, put up a draft which the Government finally approved of and published in *The Fort St. George Gazette* dated December 14, 1948. It was also suggested that, if necessary, two classes of certificates might be issued, one for universal exhibition and the other for adults only. After much deliberation, the Cinematograph (Amendment) Act 1949 was passed on May 1, 1949, and came into force on September 1, 1949. It provides for the classification of all films passed for commercial exhibition into two broad groups A and U. By this the film censors are empowered to restrict to adults above the age of 18, films of horror, sex and crime not considered suitable for children and adolescents. Films in the U category, however, are open for universal exhibition.

In the meantime, however, the Government's well-meaning but stringent policy had aroused much scathing criticism in the press as well as from the industry. On March 27, 1948, a conference was held between the Home Minister of Bombay, the Bombay Board of Censors and representatives of the Indian film industry.

At this informal conference, many of the problems facing the industry and Government were thrashed out and a truce declared on the question of censorship. The Home Minister assured the industry that "at the same time as tightening up the censorship of all objectionable features, Government would soon provide them with a comprehensive production code to help them avoid wastage of time, energy and money on features that were bound to be banned by the censors". He also suggested that they should "consider the advisability of tendering scenarios in advance to the censors for general approval."[1] The producers, however, voted against the proposal to submit scripts for pre-censorship. They

[1] *The Evening News of India,* April 13, 1948.

were of the opinion that a uniform code should be drawn up and adopted by all producers as their guiding factor.

Among the other questions discussed at that conference was the protest lodged by the industry that 'different yardsticks' were used for censoring Indian and foreign films. Regarding this, it was finally agreed that, as far as practicable, the same standards of censorship would be applied to foreign and Indian films though, of course, some consideration was due to the social habits of countries in which the pictures were made.

Though partial agreement was reached, the question of censorship was not (and is still not) finally settled.

In August 1948, a new step forward was taken to come to some solution regarding this question of questions. After much deliberation, the Bombay Board of Film Censors in consultation with the Indian Motion Picture Producers Association and with the approval of the Government of Bombay, issued to film producers a set of suggestions for guidance in the production of feature films "with a view to ensuring that the cinema industry plays its proper role in the building up of a healthy national life." Broadly speaking, the rules are in no sense new. Similar provisions have existed not only in the U.S.A. and Great Britain but in our country as well. However, the change brought about is that instead of giving instructions to film inspectors, the Board has now set forth certain suggestions for the producers to adopt, thereby hoping to avoid the initial filming of certain scenes and lessen the possibilities of deletion.

For convenience and ready reference, the suggestions have been classified under seven heads, viz:
1 Religion and Faith.
2 Peoples, Ideals and Morals.
3 History and Mythology.
4 Law.
5 Crime.
6 Sex.
7 Miscellaneous.

The instructions briefly say: "Profanity to God, or to religions, or faiths, or to their founders, or accredited Ministers, shall not be permitted; salacious incidents, obscene, ambiguous and irreverent titles, obscenity in talk, songs or gestures distasteful or prejudicial to good taste, shall not be permitted.  No picture, which will lower the moral standards of those who see it, shall be permitted.  Presentation of history, mythology, legends and classical works shall, as far as possible, be based on recognized documentary evidence.  Characters of Indian or other mythologies, of gods and goddesses, of historical heroes or of sacred personalities, shall not be presented in a frivolous manner.  Law, natural or human, shall not be ridiculed nor shall sympathy be created for its violation.  No crime shall be presented in a way which will create sympathy for it, or inspire its imitation.  Sympathy of the public shall never be thrown on the side of crime, wrongdoing or evil.  Illegal forms of sex relationship, such as free love, companionate marriage or virgin motherhood, shall not be permitted.  Adultery or illicit sex relationship, if necessary for the plot, shall not be justified nor presented attractively. Kissing or embracing by adults, exhibiting passion repugnant to good taste, shall not be shown.  Though common in Western countries, kissing and embracing by adults in public is alien to our country.  Dancing is acknowledged as an art.  It should, therefore, be presented beautifully, in keeping with the finer traditions of our country.  Incredible and crude presentation of feats in stunts shall not be shown.  The use of miracles permissible in religions and mythological pictures shall, like the exercise of supernatural powers, be severely restricted."[1]

None the less, the anamoly of a film passed by one Provincial Board being banned by another, continued. To rectify this defect, the Indian Parliament, on December 20, 1949, passed the Cinematograph (Second Amendment) Act 1949, providing, in the main, for the establishment of a Central Board of Film Censors for

[1] *Journal of the Bengal Motion Picture Association,* May 1949, pp. 19-21.

certifying and examining films meant for public exhibitions.[1] The industry had been agitating for the establishment of a Central Board. The new Act therefore, met with its widespread approval as well as that of the press.

A common system of censorship for the entire country should go a long way towards establishing uniformity in the standard and methods of censorship. It will do away with the vagaries of the various Provincial Boards. It, however, yet remains to be seen how the new set-up will work in actual practice.

The Government's laudable attempt to clear the Indian screen of all its demoralizing aspects has, however, not passed unchallenged by the press and the film industry. But being a highly controversial topic, press opinions are divided. *Filmindia* is all praise for the new policy, claiming to have suggested it. It observes: "The film censors have been pretty active last three months and have carried out most of the suggestions given by *Filmindia* to rid our pictures of their anti-social stuff. If they keep up their present watchful enthusiasm, we shall soon have a clean, instructive and entertaining screen which will help both the young and the old to get correct recreation."[2]

*The Times of India* and *Blitz*, however, have criticized the new policy. As *The Times of India*, satirically commenting on the elimination of drinking scenes from the films, says: ". . . . . . All this is very puzzling. Apparently the public are to be permitted to see scenes depicting the 'horrible' effects of drinking, but not those in which drinking is shown as a harmless social custom or in which it tends to cheer up the tired and the depressed. What the Ministry should now do is to devise a type of blinkers for the public by which they can view only those sights which are supposed to be good for them. The ministers might even offer a prize for blinkers of this description! Meanwhile, soaring prices, shortage of food and cloth, black-marketing and other trifling sins will, one supposes, continue to flourish as

[1] *Journal of the Film Industry*, December 1949, pp. 15-17.
[2] *Filmindia*, January 1948, p. 9.

usual."[1]

In fact there has been a great deal of controversy in the press about 'wet' and 'dry' films. The public is resentful of the cuts made by the censors wherever there are drinking scenes; and many have protested against it in the papers. The general argument is that the 'infuriating slip between the cup and the lip' rudely upsets the continuity of the film, makes the scenes ridiculous, results in poor art and poorer propaganda and, on the whole, the film suffers.

In defence of the Government's policy, S. A. Ayer, President, Bombay Board of Film Censors, observed: "The film distributors decide for themselves how cuts could be made to bring their films into line with the law of the land. . . . And, therefore, it is no use blaming the film censors." He also observed that: "Some films are very wet, indeed dripping wet, and these have got to be rendered as dry as possible. And if this is irksome . . . it cannot be helped, because it is the declared policy of the Government of Bombay. As for films in which the players occasionally take alcoholic refreshment, quite incidental to the motif of the story, care is taken to avoid disturbing unnecessarily the process of escapism. If actual drinking of alcoholic liquor is absolutely essential for continuity then that is also allowed to some extent for the time being. . . ."[2]

*Blitz*, realizing the need for a better standard of production, comments on the ultra-puritanism in Government's film policy as follows: ". . . . It is deplorable that at the altar of censors even films with clean and healthy entertainment have been subjected to needless puritanism by their insistence on the deletion of certain 'objectionable' (the word is badly in need of a revised definition. .!) dialogue or incidents of an innocent character which are often meant precisely to heighten or emphasize the moral by contrast.

"It is true, as the Home Minister observed, that 'there is too much frivolity' in the present day Indian film, which has got to be avoided if the film industry

[1] *The Times of India,* April 10, 1947.
[2] *Ibid,* June 10, 1948; July 27, 1948.

has to justify its claims as a medium for enlightenment and education. The Government may be under the impression that it is doing fine in the matter of helping the industry to eradicate this 'frivolity' and pave the way for the much needed qualitative betterment; but at the same time let them be warned in time, that this policy is being stretched rather too far by some of their officials —particularly on the Censor Board—and the sooner this puritanism is abandoned, the more speedy and effective will be the reforms that are being pursued on the film front."[1]

The Board's new Code of Instructions was also criticized. While *The Times of India,* judging from the censors' past actions, was sceptical about the successful application of the Code, *The Sunday Standard* dated August 29, 1948, in its editorial, lashed it in unmistakable terms. It observed: ". . . This is a very laudable motive. Film standards are indubitably very low. . . . it is therefore necessary that certain standards should be set up for the industry. But we beg leave to question the validity of the multitude of 'don'ts' tabulated by the Board. In place of a discerning analysis of the issues at stake on a cultural and artistic plane, we see the darkening and harmful influence of Mrs. Grundy at work. . . . We doubt whether the Board has thereby enhanced its reputation for reasonableness. On the contrary we think that in the excess of its zeal for purity it has only exposed itself to attack. . . . It is the negativeness of the Board's policy that is open to criticism. We suspect that it has overstepped the bounds of its jurisdiction to the extent of appropriating to itself the guardianship of public morals. . ."

The industry also has been very vehement in its criticism of the Government's policy of censorship. The vagaries of the different Provincial Boards have been frequently deplored. The *Journal of the Film Industry* has repeatedly remarked: "We are as much against vulgarity and immoral tendencies in a film as any Provincial Government. We would, however, like to see

[1] *Blitz,* February 8, 1948.

some uniformity in the standards adopted by the Provincial Government in censoring pictures. Vagaries in censorship will assist none ... Let all pictures be passed by a Central Board of Film Censors. The decision of such a Board should not be subject to revision by the Provincial Government unless for reasons of grave danger to public security."[1] In another issue, it observes that the Government has "no set rules or principles for guidance except the vague idea of improving the moral content of motion pictures."[2] Leading Indian producers and distributors have also complained about the lack of uniformity in censorship policy and strongly advocated the establishment of an all-India Board.

The present policy has been condemned as a narrow-minded one and ruinous to the future of the industry. Analysing the unsatisfactory features of the present system, a leading producer listed the following: "(1) Orthodox and narrow views on showing the true aspects of life. (2) A prudish or puritanic attitude to harmless little quickly-forgotten gaieties. (3) Lack of courageous action when necessary particularly in dealing with foreign films defamatory to the East."[3] In fact the *Journal of the Film Industry* has even gone to the extent of saying that "by prohibiting absolutely the portrayal of evil in society the Home Minister is attempting to foster complacency and putting the social conscience to sleep."[4]

As regards the proposal to submit scripts for censorship, the industry was unanimously against it. It was argued that scripts were secret documents, and thus trade secrets would be divulged in the process of pre-censorship. Besides it would not be practicable, for changes in script were often made after commencement of shooting. With more frankness, some producers confessed that in a great many cases a complete shooting script was rarely prepared in advance. Another aspect of the situation was the producers' doubt about the ability

1 *Journal of the Film Industry,* July 1947, p. 9.
2 *Ibid,* December 1947, p. 15; February 1948, p. 14.
3 *The Bharat Jyoti,* March 21, 1948.
4 *Journal of the Film Industry,* October 1947. p. 11.

of the censors to understand the technicalities of a shooting script. It was argued that without a basic knowledge of film terminology and technical devices, very few could understand a scenario with its dissolves and wipes, its fade-outs and fade-ins. The producers were therefore reluctant to hand over their scripts to the inexperienced judges, however well meaning they may be. To avoid these difficulties, they suggested that there should be an established production code to guide the producers and that it was the duty of every producer to see that his script conformed to the provisions of the code.

The question of censorship, therefore, has become a major problem to the producers and the Government. Though it cannot be denied that the standard of films has to be raised considerably if they are to become a significant social force in the new India, one is inclined to doubt the efficacy of the steps taken by the Government to achieve the purpose. Their stringent policy is at times carried too far, and scenes of harmless gaiety which are quickly forgotten are deleted on the grounds of frivolity and moral degradation.

Even in the new code of suggestions and instructions, the difficulty of intelligent and impartial interpretation is present. It would have been desirable for the industry itself to draft a code of self-regulation, adhere to it and administer it as is done in the U.S.A.

Of course the American method cannot be applied en bloc to India, but there is no reason why a system based on the PCA, but adapted to suit Indian conditions, should not be practicable. It would not only appeal to the industry, but its intelligent administration would go a long way in raising the standard of films and thereby ensuring that they played their proper role in the construction of a healthy national life.

The solution to the problem of social control of films is thus by no means easy to reach. The great potentialities of the screen have led many to argue that it should be free to depict the realities of life, normal or social. On the other hand, there are some who argue that because of this very power the film should be controlled. Between these two trends of thought, how is the motion picture to steer its course and achieve its artistic and social possibilities as a medium of mass communication?

Freedom of the screen, like the liberty of the individual, does not mean a complete lack of regulation. A free screen does not include obscenity, indecency, lying or fraud either in principle or in practice. "True freedom", as Eric Johnston observed, "is always liberty under law. Its proper exercise is never incompatible with moral principles. Those who want a lawless freedom, a freedom to do whatever they please regardless of the precepts of virtue and the welfare of the community, confuse the privileges of liberty with the indulgence of licence."[1]

Freedom and control are not conflicting but complementary terms. Control there must be in the interests of society, but what should be its basis and its extent, that is the important question? A rigid code of regulation insensitive to changing moral and social values would shackle the screen and divest it of reality. The controlling agency should be so constituted that while it protects the traditional mores of the community, it leaves the way open for change by persuasion. Such tolerance is necessary in our society where forms of conduct vary from class to class, from one area to another and between rural and urban groups.

After years of experience in Western countries, two methods—censorship and self-regulation—have been evolved to solve this problem. What are the advantages of one over the other?

Self-regulation, as practised in the U.S.A., implies that "the industry itself, rather than the Government or any other external force, supports the controlling agencies and supplies the necessary sanction...both preventive and punitive measures are used to control the contents of films and their advertising in accordance with the interpretation of a written code by an administrative body."[2]

[1] Ruth Inglis, *Freedom of the Movies*, pp. 2-3.
[2] *Ibid*, p. 174.

Self-regulation has many advantages over censorship. Here the controlling agency and its administrators are integrated with the production process and are familiar with its problems and methods. Preventive control is less expensive and more efficient than deletions and possible rejections. A rejected or a badly mutilated film is a social waste, for often the post-production changes demanded by the censors ruin films. Censorship is by its very nature negative and uncreative.

This does not mean that there are no drawbacks to this system of self-regulation. Against it can be said that it places in the hands of a few people the decision as to what the public will see. Moreover, these people are not controlled by the public and there is no outside review of self-regulation.

Experience, however, has revealed it to be the most effective means. Since control of films cannot be completely eliminated, self-discipline, as implied in a system of self-regulation, is the only solution to this dilemma.

However, merely by preventing producers from making poor grade pictures, the content of the screen cannot be raised. Ultimately, the improvement of films rests upon raising the level of audience appreciation. It is the duty of a medium of responsible public entertainment not to degrade public taste. There should be a constant effort to raise the level of entertainment and widen the scope of the screen. For this, independent criticism should be encouraged as a service to the industry.

Appreciation of better films must be taught through criticism, special audiences must be developed and interest in films must be cultivated along with economic competition and self-regulation. All this together will contribute towards the making of less stereotyped films and raising the general level of production.

# 10

## THE FUTURE OF THE FILM

THE film has arrived in the middle of the twentieth century with a little over fifty years of swiftly evolving experience behind it, at the position of a dominant form of expression. It has proved itself to be not only a means of entertainment but also a potential social force, not only an art-form but also a vivid means of mass communication; but times are moving fast and certain changes are imminent which will have serious repercussions on the future film. In view of this, it is proper to take a peep into the future.

What has the future in store for films? Astonishing things are predicted. Amongst the innumerable prophetic utterances regarding film trends of the future, there are some which foretell of technical miracles: colour to vie with all the hues and tints of nature; the sense of smell to be stimulated along with that of sight and hearing; television and radio film; stereoscopic, curved and circular screens from which characters will stand out as solid creatures; and synthetic film stars; while others go to the extent of saying that theatres will have four or five screens side by side all operating simultaneously. It seems there is going to be no escape from escapism in the future!

Whatever the technical changes, there is no doubt that the place of film in future society is assured: for a generation is quickly growing up which has never known a filmless world, and to whom the cinema is an essential factor in daily life.

Sifting through the plethora of film prophesies, one

finds that while some of them are distant and remote, others like television are just round the corner. Western countries are not merely speculating with its possibilities, but forging ahead with plans for its practical application.

Film and television are so much alike and the future of one is so closely interwoven with that of the other, that a comparison between them is inevitable. Both film and television reach their audience by two dimensional moving pictures. No doubt the screen of the latter is smaller but so is its audience, and to the viewer sitting a few feet away from the set, the size of the screen does not appear too small. Both media use a flexible camera, whereby the director can emphasize certain points. The film's conventions of cut, fade-out and dissolve apply to television also, while the subtlety of acting made possible through the use of close-up is a common requirement of both.

With these points, however, the resemblance between film and television comes to an end. For, while the film presents to its audience scenes from times past, television enables its viewers to share the excitement and the sense of actually being present at great events. In this respect, television has something in common with the theatre. Thus, one of the most important attributes of television which distinguishes it from films is 'Immediacy.' This difference of seeing a record of something which has happened (as in newsreels) and to see something which is occurring before your eyes are not only two entirely different matters but constitute the difference between make-believe and belief. For, while in the case of television there is the thrill of knowing that the performance is taking place at the instant of seeing, in the case of the screen the sense of being fobbed off with something recorded, something second-hand, is very acute.

For actors, also, the television has certain advantages over the film. Many of them have admitted that they prefer the television camera to the cine-camera. For, not only do they perform before a live audience which is known to be there, though it is unseen and unheard, but they are also able to give a more individual and homogeneous rendering of their parts in television where, from the beginning to the end, they can develop a characterization, while in a film studio they are puppets in the hands of the director, who may require his Romeo to die first and woo his Juliet afterwards. This is the fundamental difference between television and film acting.

However, as there can be no retakes in television as in motion picture, every move of the actors and cameras must be perfect and intricately mapped out before hand, for any error speeds out into space and is caught by hundreds of viewers almost before the actor or director can detect it.

The greatest handicap of television, however, according to Rudolf Arnheim[1] is that it is not possible, as it is with films, to select the best strips of scenes shot from the entire material, cut them and edit them to form a suitable sequence. Even if in television more than one camera at different distances and angles were used so that the director at the control could change the angle during the transmission and thus compensate for the possible monotony of a narrow range of action, the efficient working of such a system would depend on the experience of the director. Moreover, it would be impossible to show scenes with any departure from the actual time sequence. Besides, however efficient the director, he could not compensate for the fundamental work of selection and editing that is possible on celluloid.

What will be the repercussions of television on films? With the general use of television by the public, films also will be televised. That is, they will be broadcast from a central projecting station by wireless so that the same film will be exhibited in thousands of cinemas simultaneously and may also be seen and listened to in private homes. From a commercial point of view, therefore, television will constitute a serious rival to the cinema

[1] Rudolf Arnheim, *Radio,* Translated by Margaret Ludwig and Herbert Read, p. 287.

and the theatre. From the example of the radio, it is known that while broadcasting, on the one hand, rouses interest in music for instance, and gives a certain stimulus to concert going and record buying, it, on the other hand, replaces concerts and gramophones, and is therefore, from an economic viewpoint, bad for them. Similarly, cinemas, theatres and stadia will feel for the first time the rivalry of broadcasting when the stay-at-home will not only be able to listen, but also see.

This fear that television in the home will hold multitudes from the box-office makes some feel that this new art eventually may displace the talking picture, as the talkies wiped out the silent film. Lee De Forest, however, believes that such a complete calamity is not possible. "The large de luxe city theatres, with their super production pictures and stage-shows will always continue to draw large audiences. The human gregarious instinct will prevail."[1]   But it is highly probable that in suburban districts, adequate television screen entertainment, everyday within the home, would keep away many from the box-offices of the smaller cinemas. This would mean a lessened demand for films from the existing studios and result in the closing down of numerous unprofitable theatres.   But against this loss, it will ensure a large new market, and films designed wholly for television will come into vogue.   For apart from live subject matter programmes, it is the opinion of many television experts that film programmes will constitute the bulk of broadcasting.

Televising of films would be an economical proposition for the producer. It would dispense with the complicated delivery system by which films are despatched and collected and would result in the saving of time and labour.

The development of the new art will also keep the producer alert.   New actors will have to be found and trained. The producer will scout for new talent and hire many a television find. Production methods will be overhauled and new markets will be tapped.

[1] Lee De Forest, *Television Today and Tomorrow*, p. 55.

17

It is believed that television will make the public even more picture conscious than it is now. Possibly this increase in picture-mindedness may serve to whet the appetite for the cinema screen; for the motion picture producer will be able to flash each week into the home a few teaser scenes from the latest film stimulating the curiosity of the televiewer to see that picture. This and many other advertising messages can be put over far more effectively on the screen than by voice alone on the radio.

From the social point of view, the coming of television will purge the film of a great deal of its drawbacks. It will do away with the necessity of hundreds of men, women and children crowding together in a darkened auditorium and will thus avoid the possibility of overcrowding and all its concommitant, physical, mental and moral evils so often emphasized by the detractors of the cinema. Moreover, television though reaching audiences of a size hitherto undreamt of, will play havoc with the traditional theories of crowd formation and group thinking. There will be no touch of a neighbour's arm, no attentive posture, whispered comment, applause or mere animal warmth to influence the onlooker. Such influences, which are always present in co-acting groups , create what psychologists have termed 'social facilitation' whereby the ordinary (solitary) responses of an individual are altered or enhanced. Hadley Cantril and G.W. Allport say that "generally speaking social facilitation results in an enhancement of activity, in conservative and conventional judgment, in labile attention, in less individualistic and self-centred thought. It tends to make individuals more suggestible, less critical and more like everyone else."[1] In a congregate assembly our neighbour's laughter infects our own; in a political rally when we see the others impressed, we tend to approve of the current opinion; in theatres and cinemas the tension of others reinforces ours and their appreciation enhances our own. This social facilitation makes our own reac-

[1] Hadley Cantril and G. W. Allport, *The Psychology of the Radio*, p. 13.

tions seem less artificial, less banal, less unsocial than they would appear to us if we were alone indulging in them.

Television presentations will come unaided by social facilitation.  One will not feel the compulsion to conform to or express the feelings that others are expressing.  One will be able to respond in any way one pleases.  One will be less swayed by the crowd situation, hence one will be less emotional and more critical, less 'crowdish' and more individualistic.

And yet, on the other hand, it may lead to a greater standardization of cultural patterns and modes of behaviour, for if broadcast films become a more or less monopolistic concern as is highly probable, there will be less scope for individuality and originality than there is in the ordinary films of today.  For television, like radio, can also create crowd mentality  even without the contagion of personal contact.  When millions of people hear and see the same subject matter, the same arguments and appeals, the same music, humour, drama or story, when their attention is held in the same way and at the same time to the same stimuli broadcast from a central organization, it is psychologically inevitable that they should acquire, in some degree, common interests, tastes and attitudes.

Television is going to be a serious rival to the cinema.  By coming into homes it will do away with the necessity of going to the theatre; and yet this very factor may enhance the charm of the cinema in the eyes of some: for to them the cinema provides an escape from the restraints of the home.  Apart from the fact that the cinema provides an outlet for man's gregarious instinct, in the darkened cinema hall, each spectator is free to drift by himself into the succulent fantasy of the screen, unabashed by the presence of others.  The same fantasy displayed in the home under the critical eyes and ears of the family would often cause feelings of guilt and embarrassment.

Television will ultimately develop into an art-form in its own right, capable of being judged by its own standards of criticism as the cinema and the theatre are; while as a medium of expression and as a social force it will have no rivals. In the sphere of drama it will become as much a rival, but no more, of the cinema and the theatre as they are of one another. As David Sarnoff observes, "With the advent of television a new impetus will be given to this form of art . . . it is quite likely that television drama will be a new development using the best of the theatre and the motion pictures and building a new art-form based upon these. It is probable that television drama of high calibre and produced by first rate artists will materially raise the level of the dramatic taste . . . as aural broadcasting has raised the level of musical appreciation."[1]

The same can be said about its influence on the other visual arts like painting and architecture. The fact that television goes into homes and reaches an audience of a magnitude undreamt of before, means that more viewers can be expected for programmes of limited appeal, as for example, a visit to an art gallery elucidated by means of an interesting commentary. Casual observers can thus be beguiled into switching on an item which they would not ordinarily have gone out of their way to see.

It is often asserted that no invention, since the discovery of the art of printing, has so profoundly influenced the manner of speech and thought and our daily lives as the wireless and its kindred instruments, the talking picture and the long distance telephone. Each of these has been exerting an ever widening influence upon our homes and gregarious tendencies. Thus with wireless's latest miracle, television, no radically new or vacant field remains to be explored. But there awaits for television a new mission which none of its predecessors can accomplish. Primarily it brings into our homes all the others —the broadcast, the long distance telephone, the theatre and the cinema, and that too displayed easily and comfortably in a versatile and persuasive manner. Today the use of wireless equipment in the home, in educational

1 Lee De Forest, *Television Today and Tomorrow,* p. 168.

institutions, by business, by government, by aviation, by shipping and by the motion picture industry is constantly growing. But in the future, television will enter into all these fields not in competition, not to supplant, but to supplement and enrich.

It is difficult to over-estimate the future influence of television on the home life of all who dwell within the range of its transmitters. The cinema has contributed much towards the recreational segregation of youth. Whatever its influence on delinquent behaviour, it is certain that its general effect has been, as J. K. Folsom observes, to shift "the centre of gravity of youthful life towards unreality and vicariousness and incidentally somewhat away from the family."[1] The motion picture in the house, though it has enriched recreational life among the more privileged homes has neither substantially reduced the patronage of commercial theatres, nor attained the scope for which it was destined, mainly because of the difficulties of film supply and the botheration of setting up and taking down the projector and the screen, of threading and winding films. But with the use of television, motion pictures will be presented for two hours nightly in every home equipped with a receiver and with no more physical effort than the turning of a switch, and people will be content to linger in the family circle through hours of comfort and entertainment. If the programme directors of television select interesting and entertaining programmes, it should not be difficult for parents to induce their children to spend the evening at home in the midst of the family circle. This common and collective enjoyment of artistic and intellectual fare by a family group may supply it with some of its old world factors for continuation and solidarity. This strengthening of the home ties will ultimately lead to a healthier social and national life.

In the realm of schools, colleges and hospitals, television will go a step beyond the film. Through its use competent lecturers, authorities in their special subjects, will be able, from a central studio, simultaneously to

[1] J. K. Folsom, *The Family and Democratic Society,* p. 157.

reach large school audiences giving visual demonstration of experiments in physics, chemistry, mechanics and first aid, or illustrated talks on road safety or how to drive or show the details of an operation; in all of which even those, whether young or old, who are shut in at home, through illness or any other reason, will be able to share.

With the development of television and its entertaining, cultural and educational gifts, the new leisure of the future will not only be more wisely used but will eventually produce new outlooks on life and a new and more understanding attitude towards living.

While the prospect of television and all its implications are just round the corner for Western countries, in India it is but a distant possibility. When colour film has not yet become a commercial possibility, when we have not ventured to experiment with stereoscopic films, how can we even dream of television and televised films in the near future?

The Indian film is thirty-six years old and as such should have acquired maturity. Yet in many respects it is a struggling and insecure medium awaiting not merely public and governmental recognition but also development of its manifold potentialities.

Though, quantitatively speaking, India is the second largest feature film producing country in the world with an average annual output of about 150 feature films, the first being the U.S.A., qualitatively we are far behind. Our films can bear no comparison to the artistic and technical finish of the Western products, even of the less prolific countries. The theme of story films is stale and hackneyed and hardly any attempt is made to break new ground. This is probably due to the fact that 88 per cent of our population is illiterate. We have over 2,000 cinemas, permanent and seasonal, but they are hopelessly inadequate to cater for the growing needs of our vast population. In the industry itself things are unorganized and chaotic. Capital is shy and financial difficulties are many. We have hardly any trained technicians or directors; so far we had no unified system of censorship; nor have we fully exploited other aspects of this mass medium of communication. In view of these handicaps, here are a few suggestions for the Indian film of the future.

Hitherto there has been no serious or organized effort on the part of our producers to improve their lot. They are like a conglomeration of many adventurers each going his own way. They lack unity, organization and, above all, equipment and resources. With the exception of a few, most of them look upon the film as a means of getting rich quickly. Many of them have no knowledge of the art of the cinema and merely take to film production in the hope of minting money. We have too many independent producers whose failures, and often unscrupulous business methods, have brought general discredit to the industry. While there are 150 producers in the U.S.A. and 70 in England, there are about 350 producers in India. Such individual enterprise without any organizational basis is probably one of the greatest weaknesses of the film industry in India. What is needed is a merger of these independent producers into bigger and stabler concerns capable of withstanding competition, whose products will form a valuable contribution to film output. A pooling together of technical resources for the sake of economy and efficiency is also essential. Unity, co-ordination and organization within the industry are all the more necessary in the future with the dark shadow of the threatened monopolistic foreign invasion looming large on our film horizon.

One of the greatest stumbling blocks in the way of the progress of Indian films is the lack of financial resources. Most of the film production is undertaken on capital borrowed at exorbitant rates of interest, the repaying of which takes up the normal profits of production. Indian capital being shy, financiers as a rule are not willing to invest in the risky motion picture business, especially when the ability of a great many of the producers is dubious. This crippling financial bogey can only be overcome by the establishment of a sound Film

Corporation willing to loan capital at reasonable rates of interest.

Along with the establishment of a financing body, it is essential that the producers, directors, script writers and technicians should be trained, efficient men. No doubt there are a few training institutes for technicians, but these are not enough. A Film Academy where men and women can be given practical training in all branches of film production is a prime necessity. But till such time as this scheme can be established as a practical proposition, men who have some knowledge of films should be encouraged to go abroad, and foreign technicians should also be brought over to train Indians.

In view of the urgent need for professional training, we should also establish a Film Institute and Council on the lines of the Cinematograph Council of Great Britain. The aim of this Institute should be to conduct research in the various branches of film art and technique. Research on the production side should cover such matters as synchronization, lighting, sound recording and colour photography in all of which there is great scope for improvement. On the distribution side, the possibilities of tapping the foreign market could be investigated.

There is no production of raw film stock in India; the entire requirements are imported from abroad. For some time past the industry has felt that it is wrong to be entirely dependent on outside sources for raw stock. India has the raw materials for making film stock, and there seems little reason why, with Government help, film stock production should not be undertaken in this country. The currency restrictions and the critical period through which the country is passing has roused Government interest and this is one of the important questions to be considered by the Enquiry Committee.

Another line of future development should be in the sphere of censorship of films. Recently, it has become a major problem to the producers and Government. Government has been complaining, and often rightly, about the low standard of films, while the producers have been justifiably nettled by the vagaries of the censors. Censorship cannot be done away with, for the film, being a powerful medium of influence, can do unspeakable harm in the hands of the unscrupulous; but what we need is not a state or government controlled body of censorship but a system of self-regulation, like the Production Code Administration of the U.S.A., the provisions of which would be enforced by a single supreme Board widely representative of the industry and the educated section of society. There is no reason why such a system, if intelligently and impartially administered, should not be successful in this country. It would go a long way in achieving a higher standard of films in the new India.

The use of factual films for purposes more serious than entertainment must also be developed. Such films, if skilfully used, can change the face of future India. There is a great scope for this medium in this country. To educate, enlighten and uplift the rural and urban population, to solve the manifold and complex problems, the film is best suited because its vivid presentation and universal appeal have a special significance in a country like ours where words, whether written or spoken, often falter and fail. Government and industrial concerns must, therefore, sponsor the production of such films and establish a film library where foreign and indigenous films can be kept, and from which interested institutions and bodies can borrow films at nominal rent. The library should have its own projection facilities, and can loan films to mobile units touring villages from time to time. Our schools and colleges must also be equipped with projectors so that they can take advantage of the library facilities. The rest of the urban population can be reached through free theatrical distribution of such films in cinemas and through special shows being organized in mills, factories, workshops and similar centres.

A section of the library should be its Bureau of Information where information and books on all aspects of film should be available to the student of the cinema. This is essential, for today there is a great dearth of information and statistics about the Indian film industry.

Hitherto, the development of the industry has been stressed but the audience cannot be ignored; for it constitutes the box-office and on it ultimately depends the financial success or otherwise of a film. Because of the film industry's overriding interest in maximum financial returns, films are made to appeal to the largest number. There is no question of taking into consideration the public taste which being inarticulate, is compelled to see the fare offered.

In Western countries, to remedy this defect, film societies are formed with the general aim of the study and advancement of film art and of creating a nucleus of a more discriminating public. These film societies have been pioneers in showing Continental and other special films not shown in public cinemas.

We need to organize film societies on similar lines, where special films and old masterpieces which, because of financial reasons, are not ordinarily shown in cinema houses, can be screened and the level of public taste raised. As Forsyth Hardy says: "The function of a film society is to stimulate the progressive application of the film through creating a better understanding of the potentialities of the medium, and building up an appreciative audience for ambitious film work."[1] In addition, much could be done by such societies in making representations to local authorities on matters of hygienic conditions and sanitation in cinemas, in providing suitable film entertainment for children, in arranging courses of film appreciation and, in fact, in relating the film to the life of the community.

Another means by which the level of public taste can be raised and standards of judgment inculcated is by courses in film appreciation which would provide adults and young people, who form the majority of cinema audiences, with some guidance in their film going. In Great Britain, lectures on film appreciation are arranged by youth organizations, film societies and adult education bodies. Similar courses can be organized here for the benefit of Indian audiences.

[1] *The Sunday Standard*, November 9, 1947.

The establishment of a film library where theatrical and non-theatrical masterpieces can be seen or from where they can be borrowed; facilities to obtain books and information on films in general; the instituting of film appreciation courses in our educational institutions and the encouragement of independent criticism would go a long way towards developing a critical and more discriminating audience and would ultimately lead to the general betterment of our film fare. This improvement is essential if the industry is not to lag behind and if its potentialities as a medium of entertainment, education and expression are to be harnessed for the reconstruction of a new and independent India.

Technical progress is not the only thing essential to the future film. The future is determined by the present. So it is up to us of this generation to reshape the subject matter and reconstitute the approach of Government and producers, so that the screen is employed in the true service of mankind and forges the links of international understanding so essential to us today.

*Appendix A*

QUESTIONNAIRE SENT TO MEMBERS OF THE FILM INDUSTRY
IN BOMBAY PROVINCE

1. How many people attend the cinema in a day? What is the average attendance during a week or a month?
2. Who attends the cinemas most—children, adolescents or adults; labour, lower middle class (clerks etc.), higher middle class or professional people?
3. What is the percentage of children to adults attending?

    What is the percentage of boys to girls attending?

    What is the percentage of men to women attending?
    What is the percentage of labourers, professionals officers, military personnel, businessmen, etc. attending?
4. What proportion of their income do the various classes of people spend on the cinema?
5. What is the amount of capital invested in the Indian film industry and how much of it is invested in Bombay?
6. What are the gross and net receipts from the tickets sold during a day, a week or a month?
7. What is the average price per seat?
8. Which price seat brings in the greatest returns?
9. What is the percentage of receipts from the different classes or grades of seats?
10. What are the total receipts from Indian pictures?
11. What are the total receipts from English pictures?
12. What is the average number of films produced in India? Out of it what is the average number of films produced in Bombay?
13. What is the average number of films imported from abroad?
14. What is the average number of films exported and to which countries?
15. What is the proportion of English to Indian pictures shown in a week? Which are more popular and bring

in the greatest returns?

16. Give the names of about ten box-office hits of every year, English and/or Indian pictures included, and why do you regard them as box-office hits, (i.e. to what cause do they owe their success at the box-office).

17. What are the types of films, i.e. crime pictures, mystery pictures, love stories, war pictures, musical comedies, mythological pictures, historical pictures, social pictures, etc., and the proportion in which they are produced and how long have they run in a particular locality?

18. What is the proportion of sports and war items in news shorts to other items?

19. How many cinemas are there in India and how many of them are in Bombay Province and City? What is their seating capacity and in which localities are they situated?

20. How many producers, studios and cinema companies are there in India and, out of them, how many are there in Bombay Province and City?

21. What are the changes in the technique of production and how long does it take to shoot a film?

22. Kindly give your views on the following:—

   (a) The modern trends in Indian film industry—introduction of technicolor, tridimensional pictures, and cartoon films.

   (b) The future of the Indian film industry.

   (c) Effect of the cinema on society.

   (d) How far the cinema is responsible for crime in India and especially for juvenile delinquency.

   (e) The considerations which guide a producer in bringing forth a new film; is it merely a question of the largest financial gain?

## Appendix B

### Questionnaire Sent to Indian Film Stars

1. When did you take to the cinema line?
2. How did you come to take it up?
3. Did your parents or other members of your family object when you took up this career?
4. What is life like in your profession?
5. What are the hours of work?
6. Are you satisfied with your position and pay?
7. How does it compare with the usual earnings of stars in other countries?
8. Has your present profession affected your position in society? If so, in what way?

## Appendix C

Name of College and Class—
Age and Sex—
Occupation of Father—
Nationality and Religion—

1. How many times in a week or a month do you usually go to the cinema? How often would you like to go?
2. Which pictures do you prefer to go to: English or Indian, and why?
3. Must you ask your parents' permission before you go to the pictures? Do you ever go without their permission?
4. What do you do most frequently in your spare time? (a) Read books; (b) visit friends; (c) go to the cinema; (d) play outdoor games?
5. Which of the following types of pictures do you like the best? Mention them in order of preference—love stories, psychological dramas, comedies, musical comedies, murder and horror pictures, war and spy stories, detective and gangster pictures, 'westerns' or cowboy pictures, adventure and Tarzan pictures, historical and biographical pictures, devotional and religious pictures, mythological pictures, fantasies and cartoons, animal and travel pictures, melodramas, newsreels or documentaries.
6. State the year when you saw your first picture. How old were you then?
7. Name three of your favourite pictures, English and/or Indian giving reasons. Also name three of your favourite actors and actresses.
8. Have you at any time felt frightened after seeing a picture? If so what kind of picture frightened you?
9. Have you at any time while seeing a picture or afterwards identified yourself with the hero or heroine

or any other character in the picture? If so, give instances.

10. Does the sight of suffering or tragedy on the screen make you cry?

11. When you see a gangster picture do you—
    (a) Feel sorry for the gangster?
    (b) Feel that you want to be a gangster?
    (c) Feel that every gangster ought to be caught and punished?
    (d) Feel nothing about what you have seen?

12. What kind of pictures, if any, do you think are not true to life?

13. After seeing pictures, with what general feelings do you usually leave the picture house? Do you feel elated, disgusted, horrified, terrified, sad, bored, delighted, feel that justice has been done, or indignant at the fact that it has not been done?

14. Do you ever buy and read the small booklets (giving a synopsis of the story and the songs) sold at cinema houses? If so, do you buy them for the songs or the story or for both?

15. What kind of a film would you like to have made, if you were in a position to dictate?

## Appendix D

### INDIAN FILM CHRONOLOGY

Year

1896    The Lumiere Brothers first brought the 'Cinematograph' to India in the months of June-July, and gave shows at Watson's Hotel, Bombay. First show given at the Novelty Theatre, Bombay, on July 14, 1896. The types of subjects shown on the screen were: arrival of a train, sea bathers, parade of the guards, stormy seas and so on.

1907    Regular cinema shows were established in the country when M. Charles Pathe opened a branch of his company for the production of films and projection equipment at Bombay. Messrs. Colonello and Cornaglia of the Excelsior Cinema and P. B. Mehta of America-India gave regular shows in their tents on the Maidan in Bombay.

1911    The Delhi Durbar filmed in colour by Charles Urban of the Kinema Color Company, New York. It was the first time that a foreign producer had come to India for film material.

1913    *Harischandra:* First Indian film; produced and directed by D. G. Phalke and released at Coronation Cinema, Sandhurst Road, Bombay; length 3,700 feet.

1917    *Nala Damayanti:* Produced by J. F. Madan of the Elphinstone Bioscope Company; released in Calcutta; featured Italian artistes Signor and Signora Manelli.

1918    The Indian Cinematograph Act passed. It gave legal recognition to the industry.

1920    *Cremation of the Late Lokmanya B. G. Tilak:* The first topical short, produced by the Oriental Film Manufacturing Company, Bombay.

1925    *The Light of Asia:* Produced by the Great Eastern Film Corporation in collaboration with a German concern, Emelka Film Co., Munich; directors Himansu Rai and Frank Osten; technicians and capital mostly foreign; first Indian film to be released abroad. It had its London premiere at the Philharmonic Hall in 1926 where it ran for ten months. *Daily Express* opinion poll ranked it as the third best picture of that year.

1931 *Alam Ara:* First Indian talkie produced by Imperial Film Company, Bombay; featuring Master Vithal and Zubeida; directed by Ardeshir M. Irani; released at the Majestic Cinema, Bombay on March 14, 1931.

1934 *Amrit Manthan:* Produced by the Prabhat Film Company, Bombay, was sent to the Venice Exhibition.

1935 *Puran Bhakt, Devdas, Chandidas:* Produced by the New Theatres Ltd., Calcutta, set a high standard of film production.

*Lafanga Langoor* or *The Merry Monkey:* The first Indian cartoon picture in Hindi produced by Herr Bodo Gutschwager; released at the Majestic Cinema along with the feature film *Swapna Swayamwar.*

1936 *Bombai-ki-Billi* or *The Wild Cat of Bombay:* Produced by the Imperial Film Company and starring Sulochana, established the star system in India.

*Amar Jyoti:* Produced by the Prabhat Film Company; sent to the Fourth International Exhibition of Cinematographic Art at Venice.

1937 *Sulemani Shetranji:* Produced by the Wadia Movietone, was the first attempt to synchronize Indian songs and dances with the American silent film *Thief of Baghdad* starring Douglas Fairbanks (Sr.)

*Kisan Kanya:* Produced by the Imperial Film Company, Bombay, starring Padmadevi, Zillu, Gulam Mahomed and Nisar, directed by Moti B. Gidwani, and photographed by Rustom M. Irani; the first Indian film to be produced in cine-colour.

*Sant Tukaram:* Produced by the Prabhat Film Company, directed by V. G. Damle and S. Fatehlal, starring Vishnupant Pagnis and Gouri; was ranked among the three best pictures of the world at the Fifth International Exhibition of Cinematographic Art, Venice.

1939 The Indian film industry celebrated its silver jubilee in May.

1941 *The Court Dancer:* Produced by Wadia Movietone, directed by Modhu Bose and starring Sadhona Bose and Prithviraj; first film to be produced with English dialogue. It was sent to the U.S.A., but was released only in a few unimportant towns.

1943   Establishment of the *Information Films of India* and *Indian News Parade:* Factual films produced by the Government of India for the promotion of the war effort. *Tree of Wealth,* a documentary film produced by the Government of India and directed by A. Bhaskar Rao, was among the films considered for the coveted annual award for the best production in this field given by the Academy of Motion Pictures Arts and Sciences, U.S.A. Though it did not get the prize, it was highly commended and appreciated abroad.

*Dharti-ke-Lal* or 'Children of the Earth': Presented by the Indian Peoples Theatre Association, produced and directed by K. A. Abbas, starring Anwar Mirza and Tripti Bhaduri; a feature film based on the Bengal famine of 1943, significant for its approach and documentary method of treatment of its theme. A copy of the film was sent to the U.S.S.R. and had its preview at the Soviet Ministry of Cinematography in March 1949. This was the first time that an Indian film was seen in Moscow.

1946   *The Story of Doctor Kotnis:* Produced by Rajkamal Kalamandir, directed by V. Shantaram and starring Jayashree and Shantaram; second film to be produced with English dialogue and sent to the U.S.A. for exhibition.

*Neecha Nagar:* Produced by Chetan Anand, was awarded the Grand Prix of the International Film Festival held at Cannes in France in October 1946.

1947   *Ram Rajya, Shah Jehan* and *The Story of Dr. Kotnis* (English version) were selected by the Government of India for exhibition at the Canadian National Exhibition, Toronto, held in August 1947.

*The Story of Dr. Kotnis* was also sent to the International Cinematographic Art Exhibition held at Venice in August-September 1947.

*Sindoor:* Produced by Filmistan Ltd., directed by Kishore Sahu and starring Kishore Sahu and Shamim; awarded an 'Oscar' by the 'CIMPA' Award Committee for the best picture of 1947.

1948  *Shakuntala:*  Produced by V. Shantaram and starring Jayashree, was released at the Art Theatre, New York, on January 1948. It ran for two weeks and was acclaimed by the press and the public.

*Romeo and Juliet:* Produced by Nargis Art Concern; directed by Akhtar Hussein and starring Nargis and Sapru, a creditable attempt to put Shakespeare on the Indian screen. A rather unsuccessful effort had been made by the Stage Film Company in 1935 to put across a crude rendering of *Hamlet* under the title of *Khoon Ka Khoon.*

*Kalpana:* Produced and directed by Uday Shankar, starring Uday Shankar and Amla Shankar; was the first feature-length dance fantasy. Its unique theme and setting made it an outstanding film in spite of its many faults. It is reported to have shared the prize for 'exceptional qualities' with some films from the U.S.A. at the Second World Festival of Film & Fine Arts, Belgium, June-July 1949.

*Mother, Child* and *Community:* Three documentary films produced by the Documentary Unit India; directed by Paul Zils and sponsored by the United Nations Organization. These films are the first of a world series planned by the UNO.

*Baghdad ka Chor:* Western India Theatres' Hindustani dubbed version of Alexander Korda's *Thief of Baghdad,* starring Sabu, Maria Montez and Jon Hall, released at Excelsior and Minerva, Bombay, on August 6; marked another attempt to dub foreign films in Hindi; a great box-office success.

1949  The Indian Cinematograph (Amendment) Act, passed on May 1, made provision for granting 'A' and 'U' certificates.

*Meera:* Produced by T. Sadasivam and featuring M. S. Subbulakshmi; selected by the Government of India for screening at The Fourth International Film Festival at Prague, Czechoslovakia in August, at the Tenth International Exhibition of Cinematographic Art, Venice in August-September and at the Canadian National Exhibition, Toronto.

*Chandralekha:* A spectacular film produced by S. S. Vasan on the lines of Cecil B. De Mille's epics, selected by the Government of India for exhibition at the Fourth International Film Festival at Prague.

*Chhota Bhai:* Produced by New Theatres Ltd., Calcutta, selected for screening at the Canadian National Exhibition, Toronto.

*Tree of Wealth:* A documentary film produced by the I.F.I.; awarded the appreciation prize for giving an inspiring theme for the best utilization of an item of natural wealth, at the International Film Festival, Czechoslovakia, in August.

*The Story of Sindri, Saga in Stone, Ladakh Diary:* Documentaries produced by the Films Division, Government of India. *Tree of Wealth, Country Crafts, Handicrafts of Travancore, Bharat Natyam:* Produced by the I.F.I., represented the Indian documentary at the Documentary Film Festival, Edinburgh in August-September.

*Ajit:* Produced and directed by M. Bhavnani and released on December 16; India's second colour film; photographed on Kodachrome 16 mm film and blown up to standard size by the Ansco process in the U.S.A.; featuring Monica Desai, Premnath and Nayampally, it was based on 'Snilloc's' popular novel *Asir of Asirgarh.* Though its theme is all too familiar on the Indian screen, the novelty of colour attracted attention. The Film Enquiry Committee was appointed by the Government of India to survey the conditions prevailing in the Indian film industry.

# BIBLIOGRAPHY

*Annals of the American Academy of Political and Social Science*, November 1947.

Arnheim Rudolf, *Film*, Translated from the German by L. M. Sieveking and Ian P. D. Morrow, 1933.

Arnheim, Rudolf, *Radio*. Translated by Margaret Ludwig and Herbert Read, 1936.

Bharucha, B. D., (Edited by), *Indian Cinematograph Year Book*, 1938.

Bower, Dallas, *Plan for Cinema*, 1936.

Box, Sydney, *Film Publicity*, 1937.

Buchanan, Andrew, *Film and the Future*, 1945.

Buchanan, Andrew, *Going to the Cinema*, 1947.

Buckle, Gerard Fort, *The Mind and the Film*, 1926.

Burns, C. Delisle, *Leisure in the Modern World*, 1932.

Cantril, Hadley & Allport, Gordon W., *The Psychology of Radio*, 1935.

Carter, Huntley, *The New Spirit in the Cinema*, 1930.

Cochran, T. C. & Miller, William, *The Age of Enterprise: A Social History of Industrial America*, 1943.

Dale, Edgar, *The Content of Motion Pictures & Children's Attendance at Motion Pictures*, 1935.

Davy, Charles, *Footnotes to the Film*, 1937.

De Forest, Lee, *Television Today and Tomorrow*, 1945.

Dharap, B. V., (Edited by), *Motion Picture Year Book of India*, 1940.

Durant, Henry, *The Problem of Leisure*, 1938.

Eisenstein, S. M., *The Film Sense*. Translated and Edited by Jay Leyda, 1947.

*The Factual Film: A Survey by the Arts Enquiry*, 1947.

Fazalbhoy, Y. A., *A Plea for Indian Newseels*, 1942

Feild, R. D., *The Art of Walt Disney*, 1945.

*The Film in National Life: Report of the Commission on Educational & Cultural Films*, 1932.

Folsom, J. K., *The Family and Democratic Society*, 1945.

Ford, Richard, *Children in the Cinema*, 1939.

Forman, Henry James, *Our Movie Made Children*, 1935.

Hardy, Forsyth, (Edited by), *Grierson on Documentary*, 1946.

Harley, J. E., *World Wide Influences of the Cinema*, 1940.

Hirlekar, K. S. and Yamuna, *Film in Education and Rural Construction. What Government Can Do*, 1937.

Hirlekar, K. S., *Newsreels & Educational Shorts, What Provincial Government Can Do.*

Hirlekar, K. S., *The Place of Film in National Planning*, 1938.

Hubbell, Richard, W., *Four Thousand Years of Television*, 1946.

*Indian Cinematograph Committee 1927-28, Evidence*, Vol. I, 1928.

*Indian Cinematograph Committee 1927-28, Report*, 1928.

*Informational Film Year Book*, 1947.

*Informational Film Year Book*, 1948.

*Information Films of India Annual 1945*, 'A Brief Review of Films Produced in 1944'.

Inglis, Ruth, *Freedom of the Movies*, 1947.

Jacobs, Lewis, *The Rise of the American Film*, 1939.

Joad, C.E.M., *Diogenes or the Future of Leisure.*

Lindgren, Ernest, *The Art of the Film*, 1948.

Manvell, Roger, *Film*, 1946.

Mayer, J. P., *Sociology of Film*, 1946.

Montagu, Ivor, *Political Censorship of Films*, 1929.

*Movies at War*, Vol. 4, Annual Report of the War Activities Committee—Motion Picture Industry, 1945.

Neumeyer, M. H. & E. S., *Leisure & Recreation*, 1936.

*The Penguin Film Review Nos. 1-9.*

*Proceedings of the Motion Picture Congress*, 1939.

Quigley, Martin, *Decency in Motion Pictures*, 1937.

Ramsaye, Terry, (Edited by) *1947-48 International Motion Picture Almanac.*

Robson, E. W. and M. M., *The Film Answers Back*, 1939.

Robson, E. W. and M. M., *The World is My Cinema*, 1947.

Rotha, Paul, *The Film Till Now*, 1930.

Rotha, Paul, *Celluloid, The Film Today*, 1933.

Rotha, Paul, *Documentary Film*, 1936.

Seabury, W. M., *Motion Picture Problems: The Cinema and the League of Nations*, 1929.

Smith, Sir Hubert Llewellyn, *New Survey of London Life and Labour*, Vols. I and IX, 1934.

Spottiswoode, Raymond, *A Grammar of the Film*, 1935.

Thorp, M. F., *America At the Movies*, 1946.

Trevelyan, G. M., *English Social History,* 1944.

UNESCO, *Report of the Commission on Technical Needs in Press, Film and Radio, Following a Survey in Seventeen Countries,* 1948.

Venkatachalam, G., *Dance in India,* 1947.

Wood, Leslie, *The Romance of the Movies,* 1937.

Wood, Leslie, *The Miracle of the Movies,* 1947.

# INDEX OF FILM TITLES

# INDEX

DATE DUE

| | | | |
|---|---|---|---|
| | | | |
| | | | |
| | | | |
| | | | |
| | | | |
| | | | |
| | | | |
| | | | |
| | | | |
| | | | |
| | | | |
| | | | |
| | | | |
| | | | |
| | | | |
| | | | |
| | | | |

PRINTED IN U.S.A.